A Comparati

Suicidal Tendency and Emotional Intelligence of Higher Secondary School Students with reference to Faculty, Gender and Area differences

MW01674101

Dilipsinh V. Bihola

Contents

Chapter - 1
Introduction

Chapter -1

Introduction

1.1 Introduction:

Youth is an outstanding time of human improvement, physically as well as sincerely and subjectively. Young people are blessed with exceptional mindsets amid this period. Juvenile improvement is influenced by the recorded time. Today, kids living in confined, socially homogenous networks are presented to more extensive universes by means of TV, daily papers and PCs and can interface with this world through Internet. Mental prosperity is critical in the life surprisingly as man lives in a universe of hot-line correspondence, logical supernatural occurrences and information blast, and so on. Emotional wellness identifies with inspirational states of mind and encounters that bring advancement and happiness regarding individuals.

Different analysts and researchers have stamped pre-adulthood as a basic period, if not the most basic period in human improvement he crossroads, which everlastingly shapes an individual and humankind's predetermination.

Puberty is the time of exceptional mingling (Dube, 1991). It is at this phase the social relationship achieves uplifted hugeness. Psychological well-being issues can profoundly affect personal satisfaction. Those with more issues, for instance, reliably had lower confidence and worked less well in school and associate exercises. Mental clutters among kids and youngsters additionally had a critical unfriendly effect on the lives of guardians and families (Sawyer et al., 2000)

Pre-adulthood is a voyage from the universe of the youngster to the universe of the grown-up. It is a period of physical and passionate changes as the body develops and the brain turns out to be all the more addressing and free. The second decade of the human life is a time of self-awareness nearly as quick as the first. Ten-year-olds are still kids, albeit many are as of now presented to difficulties from the grown-up world. By the age of 20, youngsters are contributing individuals from society, securing rights at an assortment of ages to wed, vote, drive, have intercourse, battle for their nation - or to go to jail. At first look, most youths appear to be splendid and cheerful; maybe their expectations are as yet unblemished. Indeed, even social preference and familial forbiddances can't pulverize their expectations.

Youthfulness is the formative stage that traverses the progress from moderately entire youngster like dependence on guardians to about total confidence for the administration of one's own life. Youthfulness is that extensive stretch of change among adolescence and adulthood and must be recognized from the physiological parts of pubescence. It is a time of socially instigated reliance delivered by postponement of work openings, expanded instructions, the innovative procedures of mechanization and cybernation, the conundrum of military administration and casting a ballot, and the rights to wed and possess property.

So in the present examination specialist has chosen to learn about psychological wellness, self-destructive propensity and enthusiastic knowledge of the higher auxiliary school understudies.

1.2 Mental Health:

Numerous individuals when they hear the term emotional wellness for the most part consider psychological instability. In any case, emotional wellness is significantly more than the nonappearance of psychological instability. Psychological wellness is something we all need for ourselves, regardless of whether we realize it by name or not. When we discuss bliss, genuine feelings of serenity, delight or fulfillment, we are typically discussing emotional wellness. Psychological wellness needs to do with everyone's regular day to day existence. It implies the general way that the general population coexist with their families, at school, at work, at play with their associates, and in their networks. It includes the manner in which that every individual orchestrates his or her wants, aspirations, capacities, thoughts, sentiments and still, small voice with the end goal to meet the requests of life.

The World Health Organization (WHO) defines health as:

"A state of complete physical, mental and social well-being and not merely the absence of disease or infirmity" (WHO, 2001).

Mental health is described by WHO as: "... a condition of prosperity in which the individual understands his or her very own capacities, can adapt to the typical worries of life, can work profitably and productively, and can make a commitment to his or her locale (WHO, 2001a, p.l).

The rationally aggravated, counteractive action of mental issue, decrease of pressure in a distressing world, and achievement of a condition of prosperity in which the individual capacities at a dimension reliable with his or her psychological potential. As confirmed by the world Federation for Mental Health, the idea of ideal psychological wellness alludes not to a flat out or perfect state but rather to the most ideal state seeing that conditions are alterable. Emotional well-being is viewed as a state of the individual, with respect to the limits and social ecological setting of the individual. Emotional wellness is worldwide term which alludes to that state of a person which results from the ordinary association and working of his psyche. Emotional well-being can likewise be known as the procedure of human self-acknowledgment, vanity and completely effective presence. Psychological well-being of a man in addition to other things is mostly worried about his aggregate feeling of development and advancement; alteration and harmony; achievement and bliss and successful participation of a gathering of network.

As indicated by Cutts and Mosley (1941), "Psychological well-being is the capacity to modify agreeably to the different strains we meet throughout everyday life and mental cleanliness as the methods we take to accept this alteration".

Laycock (1944) expressed that "a rationally solid individual is one who has accomplished an acceptable theory of life, comprehends his or her very own issues, has accomplished social ampleness, enthusiastic development and parity, discovers delight in his/her work and has built up a decent arrangement of living propensities."

Emotional wellness and dysfunctional behavior are dictated by various and interfacing social, mental, and organic variables, similarly as wellbeing and sickness when all is said in done. The clearest proof identifies with the dangers of psychological instabilities, which in the created and creating world are related with markers of destitution, including low dimensions of training. The relationship among destitution and mental issue has all the earmarks of being general, happening in all social orders independent of their dimensions of improvement. Factors, for example, weakness and sadness, quick social change, and the dangers of savagery and physical sick wellbeing may clarify the more noteworthy defenselessness of needy individuals in any nation to psychological maladjustments (Patel and Kleinman, 2003).

Singular factors and encounters, social collaboration, societal structures and assets, and social qualities influence psychological wellness for every individual. It is affected by encounters in regular day to day existence, in families and schools, on avenues, and at work (Lehtinen et al., 1997). The emotional well-being of every individual thusly influences life in every one of these spaces and henceforth the soundness of a network or populace is additionally influenced on the loose. Ethnographic examinations in the creating scene demonstrate how conditions and social settings, for example, the ghettos of Mumbai shape neighborhood encounter and the emotional wellness of networks.

Around the world, mental and social issue spoke to 11% of the aggregate malady load in 1990, communicated as far as inability balanced life years (DALYs) (WHO, 2001b). This is anticipated to increment to 15% by 2020. Psychological wellness issues likewise result in an assortment of different expenses to the general public (WHO, 2003). Despondency was the fourth biggest supporter of the malady trouble in 1990 and is relied upon to be the second biggest after is chaemic coronary illness by 2020. However, psychological instability and emotional well-being have been ignored themes for most governments and social orders. Ongoing information gathered by WHO shows the expansive hole that exists between assets that are accessible in nations for psychological well-being and the weight caused by emotional wellness issues (WHO, 2001c). The significance of emotional wellness in the upkeep of good physical wellbeing and in recuperation from physical ailment is currently very much substantiated. Psychological well-being status is a key thought in changing the wellbeing status of a network.

Jahoda (1967) states that "there are at present two schools of pondered the significance of emotional wellness. One, to a great extent spoken to by the restorative calling, thinks that its productive to consider emotional wellness the nonattendance of mental infection. The second, to a great extent spoken to by clinicians, the showing calling, and psycho-experts, respects emotional well-being in positive terms, as the nearness of certain mental qualities. Each school has valid justifications for its methodology. To view emotional well-being as the nonappearance of mental infection is with regards to the customary assignment of medicinal calling to help and fix. Such a significant number of people experience the ill effects of psychological sickness or passionate unsettling influence that the assignment of managing their issues shows up overwhelmingly critical, even without including the entanglement of asking climate the individuals who are free from handicaps and are consequently likewise allowed to take a stab at a full and fulfilling life. This last inquiry is the real worry of the second school of contemplated emotional wellness. To consider it in positive terms keeps away from one noteworthy issue in the main methodology, that there is no broad concurrence on what comprises mental turmoil. It is simple enough to perceive serious types of psychological sickness; yet with extreme unsettling influences it is difficult to state whether a man is in reality sick or not. Also, where socially disliked conduct is worried for instance, in the present discussion about regardless of whether certain violations ought to be viewed as the consequence of mental aggravations, the way that no broad meaning of psychological sickness is accessible makes the discussion pitifully befuddled.

1.2.1 The Innate Value of Mental Health:

Emotional wellness adds to all parts of human life. It has both material and insignificant, or inherent, values: for the individual, society, and culture. Psychological well-being has a proportional association with the prosperity and profitability of a general public and its individuals. Its esteem can be respected in a few related ways:

Emotional well-being is significant for the prosperity and working of people. Without one being rationally solid, one can't work successfully. Great psychological wellness is a critical asset for people, families, networks, and countries. Psychological wellness, as an indivisible piece of general wellbeing, adds to the elements of society, and has an impact all things considered on efficiency. Just the individuals who are rationally solid can end up beneficial by upgrading others too during the time spent advancement.

Emotional wellness concerns everybody as it is created in our regular daily existences in homes, schools, working environments, and in recreation exercises. Positive psychological well-being adds to the social, human, and monetary capital of each general public. Otherworldliness can make a noteworthy commitment to psychological wellness advancement and emotional well-being impacts profound life (Underwood-Gordon, 1999).

Psychological well-being can be viewed as a substance asset, adding to the person's personal satisfaction, and can be expanded or be ebbed by the activities of society. A part of good emotional well-being is the limit with regards to commonly fulfilling and persisting connections. There is developing proof that social quality is basic for the monetary flourishing of networks and this relationship seems, by all accounts, to be common.

1.2.2 Importance of Adolescent Mental Health:

Immaturity is an especially one of a kind period in life since it is a period of serious physical, mental and psychological improvement. Emotional well-being is essential to our physical wellbeing, our personal satisfaction and our efficiency. Psychological wellness is of specific significance for kids and youngsters. Great emotional well-being of youth or youthfulness regularly supports great psychological wellness and prosperity all through life. Emotional well-being issues in these years, if not settled can have sweeping and persevering results.

The absence of regard for the emotional well-being of youths may prompt mental clutters with deep rooted result, confusions with wellbeing matters, and lessens the limit of the individual and society to be protected and gainful. Contemporary acknowledgments of kid and puberty impartial disarranges give an inevturre to blend in current information, recognize issues for future investigation, and harmonizes suitable arrangements.

The size of the weight of illnesses identified with youngster and youthfulness mental disarranges is under remained by clinical and guardians yet up to this point been hard to qualify. Instruction, under accomplishment prompting reliance, enrolment in criminal movement, the utilization of illegal medications, co sullen therapeutic conditions are nevertheless a portion of the a lot of confers that are related with young people of today.

Significance of being rationally sound has been featured in the accompanying:

- Expansive unto 20% of the youngsters and teenagers experience the ill effects of an incapacity impartial sickness (WHO, 2000).
- Expansive suicide is the third driving reason for death among young people (WHO, 2001)
- Major Depressive Disorder (MDD) frequently has a beginning in puberty, crosswise over assorted nations, and is related with significant psychosocial impedance and with of suicide (Weissman et al., 1999). There was progression and specificity identified with the juvenile which proceeded into adulthood and was related with high rates of suicide and expanded rate of mental, psychosocial debilitation, and lower instructive accomplishment.

Most of the youngsters who have great emotional well-being are those with great psychosocial improvement, the limit with regards to viable conduct, and great social and family connections. Of these, youngsters who encounter emotional well-being issues and scatters, that are moderately fleeting and require brief intercessions. A few, be that as it may, encounter more intricate and extreme challenges, which influence their capacity to appreciate life and to meet age fitting formative midis tows.

1.2.3 Factors Influencing Adolescent Mental Health:

It is evaluated that 1 percent of kids and juvenile experience the ill effects of over the top habitual confusion and a further 1 percent of young people experience the ill effects of dietary issues (Kurtz et al., 1996)

Among youngsters issues, for example, suicide, lead issue, liquor and medication misuse, wretchedness, and a lack of ability to concentrate consistently scatter, are for the most part ending up more typical, and there are expanding dimensions of maltreatment and disregard (Rutter and Smith, 1995; Zubrick, 1998 and Zubrick et al., 2000). Besides, mental disarranges (outstandingly misery) are showing up at a more youthful age and they additionally appear to increment in seriousness (Zubrick, 1998 and Zubrick et al., 2000).

Kids or youngsters with emotional well-being issues will probably:

- Report feeling exceptionally focused
- Have poor or reasonable physical wellbeing, perform underneath grade level at school, or utilize liquor or different medications, and
- Think about executing themselves (Zubrick et al., 1995; 1997).

There is expanding proof that numerous emotional wellness issues that happen in youth proceed into grown-up life, conveying with them an expanded danger of grown-up psychological well-being issue, demise, misconduct, wrongdoing, joblessness and vagrancy (Rutter, 1995; Zubrick, 1998 and Zubrick et al., 2000). At the point when these individuals moved toward becoming guardians, they are at higher danger of being imable to give a steady and secure condition for their own youngsters, so their issues will stream on to the people to come (Quinton and Rutter, 1988 and Ijzendoom et al., 1995).

In spite of the fact that a variety of hazard factors are known to be related with emotional well-being issues and disarranges, the particular reasons for most are for the most part not known. We do know, in any case, that these issues and disarranges have the potential not exclusively to influence the juvenile's present prosperity, yet in a few young people, to upset learning, improvement and prosperity over numerous years. As noticed, the effect of genuine emotional well-being issues may hold on in to adulthood and on to the psychological well-being and prosperity of the people to come.

Elements that impact the psychological wellness of pre-adult include:

- Physical wellbeing and improvements, since it is a time of fast development and advancement great physical wellbeing makes ready for the youths' great psychological well-being.
- Social and mental improvements are particularly interlinked with youths being rationally solid.
- The family and the quality and consistency of support and the youthful's association with guardians or different grown-ups; Environmental variables, both social and physical. Hereditary components to a specific degree impact the pre-adult psychological well-being.
- Social standards and desires that impact tyke raising are critical in the improvement of good psychological wellness in the youthful stages. Social effects on young people and families and being socially advantaged or hindered, including access to fundamental assets all assume a critical job in the advancement of the great emotional wellness.
- Social and ecological components are especially essential, both as supporters of hazard and as focuses for activity to diminish chance and emotional well-being issues over the network.

Basic hazard factors for mental disarranges and emotional well-being issues in teenagers are:

- Problems of organic development
- Unstable associations with guardians or with other parental figure or passing if a parent
- Inadequate child rearing abilities;
- Poor quality kid care;

- Family dissension, savagery in the family, parental partition and family breakdown, and in a few conditions, sole child rearing;
- Parents who have genuine medical issues including psychological instability as well as medication and liquor issues that influence their capacity to be compelling guardians.
- Lack of social help
- Psychological injury (E.g. misuse, mischances, bums, debacle);
- Physical disease or incapacity;
- Lack of associate help and contribution in freak peer gatherings
- Poverty (Zubrick et al., 2000; Nurcombe, 2000).

1.2.4 Factors that Protect Adolescent against Mental Health Problems:

Emotional well-being has been differently conceptualized as a constructive feeling (influence, for example, sentiments of joy, an identity characteristic comprehensive of the mental assets of confidence and authority, and as versatility, which is the ability to adapt to difficulty. Different viewpoints and models of emotional wellness add to our comprehension of what is implied by positive psychological wellness. While there are chance factors that can make emotional well-being issues; one can likewise investigate those perspectives, which advance and secure against being rationally burdened.

- Nurturing, warm and secure associations with aduUs, including a positive relationship mind no less than one parent, and a steady association with another grown-up (E.g. an educator, close relative or uncle);
- Positive, remunerating school conditions and a feeling of 'connectedness' to the school and/or network;
- Positive individual accomplishments which incorporate great scholarly exhibitions and inclusion in games and so on; It is the time of human improvement amid which a youngster must move from reliance to freedom, self-rule and development

- Involvement in genius social companion gatherings; The youngster moves from being a piece of a family gathering to being a piece of an associate gathering and to remaining solitary as a grown-up
- A positive air towards life

Youth includes a procedure, which reaches out over a huge time of a man's life. In any case, there are singular contrasts, with some youngsters traveling through youthfulness significantly more rapidly than others. Immaturity presents numerous difficulties as natural, mental and social changes are gone up against. Vital procedures of progress need to happen inside the youngster if these difficulties are to be gone up against adaptively and with progress. At the point when an immature can't go up against and manage a formative test effectively there are probably going to be unhelpful mental, enthusiastic and social results.

Immaturity is a period of progress and emergency, which might be adaptively, experienced by a few yet for others displays the likelihood of unfortunate mental, social, and passionate outcomes. The essential objective of youthful is to make the change from adolescence and adulthood. Young people need to do this while managing natural, mental and social difficulties. Further achieving adulthood effectively and solid will be affected by the different encounters, ecological anxieties and natural perils.

Over the most recent twenty years due to financial and innovative advancements, the commonness of psychological wellness among the young people has risen remarkably, which has caused to stay into this time of human improvement, hello there the current conditions, the investigation of immaturity ends up fundamental to protect, fix and enhance the emotional well-being of those teenagers who are examining in schools.

1.2.5 Programs and activities related to mental health education:

Emotional well-being training ought to grant understudies more appropriately through imaginative projects or exercises than giving just verbal learning about psychological wellness. A few projects and exercises have given as pursues:

1. Making different undertakings by understudies identified with psychological wellness.

2. Arranging rivalries and projects in schools like-critical thinking, solid eyes, splendid skin, phenomenal physical make-up, ability building projects, kid and youth advancement programs and so forth.
3. Planning for bringing in emotional wellness training through co-curricular exercises.
4. Making and showing diagrams, notices on close to home cleanliness like yogasana, diet, great wellbeing state of mind and so forth by understudies in classroom.
5. By arranging display scrapbook, cuttings, flipbook, backdrops and things identified with psychological well-being instruction.
6. Mental wellbeing exercises can be done amid the supplication meeting, in classes or in get together corridor. We can pick points based on need and current issue in the network. Different varying media helps can likewise be utilized to import psychological well-being training.
7. Day festivals like world emotional wellness day, psychological wellness preventions at work. (e.g. push avoidance programs).
8. Conducting arranged wellbeing sessions did by group of social specialist and therapeutic officer in school. Psychological well-being advanced exercises in schools. (e.g. programs supporting natural changes in schools).
9. Proper advising and follow up about psychological wellness and cleanliness to the guardians in PTA meeting.
10. Giving more accentuation on yoga and exercise since they are the essentials of good emotional well-being.

1.2.6 Role of schools developing mental health:

The school accepts extraordinary accountability during the time spent amicable improvement of identity. Kids put in six to seven hours in school. Schools are in, a situation to help in the improvement of youngsters possibilities by taking into account their necessities. The following are notice in a nutshell the different estimates which can be taken in schools for the best possible improvement of physical, mental and otherworldly capacities of youngsters.

1. **School condition**. School condition assumes an imperative job in the improvement of uplifting states of mind. The earth ought to be free from station, statement of faith or religious sentiments. It ought to give feeling of security in every last understudy regardless of their religion or financial conditions. It ought to give an appropriate domain to gaining free from dread, strain and dissatisfaction.

2. **Vote based condition**. Schools as a foundation should work on majority rule lines. Understudy's portrayal ought to be made on different advisory groups so understudies recognize themselves with the foundation. School issues ought to be talked about with instructors and understudies and choice ought to be taken by taking understudies in to certainty.

3. **Arrangement for different curricular exercises**. The school ought to sort out various curricular exercises suiting to the requirements of people to discharge their repressed enthusiastic emotions. The school may arrange customary recreations, talks, discusses, exploring, guided perusing, dramatizations, instructive presentations and well-magazines, and so forth.

4. **Instructor's job**: The educator must have the information of key standards of human conduct to handle the issues of his understudies. He should be sincerely steady and ought to have an uplifting mentality towards educating. He should appreciate understudies and their welfare.

5. **Opportunity of articulation**: Children ought to be given an open door in the class tom express their perspectives uninhibitedly on issues.

6. **Assortment of intrigue**: The educator should attempt to build up an assortment of interests in his understudies, for example, recreations, perusing, and side interests of deferent kinds which may help in the advancement of sound states of mind. The instructor ought to acknowledge and empower beneficial exercises of his understudies.

7. **Perusing for emotional well-being**: The instructor should choose books which are suitable to age levels and understudies be encouraged to peruse those books.

8. **Classes in human connections**: The school ought to compose classes in human relations. Day by day life issues ought to be talked about. The significance of how to live ought to be accentuated. Understudies ought to likewise be welcome to talk about openly their issues.

9. **Arrangement for sex education and good training**: Most of the issues of youths are worried about sex and good clashes which causes mental unsettling influence. It will be of more noteworthy utilize if sex and good instruction are made a fundamental piece of ordinary educational programs.

10. **Craftsmanship and specialty**: composing for comprehension and arrival of passionate pressures can likewise be utilized in psychological well-being programs.

11. **Direction:** Schools ought to arrange direction administrations for the advantages of understudies. Direction is of three kinds individual, instructive and professional.

1.2.7 The present Scenario of Mental wellbeing in India:

The present century has positively seen a few advancements in the field of emotional wellness in India. The lawful rules and the medicinal experts have added to words the welfare of rationally sick people. The usage of National Mental wellbeing program in 1982 was a dynamic advance toward satisfying the privileges of rationally sick people. In light of this program, in 1995 District Mental Health program was likewise propelled in 24 District in India.

The Mental wellbeing Act, 1987, however was invited around then, at present neglects to address number of applicable and appropriate issues. The Act is quiet about the social shame, training of rationally sick, business, recovery and incalculable infringement of fundamental human rights. At present 20% populace experiences emotional wellness issue.

In 2002, the Supreme Court of India coordinated to every one of the states to recognize elements implying emotional well-being care and coordinated to give offices to address the issue of such populace.

Consequently, the psychological well-being issues extending from mellow to extreme are ceaselessly on the ascent in India anticipating an answer for give alleviation to the sufferers. Thus there is a prompt requirement for changes in the leaving arrangements with the end goal to guarantee security of human rights in India.

1.2.8 Role of instructive establishments in creating emotional wellness:

Instructive establishments are now made significant arrangements for the prosperity of their understudy network by having arrangements for instructors and supporting understudies with psychological wellness issues. Yet, these endeavors are insufficient to help the necessities of the understudies with uncommon instructive requirements and understudies with mental issues. Instructive foundations need to distinguish the noteworthy deterrents and make open doors for enhancing the offices for understudies. In the event of higher instructive foundations they are as of now connected with parcel of pressure, enthusiastic requests of adapting to parental and peer weight, ponder amid the examinations and money related weights. These may add to the higher rate of passionate side effects among understudies. It is exceptionally fundamental for the instructive establishments to approach in a planned way with different associations like the essential social insurance administrations, optional psychological wellness suppliers and other applicable offices to address the issues of understudy emotional well-being and recognize the underlying side effects at the soonest proposals for the instructive foundations.

1. Mental medical problems ought to be tended to in each instructive foundation relating to enthusiastic proficiency, sexual wellbeing, substance utilize and abuse, and so on. Contingent on the development dimension of the students.

2. Websites, sees, understudy's handbook, handouts, flyers and numerous such other medium ought to be used suitably to crusade for the reason, impact and fix of psychological well-being issues among understudies.

3. Students who have been recognized to have the need of psychological well-being administrations ought to be guaranteed to get a nonstop help of emotional well-being care notwithstanding for the home region.
4. Institutions ought to select qualified psychological wellness suppliers and expert bodies to study and guide the human services needs of the understudies in the establishment. At times the understudies mental sick wellbeing probably won't be seen to be sufficiently serious for suggestion at the neighborhood psychological well-being administration.
5. Action research ought to be led much of the time to assess the execution and the results of the human services suppliers in the foundations and furthermore to give them an appropriate input.
6. Institutions must guarantee that sufficient assets are being resourced to meet the psychological well-being specialist co-ops of the foundations keeping into thought the developing needs of the understudy populace.
7. Institutions must energize positive associate relationship to such an extent that understudies might be urged to examine their challenges and discuss uninhibitedly with the wellbeing laborers the same number of understudies decide not to unveil their mental issues for the dread of dismissal.
8. Institutions should work as a team with essential wellbeing administrations. Auxiliary psychological well-being care suppliers and other significant organizations to address the issue in a planned way and should help reinforce the informal organization and social help for the understudies.
9. Create open doors for the understudies to use their spare time in the instructive foundations to be occupied with seeking after their leisure activities or inventive contemplations so they may not be defenseless against the enticements of medications and liquor.

1.2.9 Role of stakeholders in mental health:

Various government organizations: Psychological well-being clinics, Guidance and advising focuses, Jail. Restoration focuses, and so on.

Government settles on different approach choices for keep up psychological well-being in the general public and people. Government drafts and passes different bills and laws for enhance and keep up great psychological well-being. Government has a managerial group of different plans and plans for emotional wellness. It encourages financially to emotional wellness clinics, general doctor's facilities, direction and advising places for psychological well-being, assemble doctor's facilities and different foundations for psychological well-being. Government gives assets to inquire about work in the region of emotional well-being.

Non - Governmental Organizations:

Network based association; City wide associations; National NGOs; and International NGOs. NGO's fundamentally plays for mindfulness in the general public. They chip away at direct field or grass root level. They can orchestrate different social mindfulness crusades in zone of emotional wellness. A large portion of HIV constructive patients lost their psychological wellness, in these cases NGOs assumes critical job for sincerely and rationally bolster these sorts of people. NGOs are functioning as specialist organization in the general public. NGO's assume vital job in direction and guiding for influenced people.

Educational Institutes:

Schools, Colleges, Universities, professional and specialized instructive foundations, UGC, NCTE. Instruction is a precise exertion towards learning essential actualities about mankind. Furthermore, the center thought behind psychological wellness is to develop fundamental qualities in the understudies so the human advancement that trains us to oversee complexities can be continued and further created. It starts at home and it is proceeded in schools. Everybody acknowledges certain things in his/her life through different mediums like society or government.

There is a notable, substantial and industrious relationship among instruction and psychological wellness. This has been seen in numerous nations and eras and for a wide assortment of psychological wellness measures. There are different purposes behind these affiliations, in spite of the fact that it is likely that these emotional well-being contrasts are in the part the aftereffect of contrasts in conduct crosswise over instruction gatherings.

Mass Media:

Print (books, flyers, daily paper, magazines, and so on.) Recordings (gramophone records, attractive tapes, tapes, cartridges, CDs, DVDs), Cinema, Radio, Television, Internet, Mobile telephone.

Open impression of dysfunctional behavior are molded by the news and diversion in media. Research affirms that adverse pictures and generalizations in movie, TV, promoting, magazines and daily papers are straightforwardly associated with the general population's contrary states of mind toward individuals with psychological wellness issues. Negative media depictions additionally directly affect people living with psychological instability, and in addition an effect on government reactions to emotional wellness issues. Most stories in daily papers in connection to psychological sickness were for the most part about unsafe (39%). Not peril to other people but rather for the most part stories with content identified with brutal wrongdoing (25%). 13% of the tales were identified with self-destructive or self-damaging conduct, just 4% managed psychological maladjustment as a variable identified with being defrauded by wrongdoing. These accounts were generally on the first page expanding sway. Stories in the amusement area did not center on risk more frequently than different areas (Research by Dr. Stun).

Along these lines the broad communications assumes essential job keep up in the general public, it influences mindfulness, to give data, claim individuals, and so on.

1.3 Suicidal Tendency:

1.3.1 Meaning of Suicide:

Suicide is a Latin expression imitative from “suicaedere” denotation killing self or it is an act of harming oneself to end one’s life intentionally. Brown. S was the individual to make utilization of the word suicide in 1642 in his "Religio Medici", which evoked an assortment of response out in the open personalities. Suicide isn't an illness when all is said in done, yet it most likely includes a person to burrowed rationale in a condition of internal felt into medical issue accountably. Rate of suicide shift crosswise over age, sex, religion, time and practices of death enrollment which has turned into the significant reasons for death around the world.

WHO States in National Alliance on Mental Illness (2006), that more number of passing have happened by suicide among youthful grown-ups as opposed to by some other disease .A suicide is submitted at regular intervals on the planet (WHO). Each finished suicide has 20 suicide attempters. A larger part of those endeavoring to end their lives are youths. Howton (2009) reports that the tenth driving reason for death is suicide on the planet and 16 suicides/100,000 individuals, is the worldwide death rate. In the previous 45 years suicide rates have expanded in the creating nations. Youthful kids and young people are not immaculate by this plague. Along these lines immature kid's suicide turns into a noteworthy worry for the general public.

1.3.2 Epidemiology of Suicide:

Around 800,000 demises are because of suicide crosswise over world consistently (WHO 2012). Of these 1,35,000 (17%) are occupant of India (Registrar General of India 2012). The rate of suicide has expanded from 7.9 to 10.3/100,000 individuals between1987 to 2007 (Vijay, 2007). Southern and eastern parts of India have higher suicide rates. In Indian urban communities as indicated by 2012 insights, Tamil Nadu stands first in the quantity of suicides submitted, around 12.5%, Maharashtra (11.9) and West Bengal remains in third position of (11.0%) having the most astounding extents of suicides. Tamil Nadu and Kerala had the most elevated suicide rates/100000 individuals in 2012. The proportion of male and female was2:1 (Government of India, 2012).

Institutionalized suicide rate for age, in India for ladies which was the sixth position and the most elevated on the planet and 25.8 for men, and the positioning comes 22nd as per WHO 2012.Among 15-29 and 30-44 each age bunches roughly 46.000 suicides happened in India (Government of India, 2012). Among these 80% were literates which is higher than the normal national education of 74% (ADSI).

Suicide in Cities

Exactly 19,120 suicides were accounted for from real urban communities in the year 2012.

Chennai-2183

Bengaluru-1397

Mumbai-1296 pursued by

Jabalpur (Madhya Pradesh)

Kollam (Kerala). Expressing the most noteworthy rate of suicides 45.1 and 40.5/multiple times higher than National normal (ADSI-2012) expressing the most noteworthy rate of suicides45.1 and 40.5/multiple times higher than National normal (ADSI-2012).

1.3.3 Suicidal Tendency and Behavior:

Self-destructive Tendency is the affinity for a man to have self-destructive ideation or to make suicide endeavors. It might likewise allude to suicide, emergency, self-destructive ideation, Para suicides, and fizzled suicide endeavor.

Self-destructive Behavior: incorporates self-destructive arranging, self-destructive endeavors and finished suicide. Alludes to moves made by one who is thinking about or getting ready to cause his/her own demise. Characterized as a distraction or act that is centered around causing one's very own demise intentionally. Aim to cause one's passing is fundamental in the definition.

Self-destructive Ideation: alludes to considerations of suicide or needing to take one's own life.

Suicide Attempt: alludes to a demonstration concentrated without anyone else demise that is unsuccessful in causing passing.

Finished Suicide/Suicide: alludes to having deliberately caused one's very own passing.

Self-destructive ideation and endeavors predicts suicide passings emphatically which can result in damage, loss of opportunity money related weight on society (WHO 2014).Suicide is the nineteenth driving reason for infection trouble all around and sixteenth and ninth driving reason all inclusive between 15-44 years old (WHO 2008). It turns into the real need of hour to gauge suicide and self-destructive conduct, and to avoid it.

The most minimal dimension or first connection for suicide conduct is Suicidal ideation. A few examinations (Pfeffer, 1984) demonstrates that there is some security in a significant level of cases particularly half, at a 2year development, who seen that 27% of young ladies and 18.4% of young men kept up these thoughts at a multi year development.

From the above we can expect that kids, who have self-destructive ideation, will have more noteworthy likelihood of creating genuine self-destructive conduct when they achieve youth. Suicide ideation as the milder components of self-destructive conduct, which dynamically converts into more genuine types of self-destructive conduct along a continuum of conduct.

This relationship between self-destructive ideation and more genuine types of self-destructive conduct was bolstered by specialists like Lewinsohn (1996) and Shea (1998) who presumed that self-destructive ideation is a solid indicator of more genuine self-destructive acts and the level of self-hurt was straightforwardly proportionate to the level of self-destructive ideation encounters.

Bearman (2004) opines that self-destructive ideation is multiple times more predominant contrasted with real suicide endeavors. Different analysts affirming this finding in his exploration and this likewise corresponds with different investigations as well (Lix. et al 2005).Thus self-destructive propensities among youth have been the subject of broad research.

Suicide has turned into the second driving reason for death among 10-24 years age gathering. Consistently one million people are passing on from suicide. Among them 33% of deaths are in youth, in created and creating nations .Suicide endeavor is normal among young people (Swahn).Suicide rate per 100,000 people increments with age in youth from 0.02 for people matured 5-9 and 7.8 for people matured 15-29 (CDCP-2008). Suicide endeavor can be seen as ahead of schedule as at 7 years old years (Giraud, 2013). Suicide is dependably a sob for help, consideration and to escape from challenges however not a honest to goodness expectation to die.23% of teenagers who were hospitalized for suicide endeavor had backslide in their endeavors the next year (Gilbody, 1997) and 10% have kicked the bucket amid the five after years (Chan et al 2009) Adolescent self-destructive ideation has found to foresee self-destructive practices and psychopathology in adulthood.

1.3.4 Theories of Suicide:

CHALLENGES-THE IDEATION-TO-ACTION FRAMEWORK

Suicide is the main source of demise (WHO 2013). Insufficient information is accepted to be the key factor for restricted accomplishment in lessening suicides as inability to pass judgment on when self-destructive contemplations advancement to deadly endeavors. Further underneath it is clarified about the information of hole and portrays the ideation-to-activity system which can clarify the hole and guide the future age of suicide hypothesis, research and avoidance.

Misery, sadness, larger part of mental issue and impulsivity are the most well-known and regularly observed hazard factors for suicide, which additionally predicts self-destructive ideation however neglected to anticipate suicide endeavors from the individuals who encounter suicide ideation/thought without suicide endeavors (Klonsky and May, 2016) which is obvious in both epidemiological examinations and furthermore in meta-investigation. It was clarified in an examination directed in the United States where the discoveries said higher rates of mental issue was found in suicide ideators contrasted with non-self-destructive; anyway the discoveries likewise said that psychological disarranges insignificantly recognized suicide attempters from suicide ideators from attempters and without endeavors. Later and worldwide epidemiological examinations found the comparative examples (Nock et al 2012, 2013).

World Mental Health Surveys clarified over 60% of the inconstancy in suicide ideations as opposed to just 7% fluctuation in suicide endeavors among ideators. Discouragement and sadness anticipated suicide ideation as opposed to suicide endeavors among psychological sickness (May &Klonsky, 2016).

Table 1 Three theories of suicide positioned within the ideation –to-action frame work.

Theory	Main factors causing Suicidal ideation	Main factors causing Progression from Ideation to attempts
Interpersonal(Joiner 2005)	Alleged burdensomeness and disillusioned belongingness	Assimilatedaptitude for suicide
Integrated motivational volitional (O"Connor)	Downfall and set-up (aided by threat-to-self And motivational moderators.	Proficiency, impulsivity Arrangement, admittance to means, artificial and Other volitional Moderators,
Three step (Klonsky& May 2015)	Amalgamation of agony and futility especially when agonyoutdoes connectedness	Dispositional, assimilated, And concreteproviders to improvedcapability for Suicide.

It is imperative and basic in both hypothetical and clinical field to comprehend suicide and its hazard and how the movement from ideation to conduct happens. This need was reacted by Klonsky and May (2014) who proposed the ideation-to activity system. In their system the point of view of (an) improvement of suicide ideation and (b) the movement from suicide ideation to suicide endeavors were seen as particular procedures, with unmistakable indicators and clarifications.

The plan of the investigation was the principle ramifications of the system. As in greater part of studies suicide attempters are contrasted and non-suicide attempters accepting all attempters would have had ideations too before submitting endeavors. This empowering indicators of ideation to take on the appearance of indicators of suicide endeavors, asking for future examinations to stop this sort of system in their training, which ought to wind up a standard as opposed to exemption in contrasting attempters with ideators (Klonsky and May 2015, Nock et al. 2008a).

The ideation to activity outline work a customary way to deal with suicide hypothesis has accentuated numerous components which incorporates psychache, escape from aversive self-insights, social segregation (Durkheim, 1897).These speculations are of much help for animating idea, inspiring examination and aiding in propelling the field with a restriction which don't offer a different clarification for the advancement of self-destructive ideation and its movement from ideation to endeavors.

Relational scholar Joiner (2005) proposed clarifications for self-destructive want and for acting towards the longing. It clarified with seen troublesomeness and low belongingness (view of sadness about these) making want/wish for suicide, though the desire to kick the bucket should help in conquering the dread of death and torment in considering suicide endeavor. This hypothesis by Joiner was viewed as the main hypothesis of suicide in the system of ideation to activity.

O'Connor incorporated inspirational volitional hypothesis is the second hypothesis for ideation-to-activity system, in which recommendations viewing annihilation and entanglement viewed as the prime reasons for self-destructive ideations, with gained ability of different components like arranging access to deadly weapon, impulsivity anticipating to clarify the movement from ideation to endeavors.

Table 2 Showing the difference between the (*a*) traditional and (*b*) ideation-to- action approaches to suicide.

(a) Traditionalapproach (b) Ideation –to-actionframework

Risk factors for suicide	**Risk factors for suicidal ideation**	**Risk factors for suicide attempts**
Mental disorders	Mental disorders	Mental disorders(post-traumatic stress Disorder)
Depression	Depression	Access to lethal means
Hopelessness	Hopelessness	Knowledge /comfort with lethal means
Impulsivity	Impulsivity	Impulsivity
Access to lethal means	Non-suicidal self- injury	Non-suicidal self-injury
Knowledge/comfort with lethal Means		
Non-suicidal self-injury		

(a) In conventional methodology suicide chance is considered as unitary build while

(b) In ideation to-activity system indicators of ideation is recognized from indicators of movement from ideation to practices.

The table represents the system of suicide chance factors notwithstanding directing the examination and hypothesis with an end goal to move in the direction of suicide chance appraisal and counteractive action. Which intercession program helps in forestalling and treating the movement of ideation to endeavors ought to be considered.

Ideation to-activity structure recognizes indicators of ideation from indicators of the movement from ideation to practices where factors like misery, despondency and impulsivity were considered as solid associates of ideation yet these factors are the poor distinguishers of attempters from ideations without endeavors (Kessler et al.,1999, Klonsky and May, 2016).Variable access and solace with deadly means and particular impulsivity are recorded in the conduct section shows dependable distinguisher of attempters from ideation who have no previous history of endeavored suicide (Klonsky, 2015). Hardly any factors like post-awful pressure issue and previous history of Non-self-destructive self-damage are the connects of both self-destructive ideation and conduct (Klonsky et al, 2013: Nock et al 2009). The previously mentioned research is predominantly founded on relationship and further research is required to distinguish particular hazard factors for self-destructive ideation and endeavors utilizing imminent structures.

The Three-Step Theory of Suicide

Klonsky& May 2015 as of late built up the three stage hypothesis of suicide to enhance the potential in comprehension and forecast of suicide, self-destructive conduct and self-destructive ideation which uses the ideation-to-activity system, giving a miserly and testable model of suicide. Primary key components of 3ST are torment, misery, connectedness and suicide limit.

Figure 1. The three-step theory (3ST) of suicide

1. Are you in pain and hopeless?

YES NO

Suicidalideation **Noideation**

2. Does your pain exceed yourconnectedness?

YES NO

StrongIdeation **Modest ideation**

3. Do you have the capacity to attemptsuicide?

YES NO

Suicideattempt **Ideation only**

Important key constructs of the 3ST are pain, hopelessness, connectedness and suicide capacity.

Step 1.Development of suicide Ideation

It clarifies that the ideation creates with agony which can be mentally/enthusiastic torment. All practices of individuals are adapted (Skinner, 1953) typically who will participate in such practices which will be remunerated or rebuffed. On the off chance that individual's understanding of living is loaded up with agony, at that point that individual is basically rebuffed for living, which diminishes the motivations to live. The hypothesis require not determine the idea of the torment. Diverse wellsprings of torment can be caused by a noisy clamor, an electric stun, or social rejection (Durkheim, 1987), difficulty and low belongingness (Joiner, 2005), physical affliction and negative self-discernments and different other aversive musings, feelings, sensations and articulation may prompt reduction the craving to live which can have a job in initial step of forming into self-destructive ideation paying little heed to its source.

Anyway torment alone won't be the reason for suicide ideation. Absence of expectation when a man is in agony and sees no enhancement of torment in future may not consider suicide. In this regard sadness is likewise required to create suicide ideation with blend of agony. Some examination discoveries uncovered suicide inspirations discovered suicide endeavors are incited by torment and misery more than whatever other elements which likewise included difficulty, foiled belongingness, want for help to impart and impulsivity whish are recreated in both clinical and in non-clinical youths and grown-up tests (May and Klonsky 2013). In an examination consider by Klonsky (2016) who overviewed two gatherings, one gathering with people who lost somebody and people who made a suicide endeavor requiring hospitalization. A rundown of 42 factors were recognized for suicide chance like sleep problems, tumult, giving without end belonging, family struggle, separation from social exercises outrage and antagonistic vibe, blame or disgrace. The discoveries were corresponded with 3ST. Agony and misery were the two components distinguished among two gatherings that go before suicidal deaths and attempts.3ST accentuates the mix of torment and sadness which achieves self-destructive ideation. It clarifies that somebody with torment however with seek after a superior future will keep on connecting with life, comparatively somebody with sad about future yet without agony won't feel self-destructive.

Step 2. Strong versus Moderate Ideation

The second of 3ST worked with lethal suicidal comportment when agonyoverdoes connectedness.

Here the term connectedness implies association with other individuals, an intrigue, a job, an undertaking, reason or the things/which means which keeps one keen on life. A person who has both torment and sadness and consider suicide will have moderate ideation if connectedness stays more noteworthy than the torment. Be that as it may, ideation ends up solid if torment overpowers connectedness. For instance guardians who encounters day by day agony and misery yet at the same time put resources into life and associated with their youngsters. On the off chance that parent"s connectedness surpasses the torment, the individual may at present have detached ideation yet it may not advance to dynamic want for suicide. Nearness of both torment and connectedness is overshadowed by torment, influences the person to encounter solid ideation and effectively to think about closure his life.

Disturbed connectedness (low belongingness and troublesomeness), is like Joiner's relational hypothesis, however it works contrastingly in the 3ST. Belongingness and difficulty are straightforwardly identified with self-destructive ideation in relational hypothesis, Whereas connectedness assumes a job of assurance in raising self-destructive ideation among people with agony and misery as indicated by the 3ST. In the 3ST hypothesis, upset connectedness isn't seen as a vital segment for creating agony or misery or for the improvement of self-destructive ideation.

From 3ST hypothesis numerous individuals with self-destructive ideation don't have disturbed connectedness, and upset associated people don't create self-destructive ideation. Research by Klonsky and May (2015) bolsters the second step of the 3ST hypothesis where connectedness goes about as a defensive factor against ideation among the individuals who had high torment and in addition sadness which was insignificantly identified with ideation in others. Torment, sadness and connectedness are by all account not the only factors talked about in stage 2 of 3ST hypothesis, different components like gloom, self-feedback, identity characteristics, personalities and encounters are additionally considered very applicable to self-destructive ideation. The 3ST proposes these elements are adding to torment, misery or potentially connectedness.

Step 3. Progression from Ideation to Attempts

Most people with ideation don't make suicide endeavor, in view of this presumption the third step of 3ST tends to the conditions under which solid ideation prompts suicide endeavor. Limit of the individual as indicated by Joiner (2005) turns into the key determinant of suicide endeavor. Solid ideation additionally does not prompt endeavor except if the individual has built up the ability to defeat the solid hindrance which is dread of death, as indicated by Joiner. The 3ST echoes this point and clarifies in two different ways. Joiner's hypothesis underlines obtained ability while the 3ST widens the idea and talks around three classes of factors (a) dispositional, (b) procured and (c) handy which are adding to suicide limit.

Dispositional are the significant variable we are conceived with. For instance people with high and low torment affectability (Young et al 2011).Persons with lower torment limit will have higher limit with respect to suicide endeavor. It was bolstered by Joiner and others proposing the job of hereditary qualities (Smith et al 2012) in the capacity of conveying suicide endeavor. The second giver, habituation to encounters is related with torment, damage and passing can prompt higher limit with respect to an endeavor. The last and third factor is concrete and viable facto like information in regards to deadly weapons could follow up on self-destructive contemplations significantly more effectively a person without the learning of deadly means. This progression is likewise upheld by Klonsky and May, 2015) in their examination where an extensive number of ideators and attempter's dispositional, gained and reasonable supporters of suicide limit were identified with suicide endeavors history controlling past self-destructive and current self-destructive ideation. The discoveries were steady with the 3ST each of the three parts of suicide endeavor whish foresee suicide endeavor well beyond ideation.

Future directions

Ideation-to-activity structure and ideation-to activity hypotheses are promising advancements in giving significant learning and avoiding suicide. Be that as it may, the key learning hole remains, which restricts our capacity to comprehend and lessen suicide, so the attention ought to be on escalated examine in future.

It is anything but difficult to recognize what are the suicide ideation hazard rather which ideators are in danger for endeavors. Demonstrating the job of obscure factors in a person's progress from ideation to endeavor ought to be distinguished and comprehended. The second future point is to gather data in regards to factors that anticipate suicide at longer versus shorter time scale for people with previous history of self-destructive idea and conduct is imperative from clinical hazard appraisal and treatment viewpoint. The third future point is to apply proof based speculations of suicide to hazard appraisal and anticipation. Holes with respect to deadly and non-lethal endeavors of suicide ought to be considered in future research thinks about as it is extremely hard to survey the deadly suicide endeavors where passing is 100%, however just minorities of suicide attempters kick the bucket by suicide in their first endeavor itself. It is imperative to think about the distinctions in clinical introduction, inspiration and other hazard factors for deadly and nonfatal suicide endeavors in future research examines.

Social Theories of Suicide

Durkheim is the organizer of exact research in human science and suicidology, speculated that Suicide rates fluctuate contrarily with the dimension of social combination of individual gatherings in his book suicidology in 1897.Also featured the job of religious incorporation and family conditions. From that point forward numerous social models of self-destructive conduct have included family capacities and social encouraging groups of people,, advancing the social attachment and recognizable proof with estimations of society in improving emotional wellness as a rule and in avoiding suicide specifically. Character the crucial component in teenagers can be accomplished by taking an interest in youth developments, social clubs, sports exercises and national administration.

1.3.5 What causes adolescents to attemptsuicide?:

Puberty is a formative stage where physical, physiological and mental changes will happen separated from parcel of pressure, changes in considerations, disarray, dread and vulnerability and strain to succeed, and needs to be more imaginative and not quite the same as others settle on them poor chiefs and issue solvers. Aside from formative changes in young people, any adjustments in condition like trouble in school/school, loss of friends and family, moving to an alternate network partition of guardians make them agitated and hard to adapt up to these issues. Suicide is by all accounts the answer for few of them to leave the emerged issues throughout their life.

Full of feeling deregulation winds up one more contributory factor for suicide ideation among school going young people (Plattner et al 2007), which is set apart by a failure to control their feelings suitably thusly making them more vulnerable to crabbiness and contrary effect (Mezzich, Tarter, Giancola et al., 2001). Tarter, Reynolds (2004), demonstrated relationship between full of feeling dysregulation and suicide chance.

Family Environment

Family assumes an imperative job in the transmission of suicide endeavors among mental ailment issues in the family independently.(Brent, Perper and Goldstein, 1988).

More number of submitted suicides inside the family was related with parent psychopathology, their age (more youthful than 20yrs), single parent families; family disharmony (Brent et al 1988), Parents not alive and those whose moms were working and poor social help (Keer, Preues and King, 2006). This shows the job of parental help and accessibility of guardians assuming a vital job in guaranteeing the teenagers ability to beat different worries in their lives.

Suicide endeavors aversion ought to be performed in early pre-adulthood and consider sex and family contrast and the job of financial status, school and wellbeing related challenges among juvenile's relatives were related among young people with self-destructive ideation.

Family utilitarian debilitation, negative life occasions demonstrated higher hazard for self-destructive ideation among teenagers (Zhang et al 2014).

Lower view of the association with the guardians, parental relationship, family union and parental control were related for young ladies self-destructive ideation (Franic et al, 2011).The family factors for self-destructive ideation varies for both young men and young ladies. Lower maternal instruction, swarmed families, birth arrange, parental war support, physical battling, being harassed and substance utilize were related for young men.

It is imperative to caution guardians on their duty in childhood and creating of their grown-ups. Young people with relatives ordinarily show suicide endeavors/conduct which high light the significance of considering family ecological elements while surveying suicide chance.

Social Support

Impression of unsupportive condition among youth came about for endeavored suicide hazard contrasted with the individuals who saw their condition as steady. A more steady condition was fundamentally connected with less suicide endeavors (Hatzenbuchler, 2011). Social help and social setting importantly affect self-destructive conduct (Farrell et al, 2015). Impression of higher family support and companion bolster are related with (diminished) bring down suicidality (Matlin et al, 2011).

Farrell (2015) reports in his investigation that parent and school bolster are moderately critical than associate help in understanding self-destructive considerations and history of self-destructive conduct.

The relative's and informal community's help gotten by the self-destructive youths goes about as an asset for treatment. Better working and social help go about as defensive variables (Compton, 2005). Poor social aptitudes, maladjustment, trouble making companions and normal experience of hostility are connected with associate issues which may have negative results on their expert accomplishments.

Slavin and Rainer (1990) examined the help of non-relatives on young people working. Non relatives, for example, instructors, family companions and companion's folks who offered extra social help to young people where young ladies had lesser manifestations of sorrow. Bolster accessible from non-family grown-ups is a promising asset in the treatment of self-destructive youth (King in press). Young ladies lacking social exercises are related with suicide hazard similarly to young men (Peltzer 2008) Perception of expanded companion bolster, instructor support and great individual controlled youths, demonstrated diminished suicidality contrasted with young men (Peltzer, 2008).

Juvenile young ladies will in general report more fulfillment than young men with the help they get (Valery, O'Connor, 1997), measure of time spent on them, offering their sentiments of individual worries to other people (Mohan, Yarcheski & Yarcheski, 1994).

Passionate help is considered as a critical factor for young ladies (Piko 1998).Several of the investigations looked into in such manner are reliably finding the sex contrasts in young men and young ladies view of their associations with others and furthermore between social builds and youthful suicidality.

Social Support and Suicide

The Social help getting from the informal organization and relatives particularly for self-destructive young people goes about as a potential asset of treatment, which likewise goes about as a cradle against stressors. Social help is critical for self-destructive young people who have encountered horrible mishaps and life stretch regularly in their life (De Wilde, Kienhorst, Diekstra, and Wolters, 1992). Self-destructive young people see their families as less drew in, tender and trusting than non-self-destructive teenagers and discouraged youths (Kerr, Preussand, King, 1993).Multiple variables play and affect powerless teenagers, without moderating impacts of a sincerely steady system. Improvement of social help might be focused for mediation for self-destructive young people. Genuine encounter of social encouraging group of people by self-destructive young people is minimal known.

1.3.6 Suicidal ideas:

May seem similarly also in energetic individuals; notwithstanding, secure a neurotic status when they happen with regards to disease, e.g., gloom or long physical sickness.

1) Biological status to act (impulsivity):

This alludes to a neuro-biochemical and hereditary turmoil including lack of caution and conduct control, which shows itself on the neuro-biochemical dimension predominantly in a focal serotonin unsettling influence (Praag, Van., 1986). In specific conditions, this natural preparation to act can likewise be initiating by psychosocial or psycho-dynamical means, anyway additionally by organic, i.e., medicament we mean. For instance, see the exchange on —suicide advancement" caused by antidepressants.

2) Current psycho-responsive activating variables:

In this segment, specific significance is ascribing to the psychoanalytic and inside-mental thought of self-destructive propensity as the indication of a narcissistic emergency (Reimer, 1986) of a critical good example. Misfortune, affront, existential certainty all assumes a crucial job in this involvement.

3) Despair, sadness and powerlessness:

Feelings of lacking prospects for the future and the difficulty of changing this perspective are focal psychopathological marvels that shape the edge between self-destructive thoughts and self-destructive activity (Beck, 1990).

1.3.7 Symptoms: Suicide cautioning signs or self-destructive considerations include:

- Frequent discussion about suicide with — for instance, making articulations, for example, "I will execute myself," "I want to be dead" or "I wish I wasn't conceived"
- Getting the way to take your own life, for example, purchasing a weapon or amassing pills
- Withdrawing from societal contact and needing to be disregarded

- Frequent inclination swings, for example, being candidly high one day and profoundly debilitated the following
- Giving ceaselessly possessions or getting undertakings all together when there's no other consistent clarification for doing this
- Being distracted with sentiments of death, kicking the bucket or viciousness
- Feelings caught or miserable about a circumstance
- Over utilization of liquor or medications
- Changing in their ordinary propensities, including eating or dozing designs
- Doing unsafe or pointless undertakings, for example, utilizing medications or driving rashly
- Saying farewell to individuals as though they won't be seen once more
- Developing identity changes or being extremely on edge or disturbed, especially while encountering a portion of the notice signs recorded previously

Cautioning signs aren't constantly self-evident, and they may change from individual to person. A few people demonstrated their aims clear, while others keep self-destructive contemplations and sentiments mystery.

1.4 Emotional Intelligence:

We as a whole need to be effective. A significant number of us define objectives around getting to be incredible, fruitful pioneers. We are for the most part searching for the means, techniques or potentially recipes that fit us best. The business is loaded up with creators, speakers, mentors and different experts that talk about insider facts to progress. Also the tapes sound and Internet assets accessible. Achievement in the business and the world universally looks to another and changed kind of initiative. Authority that mixes information (IQ) with passionate insight share (EQ).

In 1990, in my job as a science correspondent at The New York Times, Goleman risked upon an article in a little scholarly diary by two therapists, John Mayer, now at the University of New Hampshire, and Yale's Peter Salovey. Mayer and Salovey offered the principal definition of an idea they called "enthusiastic knowledge."

Those were days when the overwhelming nature of IQ as the standard of greatness in life was unchallenged; a discussion seethed about whether it was set in our qualities or because of experience. Be that as it may, here, abruptly, was another state of mind about the elements of life achievement. Goleman was energized by the thought, which he composed on the cover sheet of the book i.e. Enthusiastic Intelligence: why it can matter more than IQ, in 1995. Like Mayer and Salovey, he utilized the expression to integrate an expansive scope of logical discoveries, drawing together what had been isolated strands of research-assessing their hypothesis as well as a wide assortment of other energizing logical improvements, for example, the principal products of the early field of full of feeling neuroscience, which investigates how feelings are directed in the cerebrum.

Goleman had the idea, just before this book was distributed ten years age, that on the off chance that one day he caught a discussion in which two outsiders utilized the expression passionate insight and both comprehended what it implied, he would have prevailing with regards to spreading the idea all the more generally into the way of life. Much to his dismay?

The expression passionate insight, or its easygoing shorthand EQ, has turned out to be omnipresent, appearing in settings as impossible as the animation strips Dilbert and Zippy the Pinhead and in Roz Chast's consecutive workmanship in The New Yorker. He has seen boxes of toys that guarantee to support a tyke's EQ; lovelorn individual advertisements in some cases trumpet it in those looking for forthcoming mates. He once found a jest about EQ imprinted on a cleanser bottle in his lodging room.

What's more, the idea has spread to the furthest corners of earth. EQ has turned into a word remembered, he has told, in dialects as various as German and Portuguese, Chinese, Korean, and Malay. (All things considered, he inclines toward EI as the English shortened form for enthusiastic knowledge). In his email inbox frequently contains questions, from, for instance, a doctoral understudy in Bulgaria, a teacher in Poland, an undergrad in Indonesia, a business in Shanghai. Business understudies in India read about EI and authority; a CEO in Argentina prescribes the book he later composed on the subject. He has likewise gotten notification from religious researchers inside Christianity, Judaism, Islam, Hinduism, and Buddhism that the idea of EI reverberates with standpoints in their own confidence.

Most satisfying for him has been the means by which passionately the idea has been grasped by teachers, as projects in "social and enthusiastic learning or SEL. In 1995 he could discover just a bunch of such projects showing passionate knowledge aptitudes to youngsters. Presently, after 10 years, a huge number of schools overall offer kids SEL. In the United States numerous regions and even whole states right now make SEL educational modules necessity, ordering that similarly as understudies must accomplish a specific dimension of ability in math and dialect, so too should they ace these fundamental aptitudes for living.

In Illinois, for example, particular learning principles in SEL capacities have been set up for each review from kindergarten through the most recent year of secondary school. To give only one case of an astoundingly itemized and far reaching educational modules, in the early rudimentary year's understudies should figure out how to perceive and precisely mark their feelings and how they lead them to act. By the late basic years exercises in sympathy should make kids ready to distinguish the nonverbal pieces of information to how another person feels; in middle school they ought to have the capacity to break down what makes worry for them or what inspires their best execution. What's more, in secondary school the SEL aptitudes incorporate tuning in and talking in manners that settle clashes as opposed to raising them and consulting for win-win arrangements.

Around the globe Singapore has attempted a functioning activity in SEL, as have a few schools in Malaysia, Hong Kong, Japan, and Korea. In Europe, the U.K. has driven the way, however in excess of twelve different nations have schools that grasp EI, as do Australia and New Zealand, and all over nations in Latin America and Africa. In 2002 UNESCO started an overall activity to advance SEL, sending an announcement of ten essential standards for executing SEL to the services of instruction in 140 nations.

In a few states and countries, SEL has turned into the sorting out umbrella under which are accumulated program in character training, savagery counteractive action, antibullying, medicate aversion and school discipline. The objective isn't simply to diminish these issues among school kids however to upgrade the school atmosphere and, at last, understudies' scholastic execution.

In 1995, he plot the primer proof recommending that SEL was the dynamic fixing in projects that upgrade youngsters' learning while at the same time forestalling issues, for example, viciousness. Presently the case can be made logically: helping youngsters enhance their mindfulness and certainty, deal with their aggravating feelings and driving forces, and increment their sympathy satisfies in enhanced conduct as well as in quantifiable scholastic accomplishment.

This is the enormous news contained in an as of late finished meta-examination of 668 assessment investigations of SEL programs for youngsters from preschoolers through secondary school. The monstrous overview was led by Roger Weisberg, who coordinates the community oriented for Academic, social and passionate learning at the University of Illinois at Chicago—the association that has driven the path in bringing SEL into schools around the world.

The information demonstrate that SEL programs yielded a solid advantage in scholastic achievement, as exhibited in accomplishment test results and grade-point midpoints. In taking an interest schools, up to 50 percent of youngsters demonstrated enhanced accomplishment scores and up to 38 percent enhanced their review point midpoints. SEL programs additionally made schools more secure: episodes of rowdiness dropped by a normal of 28 percent; suspensions by 44 percent; and other disciplinary activities by 27 percent. In the meantime, participation rates rose, while 63 percent of understudies showed fundamentally more positive conduct. In the realm of sociology inquire about, these amazing outcomes for any program advancing conduct change, SEL had conveyed on its guarantee.

In 1995 he additionally recommended that a decent piece of the viability of SEL originated from its effect in molding youngsters' creating neural hardware, especially the official elements of the prefrontal cortex, which oversee wording memory—what we hold at the top of the priority list as we learn—and hinder problematic passionate motivations. Presently the main fundamental logical proof for that idea has arrived. Stamp Greenberg of Pennsylvania State University, a co-designer of the PATHS educational modules in SEL, reports not just that the program for primary school understudies flaunts scholastic accomplishment at the same time, considerably more altogether, that a great part of the expanded learning can be credited to upgrades in consideration and working memory, key elements of the prefrontal cortex. This firmly recommends neuroplasticity, the molding of the cerebrum through rehashed understanding, assumes a key job in advantages from SEL.

1.4.1 IQ's shortcoming:

In the event that there is anything near an agreement in the comprehension of insight. It is that the Intelligence Quotient or "IQ" does not completely represent a person's prosperity or disappointment on the planet. Truth be told, most social researchers who think about insight gauge that IQ represents just 20 to 30 percent of result. Regardless of whether, as advocates state, IQ is the "best known indicator" of things like money related achievement, these numbers are not the thoughtful you would need to bet on.

The mission to find what represents whatever is left of our identity and what we do-the rest of the 70 to 80 percent-is presently what drives the field. So we can state that IQ isn't the general indicator of the accomplishment in a person. It requires different elements for the achievement, in different elements passionate knowledge is one of the most compelling motivation in making the progress.

1.4.2 The Birth of Emotional Intelligence:

In 1990, Dr. Peter Salovey of Yale University and Dr. John Mayer of New Hampshire started distributing articles about something they called "enthusiastic knowledge". They tried how well individuals could distinguish feelings in faces, dynamic structures and hues, and from these examinations, they trusted they found a kind of widespread bent of feelings. They inevitably distributed an article in which they delineated what passionate insight was, drawing together under one umbrella a progression of what appeared to be random aptitudes.

It was not until 1995, notwithstanding, when New York Times science essayist Daniel Goleman composed a well known book called Emotional Intelligence: why it can matter more than IQ that the possibility of passionate knowledge got on vigorously. What has occurred since is a change in perspective in American culture, especially in the regions of training and corporate business where Goleman's book—and a subsequent book called working with enthusiastic insight—has shaken up the old request and brought the dug in mid-century methods for educating and business under investigation.

The possibility of passionate insight lies in a bunch of essential standards. Sincerely canny individuals, Goleman says, can marshal their passionate motivations (or, at any rate, more so than the individuals who are not candidly savvy); they have a mindfulness to comprehend what they are feeling, and can consider and express those things; they have compassion for the sentiments of others and knowledge into how others figure; they can do things like defer delight; they are gathering, and, most vital, where they fit inside that gathering.

About Daniel Goleman

Daniel Goleman is a globally known therapist who addresses habitually to proficient gatherings, business groups of onlookers, and on school grounds. Filling in as a science writer, Goleman gave an account of the mind and conduct sciences for The New York Times for a long time. His 1995 book, Emotional Intelligence (Bantam Books) was on The New York Times smash hit rundown for eighteen months; with in excess of 5,000,000 duplicates in print worldwide in 30 dialects, and has been a blockbuster in numerous nations.

His most recent book, Social Intelligence: The New Science of Human Relationships will be distributed on Sept. 26, 2006. Social insight, the relational piece of enthusiastic knowledge, would now be able to be comprehended as far as ongoing discoveries shape neuroscience. Goleman's book depicts the numerous ramifications of this new science, including for selflessness, child rearing, love, wellbeing, learning and authority.

Goleman was a prime supporter of the Collaborative for Academic, Social and Emotional Learning at the Yale college Child Studies Center (now at the University of Illinois at Chicago), with a mission to enable schools to present enthusiastic proficiency courses. One characteristic of the Collaborative - and book's-affect is that a huge number of schools the world over have started to execute such projects.

Goleman's 1998 book, working with Emotional Intelligence (Bantam Books), contends that work environment abilities dependent on enthusiastic knowledge assume an extraordinary job in star execution, and that the two people and organizations will profit by developing these capacities. Goleman's book, Primal administration—figuring out how to lead with Emotional Intelligence (co-created with Richard Boyatzis and Annie Mckee), investigates the urgent job of enthusiastic insight in authority. Goleman is co-administrator of The Consortium for Research on Emotional Intelligence in Organizations, situated in the Graduate School of Applied and Professional Psychology at

Rutgers University, which prescribe bests rehearses for creating passionate knowledge capacities, and to advance thorough research on the commitment of enthusiastic insight to working environment adequacy. Goleman's book Destructive Emotions relates a logical discourse between the Dalai Lama and a gathering of analysts, neuroscientists, and logicians. He is an individual from the governing body of the Mind and Life Institute, which supports and continuous arrangement of such exchanges, and encourages important research.

Goleman has gotten numerous honors for this composition, including a Career Achievement grant for reporting from the American Psychological Association. In acknowledgment of his endeavors to impart the conduct sciences to the general population, he was chosen a Fellow of the American Association for the Advancement of Science.

1.4.3. What is Emotional Intelligence or EQ?:

The term EQ includes the accompanying five qualities and capacities:

1. Self-mindfulness knowing your feelings, perceiving feeling as they happen, and separating between them.
2. Mood administration dealing with emotions so they are significant to the present circumstance and you respond properly.
3. Self-inspiration "getting together" your sentiments and guiding yourself towards an objective, in spite of self-uncertainty, idleness and lack of caution.
4. Empathy-perceiving emotions in others and tuning into their verbal and nonverbal signs.
5. Managing relationship-taking care of relational association, compromise and transactions.

These five attributes or areas of passionate knowledge are the indicator of the enthusiastic insight remainder or EQ.

1.4.4. What does it mean to be Emotional Intelligence?:

In Emotional Intelligence, Daniel Goleman recounts the account of an examination done at AT&T's Bell Labs, a New Jersey-based research organization brimming with specialists who were all extremely effective at school and who all scored very on IQ tests. In the investigation, supervisors and associates named the best 10 to 15 percent who emerged as extraordinary, at that point the explores looked into the records of those individuals, watched them working, talked with them—all to perceive what it was that could isolate them from such hardened rivalry.

What they found was that the stars will probably include effectively assembled systems inside the lab which they could depend on when they required it to. They were the unrivaled coordinated efforts, the most famous Emotional Intelligence in a major manner is tied in with being socially proficient, even modern at work or at play. "Well known and enchanting," composes Goleman, "are terms we use for individuals whom we jump at the chance to be with on the grounds that their enthusiastic aptitudes make us feel better".

These well-known and beguiling individuals, EI defenders would contend, have a more unobtrusive power over their passionate mind, despite the fact that "control" may be a deceptive word. Basically, their minds are more averse to end up commanded by passionate driving forces. Also, however the issue is confused, it isn't generally their will the isolates them; more than likely, it is in some extensive part nature they have been presented to, the sorts of individuals, the circumstance, their childhood. EI advertisers in no way, shape or form attest that passionate knowledge is a totally learned marvel, or that it is autonomous from heredity. Based, however, on what we are aware of the manner in which the mind creates in the initial two decades, it appears that somehow or another the neurological wiring to have the capacity to peruse the feelings of others isn't so unique in relation to the wiring that controls your fingers and arms as you play violin: the neural pathways that last are the ones we utilize, the ones we have to get on the planet.

1.4.5. Meanings of Emotional Intelligence:

As indicated by Daniel Goleman (1995). "The limit with regards to perceiving our very own sentiments and those of others, for spurring our-selves, and for overseeing feelings well in our-selves and in our connections."

As indicated by Daniel Goleman (1995). "Passionate Intelligence is an ace fitness, a limit that significantly influences every single other capacity."

As indicated by John D. Mayer and Peter Salovey (1995); "Passionate Intelligence might be characterized as the ability to prevail upon feeling in four zones: to see feeling, to incorporate it in thought, to comprehend it and to oversee it."

As per the perspectives of YettaLautenschlanger (1997); To be candidly insight, I present that you should wind up capable in the four regions of enthusiastic knowledge i.e. Mindfulness, Acceptance, Attitude and Action. Mindfulness implies recognizing what you are feeling when you are feeling it. Acknowledgment implies trusting that feelings are a natural procedure occurring in the body and the cerebrum and that isn't constantly sane. It implies having the capacity to feel a feeling without making a decision about it. Dispositions are convictions that are appended to feelings. These are times when the feeling pursues the state of mind, or is hued by a demeanor. Except if the state of mind is tested, the feeling will keep on being felt a similar way. Activity is the conduct you take dependent on feeling and disposition.

As indicated by definition given by Mayer and Salovey (1995), all of us might be found to have fluctuating limits and capacities as to one's managing feelings. Contingent on the idea of this capacity, he or she might be said all the more candidly keen or lesser, in a correlation with others in the gatherings.

In view of these, we may comprehend one's enthusiastic insight as a unitary capacity (identified with, however free of standard knowledge) accommodating in knowing, sentiments and making a decision about feelings in close participation with one's reasoning procedure to act appropriately, for a definitive acknowledge of the satisfaction and welfare of oneself tuned in to other people.

1.4.6. For what reason do we require Emotional Intelligence?:

Research in cerebrum based learning recommends that enthusiastic wellbeing is basic to successful learning. As indicated by a report from the National Center for Clinical Infant Programs, the most basic component for an understudy's accomplishment in school is a comprehension of how to gain from "Passionate Intelligence" by Daniel Goleman. The key elements for this comprehension are:

- Confidence
- Curiosity

- Intentionality
- Self-control
- Relatedness
- Capacity to impart
- Ability to participate

These attributes are for the most part parts of Emotional Intelligence. Qualities that is enter in close to home and expert improvement and getting to be fruitful. Fundamentally, an understudy who figures out how to learn is considerably more well-suited to succeed. Enthusiastic Intelligence has demonstrated a superior indicator of future accomplishment than conventional strategies like the GPA, IQ, and state administered test scores.

As of late, the incredible enthusiasm for Emotional Intelligence with respect to companies, colleges, and schools across the nation. The possibility of Emotional Intelligence has enlivened research and educational modules advancement all through these offices to enhance instructive educational modules and consolidate these standards in learning for understudies. He turned out to be extremely inspired by Goleman's work in 2000, alongside crafted by Howard Gardner and his Theory of "Different Intelligence" as a device for giving achievement.

Building one's Emotional Intelligence has a long lasting effect. Numerous guardians and instructors, frightened by expanding dimensions of contention in youthful school youngsters—from low confidence to early medication and liquor use to misery, are surging t show understudies the aptitudes vital for Emotional Intelligence. Also, in companies, the consideration of Emotional Intelligence in preparing programs has helped utilizes participate better and rouse more, in this way expanding profitability and benefits, Researchers have inferred that individuals who deal with their own sentiments well and arrangement viably with others will probably live substance lives. Also, upbeat individuals are more able to hold data and do as such more successfully than unsatisfied individuals.

As should be obvious EQ is in excess of a grin and an empowering word, it's an arrangement of capacities that recognize star entertainers from normal pioneers, the nonattendance of which wrecks vocations. As expressed by Daniel Goleman in his book Emotional Intelligence and Primal Leadership, and The Center of Creative Leadership. Fortunately dissimilar to IQ, your enthusiastic knowledge, or EQ, can be created.

1.4.7 Emotional Intelligence's deficiencies:

Goleman contends that encouraging passionate insight is for the last time the response to the issues that afflict us-from secondary acts of mass violence to conjugal issues and uncommunicative sweethearts. It represents, Goleman demands, an extraordinary larger part of what IQ does not. In any case, at last, one needs to ask: how not the same as IQ is passionate insight. Despite the fact that Goleman never utilizes the condensing in his book, EQ (short for enthusiastic remainder) has unavoidably sprung up and discovered its way into a few book titles in the short a long time since Emotional Intelligence was first distributed. Goleman himself has composed two "informal" EQ tests, one for USA Today, the other for UTNE Reader, with inquiries like: "you are endeavoring to quiet down a companion who has worked himself up into a fierceness at a driver in another vehicle who has cut perilously close before him. What do you do?" The different decision answers that pursue incorporate potential outcomes like "Instruct him to overlook he's alright now and it's no major ordeal." Or "Go along with him in putting down the other driver, as a show of compatibility. "It appears to be inescapable, in light of the historical backdrop of insight testing, that the idea of passionate knowledge will in the long run be lessened to a number and used to track youngsters or vilify them. It surely matters little when critical researchers and savvy people—including Alfred Binet, the man credited with making the insight test-took a stand in opposition to such utilization of the early tests.

1.4.8. Critics of Emotional Intelligence:

A portion of the scientists undoubtedly caution against the risks of treating enthusiastic knowledge like a panacea. Harvard analyst Jerome Kagan, whose youngster-advancement examine Goleman uses to discuss the idea of modest and gregarious children, cautions that passionate insight has indistinguishable vulnerable sides from IQ and a few people "handle outrage well, however can't deal with dread. A few people can't take bliss. "A shrewd methodology, Kagan clarifies, is look at feelings in an unexpected way, and to not envelop them in one slick bundle of passionate knowledge. Another feedback of passionate knowledge is that it presumes a right reaction to specific circumstances, when in truth an assortment of enthusiastic reactions are substantial. In a 1995 Time Article, Dr. Paul McHugh, executive of psychiatry at Johns Hopkins University School of Medicine, lashed out at showing enthusiastic insight, which he sees as a poor endeavor to reevaluate the experience gathering. "The creator is assuming that somebody has the way to the correct feelings to be instructed to youngsters," he says. "We don't realize the correct feelings to be educated to grown-ups. Do you truly think a tyke or eight or nine truly comprehends the distinction among forcefulness and emphaticness?" surely appears to have gone along at the correct time. Goleman alludes in his book to the 1989 slaughter at a grade school in Stockton, California, as by one way or another the apex of what can turn out badly with a general public not in contact with its feelings. As we as a whole; know now, this apparently segregated occasion was only the introduction to a long and grisly series of shootings that have happened since 1995, when the book was distributed, all of which appear to help different thoughts in enthusiastic knowledge, that regardless of whether there isn't one appropriate reaction to feelings like tension, blame or outrage, there are positively improper reactions. What's more, looking at it with regards to the long history of insight think about, passionate knowledge—like the models displayed by Gardner and Sternberg—while not a correct science (or even much want to be), appears to exhibit the model of a more dimension playing field, and maybe a more complex perspective of insightfulness. In the event that passionate insight isn't appropriated so far another device of rejection and that threat positively lingers it might just improve the world a place, and that is not something numerous individuals would tragically say about the knowledge test.

1.4.9. Areas of Emotional Intelligence:

What are the fixings that make up predominant entertainers' in our associations? Must they be savvy? Know their stuff? Have steady drive? Be agreeable? Late research demonstrates dark issue and specialized/work learning are nevertheless limit skills. What separate the "stars" are the individual characteristics, the purported "delicate aptitudes." It gives the idea that Antoine de St. Exupery maybe took care of business in The Little Prince when he stated, "What is fundamental is imperceptible to the eye."

The main two reasons supervisors are "crashed" in their vocations, as per the Center for Creative Leadership, are

1. Inability/reluctance to adjust and
2. Failure to build up and keep up community oriented working connections.

Goleman's theory is that somewhere close to 75% to 90% of powerful execution, especially on account of directors and pioneers, is inferable from "passionate knowledge" (EI). What is EI? He characterizes it as, "the limit with regards to perceiving our very own sentiments and those of others, for rousing ourselves, and for overseeing feelings well in ourselves and in our relationship." He dedicates 66% of the book to spreading out in detail 25 capabilities, assembled into five spaces, the initial three reflecting how we oversee ourselves and the last two how we handle our associations with others. These spaces are:-

1. Self-Awareness

   A capacity to see what you are feeling at the time and to take advantage of your natural self as you manage the every day choices and difficulties of hierarchical life. It incorporates practicing a fearless, authentic receptiveness to input about your qualities, your vulnerable sides and where you have to develop.

2. Self-Regulation

   Dealing with your more profound feelings and driving forces properly, as opposed to liberally (know any individual who permits himself/herself to "become violently unhinged" and lash out at others?). It incorporates situating these emotions against the more extensive point of view of your more extended term objectives and the interests of others and the association on the loose. "stretch strong" people are the individuals who have aced the capacity to remain centered and productively empowered in the midst of pressure. This area is additionally about being dependable ("strolling your discussion") and permitting space in your reality for equivocalness and for the (regularly extraordinary) thoughts of others.

3. Motivation

   A mix of an inside created drive to accomplish, an enthusiastic duty (regularly called enthusiasm) to objectives (both your very own and the associations'), an ability to assemble yourself as well as other people to activity, at the same time putting an idealistic "turn" on difficulties and misfortunes you confront.

4. Empathy

This is a flat out key to setting up working connections. It expands on the initial two spaces. You can't check out others in the event that you are distracted by your very own upsetting emotions. Sympathy implies having a certifiable enthusiasm for, and affectability to, the points of view, concerns and needs of others. In organizations, it incorporates an administration introduction to the client and also a solid attunement to the predominant authoritative governmental issues.

5. Social aptitudes

Affecting others is an essential to your prosperity. To impact, you manage the enthusiastic condition of others. With people, you manufacture affinity, impart resolve contradiction, and motivate them towards your vision and thoughts. With gatherings and groups, you organize (it's an action word presently), work together, make a feeling of the group's character, and encourage the cooperative energy from the quest for aggregate objectives.

Goleman trusts the majority of the enthusiastic abilities can be created. This is done, he says, by supplanting old, instilled propensities for thought, sentiments and conduct with new propensities. You do it by rehearsing the new propensities, after some time connecting new neural pathways in your mind as you introduce your new, more fitting default reactions. He plots a 14-point process for doing this to reinforce your association's "safe framework" that keeps it solid, flexible and ready to exploit openings that develop.

The creator puts forth a solid defense for the high use picked up by concentrating on the delicate aptitudes that support and drive "hard" business and hierarchical outcomes. He attracts our thoughtfulness regarding the significance of what he calls the "imperceptible relational economy" that exists in associations. Your high performing pioneers and individual supporters are the individuals who comprehend and work adequately with the "money" of this parallel economy—the feelings that are connected to the necessities, expectations and fears of all who work in your association.

All in all, what does this book mean for directors? I trust Daniel Goleman has taken advantage of some basic certainties about human execution in associations. He has spread out the guide. We have to center the speculation of our kin improvement dollars in these enthusiastic capabilities that so regularly get just lip benefit in business today.

This requires confidence: the arrival on speculation requires significant investment. Why? Since a significant number of our old propensities are all around settled in, frequently since youth. A significant number of these skills are established somewhere down as a part of our identity. However, we realize they hold the way to singular execution and adequacy. What Daniel Goleman has done is draw us one stage nearer to that question we should in the long run answer in administration preparing: Can we, indeed, create solid entertainers without tending to the human cognizance itself?

1.4.10Emotional Intelligence in schools:

School as living organism

There is presently an inclination to consider schools as natural wholes that develop and create, and inside which every one of the performers, their activities and their insight are interrelated and cooperate with the encompassing condition, this natural allegory for organizations is taken up by the individuals who look to expand the effectiveness of schools as spots of learning. In addition to other things, in illustration a parallel with the working of living beings, they push inside correspondence and specifically the effect of day by day transactions between the performing artists concerning ways and methods for running the school. They contend that just a far more noteworthy joint effort between every one of the on-screen characters can prompt genuine enhancement of school exhibitions. They additionally observe the school as a place where students can master something of their future social conduct from these trades. However they hold back before indicating the requirement for a more efficient way to deal with specific aptitudes identified with understanding feelings in oneself and in one's associations with others.

The fundamental exercises of the present schools

The hidden exercises of the current instructive worldview have little to do with the particular substance of training, yet rather are firmly identified with teaching market rationale and re-implementing the attendant drive to expanded independence. They show

- Attributing quantitative qualities to subjective marvels allows us call it putting a cost on execution. You will perceive the every inescapable stamp framework which quickly turns into the prevailing objective of students;
- Encouraging singular rivalry as opposed to amass cooperation and solidarity;
- Making trust that learning is a rare ware, that takes puts just in given spots at particular occasions, with pre-characterized subjects and with the assistance of specialists.
- Emphasizing objectivity and rationale while dismissing feelings and connections.

Learning in schools is a dynamic, arranged movement cast in the light of the solidly held conviction that youngsters are not the same as grown-ups and that they should be set up for the grown-up world in the meantime as they should be shielded from it. This origination of learning and the simple thought of youth are ongoing innovations. There are motivations to trust that, with the approach of an electronically organized society, the reasonable qualification among youth and adulthood is vanishing. One thing is sure, regardless of whether it is by means of the media or specifically in their lives, kids are progressively exposed to the entire scope of feelings known to grown-ups, also a wide assortment of connections spreading from the best to the most noticeably awful.

1.4.11 Significance and importance of thinking about one's Emotional Intelligence:

The thinking about one's enthusiastic insight as far as his passionate knowledge remainder has more extensive instructive and social ramifications for the welfare of the individual and the general public. This reality has now been perceived and given useful shape and suggestions all-round the globe. The credit of giving due exposure and familiarizing the total populace with the significance and criticalness of enthusiastic knowledge goes to the well-known American clinician Dr. Daniel Goleman through his smash hits like Emotional Intelligence—why it can matter more than I.Q. what's more, working with passionate insight, and so forth. He has conveyed to the bleeding edge the accompanying focuses with respect to the significance of passionate knowledge and its measure through his compositions.

- Emotional knowledge is as incredible, and on occasion more groundbreaking than IQ. While IQ contributes just about 20% to achievement throughout everyday life, the other contribute the rest. We can construe that passionate insight, fortunes and social class are among those different variables.

- Unlike IQ, enthusiastic knowledge might be the best indicator of accomplishment throughout everyday life.

Candidly clever individuals will probably prevail with regards to all that they embrace in their lives.

- Unlike what is guaranteed about IQ, we can instruct and enhance in youngsters and any individual some critical passionate skills preparing for expanding their enthusiastic knowledge and therefore making their lives more advantageous, more agreeable and fruitful in the coming days.

- The idea of passionate knowledge is to be cheered, not on the grounds that it is absolutely new but rather in light of the fact that it catches on one convincing term the quintessence of what our youngsters or we all need to know for being beneficial and upbeat.

- IQ and even Standard Achievement Test (SAT) scores don't anticipate will's identity effective throughout everyday life. Indeed, even school achievement can be anticipated more by enthusiastic and social measures (e.g. acting naturally guaranteed and intrigued, following headings, swinging to instructors for help and communicating needs while coexisting with different partners) than by scholastic capacity.

- One's enthusiastic insight encourages him much in every one of the circles of fife through its different constituents or segments to be specific learning of one's feelings (mindfulness), dealing with the feelings, inspiring oneself, perceiving feelings in others (sympathy) and taking care of connections. The accomplishment of the final products as far as better treatment of shared connections is very fundamental and huge in one's life. It must be conceivable through one's capability of passionate insight and its legitimate improvement.

The perspectives and thoughts spread by Daniel Goleman have gotten an upset the field of youngster minding, home, school and work put administration. It has likewise given adequate help to the direction and guiding administrations including physical and emotional wellness programs. Despite the fact that these may appear a bit misrepresentation in the tall case that passionate insight is a certain certification for unfit favorable position throughout everyday life, yet there is no preventing from securing the way that one's enthusiastic make-up checks significantly towards one's capacity to bargain effectively with other individuals and with one's own sentiments. Since these characteristics include fundamentally towards one's prosperity one's territory of accomplishment, it might assist one with stepping in for the required achievement. A large portion of the issues throughout our life whether adolescence or immature issues, home and family issues, work circumstance issues or political, territorial or worldwide issues are the consequence of the misusing of the included suppositions, sentiments and feelings of the people concerned, gathering of people, society and the countries. On the off chance that appropriate instruction, openings and endeavors are made for the preparation of feelings and advancement of legitimate enthusiastic knowledge potential among the general population ideal from their adolescence, at that point it will without a doubt help in bringing shared passionate comprehension, sympathy went with right activities and conduct with respect to the people and gatherings for having a superior existence with harmony and collaboration.

To advance and given others a chance to advance and to live and given others a chance to live are in this manner a definitive objectives of any instruction or preparing accommodated building up one's capability of passionate insight. Give us now a chance to view such measures as embraced for the welfare of the adolescents and candidly influenced people.

1.4.12 How to help in the proper development of Emotional Intelligence?:

The accompanying measures may demonstrate accommodating toward this path:

- Try to encourage yourself and the adolescents build up the capacity to effectively see emotions both in one and others.
- Try to surrender the second thoughts and misperception of the emotions in others. It prompts an antagonistic attribution predisposition. Keep in mind that adoration

dependably brings forth love, while doubt, heartedness and hostilities are remunerated in like manner.

- In all circumstances, mindfulness of the sentiments and feelings is generally critical. Attempt to show the kids and grab realize what you are feeling when you are feeling it at a specific time.
- For understanding others and their sentiments, build up the characteristics of a decent audience.
- People who have a high EQ (enthusiastic remainder) additionally have a high score on compassion and sympathy comes through successful tuning in.
- Try to get rid of the wrong idea that musing is most suitable when not blurred by feelings. Endeavor to take in the joining of contemplations and feelings, heart and brain for the suitable conduct at the correct time. Thusly, don't attempt to smother feelings (as each inclination has its esteem and centrality) yet to strike a harmony between normal considerations and feelings.
- Teach the kids and yourself that all feelings are solid (since feelings are what join the heart, mind and the body). Outrage, fear, misery, the purported negative feelings are as sound as harmony, boldness and euphoria. The imperative thing is to take in the craft of communicating one's sentiments or feelings attractively at an alluring time in an alluring sum. In this association, have this comment of the Great Greek Philosopher Aristotle as a rule.

"Anybody can wind up irate—that is simple. In any case, to be furious with the ideal individual, to the correct degree, at the opportune time, for the correct reason, and in the correct way—that isn't simple."

- Try to practice and show the youngsters the craft of dealing with the sentiments and feelings as sufficiently as could reasonably be expected. This is particularly essential for the troubling feelings of dread, torment, outrage and so on.
- Don't enable the feelings and sentiments to create as obstruction and hindrances in your way. Utilize them us a propelling specialist or power for accomplishing your objective.
- Teach yourself and your kids the exercises of sympathy, i.e. building up a feeling of what another person is feeling.

- Have measures for the best possible improvement of social abilities for better correspondence and relational association with others. Try not to break the correspondence channel and express your sentiments with an equivalent feeling of visiting and tuning in to other's affections for the better administration of relationship.
- Try to give additional time and endeavors to creating intellectual expert abilities as well as full of feeling aptitudes for the advancement of enthusiastic knowledge.
- Last yet not the minimum is to give you as a model or sidekick for keeping up legitimate enthusiastic bonds. On the off chance that you have created yourself as a candidly canny individual, you may move or lead others to wind up so. In any case, it isn't basic to be impeccable or finish for directing others as guardians, instructors or supervisors. One simply needs to perceive what others require, and be there for addressing their necessities.

1.5 Organization of the report:

Analyst has isolated this investigation report in three guideline zones:

In any case is preliminary region. This zone include with cover sheet, duty, hypothetical, confirmation, declaration, certification, record, summary of table and once-over of figure.

Second fragment is essential collection of research report. This region has been coded in all around five segments. The beginning area joins Concept of Mental wellbeing, Suicidal Tendency and Emotional Intelligence. This part moreover oversees centrality of the survey. The section two is review of the open composition on thriving; work satisfaction and word related stress of teacher and related other calling. The systems used, decree of the issue, focus of the survey, theory, factors, test for the audit, information about gadgets and Statistical methodology are inspected to a limited extent three. The results got are presented and discussed to a limited extent four. The fifth area joins the completions of the audit, and furthermore the recommendations for future research and practice.

Third portion is named as references; it includes with addendums and references of related present research report.

Chapter - 2
Review of Related Literature

Chapter 2
Review of Related Literature

2.1. **Introduction**

2.2. **Studies Related to Mental Health**

2.3. **Studies Related to Suicidal Tendency**

2.4. **Studies Related to Emotional Intelligence**

2.1 Introduction:

The essential point of the investigation was to look at the psychological wellness, self-destructive inclination and enthusiastic insight among higher auxiliary school understudies with various social culture factors. Research in the past has differed recognition on the pretended by family, peers and numerous different components and social encouraging group of people on self-destructive propensity of youths. Audit of writing gives an introduction towards alternate points of view of psychological wellness, self-destructive propensity and enthusiastic insight of higher auxiliary school understudies with various socio social components; helping in the basic role of satisfying the past goals of the examination. To encourage better comprehension of elements which are influencing psychological well-being, self-destructive propensity and passionate insight of high optional school scholars.

2.2 Studies related to Mental Health:

Positive emotions about self amid advancement have been contended to advance mental prosperity and solidness (Harter, 1990). The significance of self-upgrade has been contemplated; it advances emotional wellness and mental wellbeing (Cowen, 1994). Positive confidence has been related with mental prosperity (Osborne, 1996).

Families were more powerful in emotional well-being area and familial connections had a critical impact in helping the juvenile to have positive psychological wellness (Cook et al., 2002). It is assessed that 1 percent of youngsters and juvenile endure from over the top enthusiastic turmoil and a further 1 percent of youths endure from dietary problems (Kurtz et al., 1996).

Among youngsters' issues, for example, suicide, lead issue, liquor and medication misuse, sadness, and a lack of ability to concentrate consistently scatter, are for the most part ending up more typical, and there are expanding dimensions of maltreatment and disregard (Rutter and Smith, 1995; Zubrick, 1998; Zubrick et al., 2000). Moreover, mental scatters (quite wretchedness) are showing up at a more youthful age and they additionally appear to increment in seriousness (Zubrick, 1998; Zubrick et al., 2000).

Kids or youngsters with emotional wellness issues will probably report feeling exceptionally focused, have poor or reasonable physical wellbeing, perform underneath grade level at school, or utilize liquor or different medications, and consider executing themselves (Zubrick et al., 1997).

There is expanding proof that numerous psychological well-being issues that happen in youth proceed into grown-up life, conveying with them an expanded danger of grown-up emotional well-being issue, demise, wrongdoing, wrongdoing, joblessness and vagrancy (Rutter, 1990; Zubrick et al., 2000). At the point when these individuals progressed toward becoming guardians themselves, they are at higher danger of being notable give a steady and secure condition for their own kids, so their issues will stream on to the people to come (Quinton and Rutter, 1988; Ijzendoom et al., 1995).

Formative scholars have noticed that cozy associate "coteries" is vital for immature socio passionate development (Youniss and Haynie, 1992). Prohibition and disconnection would thus be able to be injurious (Windle et al., 1991). Parental help is likewise thought to be defensive against youthful issue conduct, in view of parent-child connection or parental socialization (Barrera et al., 1993).

Social help would subsequently be defensive to the degree that it could help reinforce a person's self-esteem. Both companion and parental help seem to add to young people's general mental prosperity, with parental help being to some degree more successful (Wills, 1990; Bemdt, 1992).

Research demonstrates that teenagers who are in danger are the individuals who have high family shakiness, for example, an abnormal state of contention among companions and their youths; low financial status; absence of chapel participation; absence of fitting parental administration of the immature; absence of social associations with associates; and low evaluations (Ek and Steelman, 1988).

Youngsters seem to invest the lion's share of their energy with relatives, regularly in the family compound, however young men are commonly more liberated to invest time with associates from home as they get more seasoned (Schlegel and Barry, 1991; Verma and

Saraswathi, 1992; Whiting and Edwards, 1998). Normally, additional time is spent within the sight of moms than dads.

The one speculation that can be made is that in these populaces, and also in educated populace, young men will in general invest more energy with associates than do young ladies, a distinction identified with young men regularly being less intently observed than young ladies, having more noteworthy opportunity of development, and investing additional time away shape home (Newson and Newson, 1976).

Sam (1999) found in an example of 200 hundred juvenile young ladies from urban territory that emotional wellness was connected with sex segregation and young ladies endured distress, which was mental in nature. Sinha and Singh (1998) discovered that parental fondness was fundamentally connected with home modification of the young people.

Basumalik and Bhattacharya (1980) discovered that prominent data in emotional well-being territory was very much solidified. No huge culturally diverse contrasts were found among Indian and American subjects with the exception of that the two specialists and laymen laid more accentuation on the earnestness of psychological well-being issues.

Mangotra (1982) seen that the psychological well-being of young men and young ladies seemed, by all accounts, to be impressively affected by the two factors to be specific knowledge and physical wellbeing. The emotional well-being of young men was ruled by the sentiments of sadness and masochist conduct, then again young ladies were observed to experience the ill effects of a feeling of weakness and nervousness.

Mohebali (1982) examined the socio-mental relates of emotional well-being. The motivation behind the investigation was to decide the effect of social contrasts, age hole, sex and emotional wellness. Further examinations were made among Indian and Iranian kids concerning emotional wellness, esteem introduction and disappointment modes. It was discovered that the most extreme abdication dissatisfaction was found in Indians, though greatest relapse was found in Iranians. Females would in general be forceful, though guys were backward and designative. The declaration of disappointment in animosity prompted balance mental status whereas that in the relapse brought about neuroticism. Young people of India and Iran both had more hostility dissatisfaction in correlation with their grown-up partners. Indian females had transcendently more hostility whereas Iranian females had relapse.

Dhoundial (1984) did an investigation on the example of 276 candidly exasperates immature young men to investigate the impacts of components like home condition and social condition. The subjects were recognized from country and urban territories of Almora area by utilizing Emotional Disturbance Inventory. He exposed a huge actuality that kids who take an interest in school wellbeing, sports or amusement programs showed lesser recurrence in event of enthusiastic unsettling influence spells.

Prassana (1984) discovered that all the psychological well-being factors segregated among high and low achievers. In the majority of the gatherings high achievers had high mean scores than low achievers for all the 16 emotional wellness factors thinks about.

Kumar, Pathak and Thakur (1985) investigated varieties in psychological wellness of individual competitors, group competitors and non competitors. These gatherings were coordinated on age and financial status. Examination yielded fundamentally poor psychological wellness for non-competitors than the group competitors and individual competitors.

Aldwin and Revenson (1987) directed a longitudinal network study of 291 grown-ups to investigate the connection between adapting techniques and mental manifestations. Respondents finished the overhauled Ways of Coping Scale (Lazarus and Folkman, 1984) for a self named upsetting scene. Factor examination delivered eight adapting factors: three issue engaged, four feeling centered, and one help assembly that contained components of both. Various relapse investigations shown bidirectionality in the connection among adapting and mental side effects. Those in poorer psychological well-being and under more noteworthy pressure utilized less versatile adapting methodologies, for example, idealism, however adapting endeavors still influenced emotional wellness autonomous of earlier manifestation levels and level of pressure. They thought about primary versus intelligent impacts models of pressure buffering. Principle impacts were restricted fundamentally to the feeling centered adapting scales and demonstrated close to nothing or negative effects of adapting on emotional well-being; intuitive impacts, however little, were found with the issue centered scales. The course of the connection between issue centered deals and indications may depend partially on seen adequacy, or how the respondent idea he or she dealt with the issue. Suggestions for the estimation of versatile methods for dealing with stress and their logical suitability are examined.

Singh and Madhu (1988) led an investigation on twenty male subjects in age amass 18-20 years to examine the effect of yogic activities on emotional wellness factors. They utilized the accompanying instruments: (I) Cattle's Anxiety Questionnaire, (ii) Tiwari and Singh's Security and Insecurity Inventory, (iii) Hand Steadiness Apparatus, and (iv) Trigram's Short-Term Memory Test. The analysis was led for a half year. They found that because of yogic practices, here and now memory and hand unfaltering quality had enhanced and a reduction in tension dimension and in sentiments of weakness was additionally watched. Along these lines, a beneficial outcome of yoga was accounted for on the previously mentioned factors of their investigation.

Ware and Sherbourne (1992) built a 36 things short-shape (SF-36) to review wellbeing status in the Medical Outcomes Study. The SF-36 was intended for use in clinical practice and research, wellbeing approach assessments, and all inclusive community overviews. The SF-36 incorporates one multi-thing scale that surveys eight wellbeing ideas: 1) restrictions in physical exercises as a result of medical issues; (2) impediments in social exercises in view of physical or passionate issues; (3) constraints in common job exercises due to physical medical issues; (4) substantial agony; (5) general psychological wellness (mental trouble and prosperity); (6) confinements in normal job exercises due to enthusiastic issues; (7) legitimacy (vitality and weakness); and (8) general wellbeing recognitions. The study was built for self-organization by people 14 years old and more seasoned, and for organization by a prepared questioner face to face or by phone.

Zahner et al (1992) directed a cross sectional overview to survey youngsters' psychological wellness benefit needs and use designs for a state arranging exertion, which included example of 822 kids matured 6 to 11 of a metropolitan focus. At the point when reports of guardians and educators were joined, 38.5% of kids were screened to be in danger of mental aggravation. Just 11% of youngsters in danger gotten treatment in Mental Health settings, less than in schools (37%) or medicinal setting (13%). The discoveries represent the significance of interagency joint effort and the need to think about reports of guardians and instructors and diverse elements of psychopathology in future arranging and research.

Dalgard et al (1995) directed an investigation on psychological well-being in which in a 10-year follow-up of an overview from Oslo, 503 people were reinter seen utilizing a similar poll. The poll incorporates data about social help, locus of control and emotional wellness and additionally negative life occasions and dependable mental strain amid the year preceding the development. The investigation affirmed the "cushion theory", that social help secures against the advancement of mental issue just when the individual is presented to stressors, similar to negative life occasions. This buffering impact was particularly solid for gloom. The buffering impact just applies to the 'facades' - the individuals who have identity - related sentiments of feebleness and absence of command over their very own lives. The internals don't have a similar requirement for social help to adapt to life stressors, and have low indication scores notwithstanding when negative life occasions are joined with relative feeble social help.

Kawachi and Berkman (2001) have called attention to that it is by and large concurred that social ties assume an advantageous job in the support of mental prosperity. In this focused on audit, they feature four arrangements of bits of knowledge that rise up out of the writing on social ties and emotional wellness results (characterized as pressure responses, mental prosperity and mental misery, including burdensome manifestations and tension). In the first place, the pathways by which informal organizations and social backings impact psychological wellness can be depicted by two option (despite the fact that not fundamentally unrelated) easygoing models - the principle impact display and the pressure buffering model. Second, the defensive impacts of social ties on emotional well-being are not uniform crosswise over gatherings in the public eye. Sexual orientation contrasts in help got from interpersonal organization support may mostly represent the higher commonness of mental misery among ladies contrasted with men. Social associations may incomprehensibly expand dimensions of dysfunctional behavior side effects among ladies with low assets, particularly if such associations involve job strain related with commitments to give social help to other people. Third, egocentric system are settled inside a more extensive structure of social connections. The thought of social capital grasps the embeddedness of individual social ties inside the more extensive social structure. Fourth, regardless of a few victories detailed in social help intercessions to improve psychological wellness, further work is expected to develop our comprehension of the structure, timing, and portion of mediations that work, and in addition the attributes of people who advantage the most.

Sharma (2005) did an investigation to discover the impacts of physical movement program on the emotional well-being of extraordinary youngsters. He controlled particularly structured physical action program to the unique youngsters and assessed its consequences for their psychological wellness by overseeing the Mental Health Battery (Singh and Gupta, 2000). The outcomes showed critical enhancement in the psychological wellness of the unique youngsters who had experienced the physical action program when contrasted with the control gather which was not exposed to the physical action program.

2.3 Studies related to Suicidal Tendency:

Thakur et al (2015) examined the pervasiveness rate and indicators of self-destructive ideations among school going teenagers in a sloping district of Shimla (Himachal Pradesh), in India. Poll technique was utilized to gather information from 218 senior auxiliary school going understudies. Discoveries demonstrate 30.9% of understudies had self-destructive ideation. Talking about issues with guardians, having great relations with teachers and accommodating schoolmates brought down self-destructive thoughts. Youths with stressing issues in family, verbally/physically manhandled and self-perception cognizant had expanded self-destructive ideation among teenagers.

Arun and Chavan (2010) contemplated the connection between high feeling of anxiety and high rate of conscious self-hurt among school going understudies in Punjab, India. Connection between's pressure, mental wellbeing and self-destructive thoughts was contemplated. In a cross sectional examination information was gathered from 2402 understudies from classes eighth - tenth standard from Chandigarh of Punjab state, India.

Results demonstrated that Out of 2402 understudies, 1078 (45.8%) had mental issues, half (1201 understudies) seen issues in their job as understudies, 930 (45%) revealed scholarly decay, 180 (8.82%) understudies detailed that life was a weight, 122 (6%) announced self-destructive thoughts and 8 (0.39%) understudies announced self-destructive endeavor. Understudy's impression of life as weight and the class they were considering, mother's working status, mental issues and issue with associates was essentially corresponded. Understudies with unsupportive home condition, scholarly issues and seeing life as weight had higher rates of self-destructive ideations.

Pillai's (2009) assessed the predominance rate of suicide hazard factors among young people in Goa of India. Tests of 3662 from provincial and urban Goa district matured between 16-24 years were considered for the examination. Self-destructive conduct and its related variables from recent months were evaluated in a meeting strategy. 3.9% youth detailed self-destructive conduct. Self-destructive conduct was observed to be related with female sex chances proportion, not going to class or school, free basic leadership, pre-marriage sex, physical maltreatment at home, life time understanding of sexual maltreatment and likely normal mental clutters. Sexual orientation isolated examination discovered free basic leadership, country living arrangement and pre-marriage sex held relationship with self-destructive conduct just among females.

Siddhartha (2006) found the predominance of non-lethal self-destructive conduct and other related conduct and furthermore recognized the hazard factors for non-deadly self-destructive conduct. Test included 1205 young people matured 12 to 19yrs from two schools. Results report the commonness of self-destructive ideation forever time (21.7%), for a year ago (11.7%) and suicide endeavors forever time (8%), suicide endeavor for a year ago (3.5%). Religion, female sex, more seasoned young people, physical maltreatment by guardians, feeling dismissed by guardians, history of fleeing from school, history of suicide by a companions, passing wish and DSH were found as critical hazard factors for non-deadly self-destructive conduct.

In an examination done by Arthur et al. (1968), Clinical and social contrasts among suicides and coordinated control patients are analyzed at the purpose of first admission to doctor's facility. A scoring framework is proposed which, in this arrangement, permits 58 of 74 (78 percent.) suicides and controls to be effectively apportioned.

Suicide rates are higher among more seasoned grown-ups than some other age gathering and self-destructive ideation is extraordinary compared to other indicators of finished suicide in more seasoned grown-ups. Regardless of this, few examinations have assessed indicators of self-destructive ideation and different corresponds of death by suicide among more seasoned grown-ups. Indeed, even less examinations on this theme have been led among tests portrayed as poor responders to medications. The reason for this examination was to inspect adapting styles and thought concealment as indicators of a suicide hazard composite score in an example of discouraged more established grown-ups with co-happening identity issue. In view of the surviving writing, it was speculated that maladaptive adapting and interminable idea concealment would essentially anticipate suicide chance. The aftereffects of this investigation shown that lifted enthusiastic adapting and thought concealment were related with expanded suicide hazard. As opposed to speculations, bring down evasion adapting was related to expanded hazard, in spite of the fact that this finding is directed by Axis II determination Thus, medicines that attention on diminishing enthusiastic adapting and incessant idea concealment may result in diminished self-destructive ideation and misery for more established grown-ups with sadness and Axis II pathology. (Cukrowicz et al., 2008).

Sokero et al. (2005) examined to explore hazard factors for endeavored suicide among mental out-and in-patients with significant burdensome confusion in the city of Vantaa, Finland. The Vantaa Depression Study included 269 patients with DSM– IV real burdensome confusion analyzed utilizing semi-organized meetings and followed up at 6-and 18-month interviews with an actual existence graph. Amid the 18-month development, 8% of the patients endeavored suicide. The overall danger of an endeavor was the general danger of an endeavor was 2.50 amid incomplete reduction and 7.54 amid a noteworthy burdensome scene, contrasted and full abatement. Various components were related with this hazard, yet deficient with regards to an accomplice, past suicide endeavors and aggregate time spent in real burdensome scenes were the most vigorous indicators. Suicide endeavors among patients with real burdensome confusion are emphatically connected with the nearness and seriousness of burdensome side effects and anticipated by absence of accomplice, past suicide endeavors and time spent in melancholy. Decreasing the time spent discouraged is a tenable preventive measure.

Kessing (2004) in his examination on seriousness of burdensome scenes as indicated by ICD, planned to approve the ICD-10 order of seriousness of wretchedness by evaluating its prescient capacity on the course of sickness and self-destructive out comes. All mental in patient in Denmark who had gotten an analysis of a solitary burdensome scene at their first release somewhere in the range of 1994 and 1999 were distinguished. The danger of backslide and the danger of suicide were contrasted for patient release and an ICD-10 conclusion of a solitary gentle, moderate or extreme burdensome scene. At their first release 1103 patients had an ICD-10 determination of gentle burdensome scene, 3182 had a conclusion of moderate burdensome scene and 2914 had a finding a serious burdensome scene. The danger of backslide and the danger of suicide were essentially extraordinary for the three kind of sorrow expanding from mellow to direct to extreme burdensome scene. The ICD-10 method for evaluating seriousness is clinically helpful and ought to be protected in future variants.

This examination researched character improvement in clinician overcomers of customer suicide. The investigation's idiographic methodology encouraged the examination of every clinician survivor's personality redefinition. The Identity Structure Analysis theoretical system, enlarged by semi-organized meetings, gave a solid procedure to obtaining and investigation of essential information from 23 respondents in three partners – clinician survivors (target), clinician survivors as a substitute (examination) and non-clinicians (control). Customer self-destructive conduct was appeared to balance clinicians" character forms over a scope of settings. Results shown that the reaction of every clinician survivor to their misfortune encounter was novel to that singular specialist. Partners of clinician survivors, whose encounter was backhanded, or as a substitute, were appeared to encounter changed highlights of personality redefinition. It was discovered that clinician survivors" introduction towards their social world, regardless of whether „defensive" or „open", would impact the degree and nature of their reaction. Further, clinician survivors" possess dimensions of suicidal tendencies were appeared to be an element of their distinguishing pieces of proof with a customer's affinity to suicide. Once more, clinician survivors" character improvement influenced their frameworks of qualities and convictions, balancing their adapting assets as they fought with coordination of their misfortune encounter. In spite of the fact that customer misfortune by suicide was for quite some time viewed as a word related or proficient risk for clinicians, an individual customer suicide occasion couldn't be anticipated with any sureness. Further, clinicians were accepted to encounter customer suicide both actually and as experts. Thus, a related key result – the basic significance for clinical results of clinicians" ability in evaluation of customers for self-destructive conduct – was underscored. The investigation's general discoveries ought to hence illuminate clinicians" training, development, proficient practice and supervision, with regards to working with customers in danger of self-destructive conduct, taking note of every clinician survivor's inclination to react particularly to their genuine misfortune encounter and arranging any related individual aftercare needs in like manner. (O'Keeffe, 2010).

The crucial structure of self-destructive inclinations, the of self-destructive conduct is examined inside and out, specifically suicide and endeavored suicides of patients experiencing gloom in both the all-inclusive community and patients experiencing clinical treatment. Specific accentuation is set upon the subject of average psychopathology as a high hazard factor, i.e. those psychopathological wonders that different self-destructive from non-self-destructive burdensome patients. It is seen that exceptional significance is ascribed to considerations of uselessness, blame, lose hope, burdensome silly manifestations, inward fretfulness and fomentation, freeze assaults and conditions of tension, rest issue and past self-destructive conduct. (Wolfersdorf, 2009)

An examination led by LaxmiVijaykumar (2010), the suicide rate in India is 10.3. Over the most recent three decades, the suicide rate has expanded by 43% yet the male female proportion has been steady at 1.4:1. Greater part (71%) of suicide in India are by people underneath the age of 44 years which forces a gigantic social, passionate and monetary weight. Fifty four articles on suicides have been distributed in IJP. A few examinations uncover that self-destructive practices are considerably more predominant than what is formally detailed. Harming, hanging and self immolation (especially ladies) were the techniques to submit suicide. Physical and psychological instability, exasperates relational connections and financial challenges were the significant purposes behind suicide. The powerless populace was observed to be ladies, understudies, ranchers and so forth. A social and general wellbeing reaction notwithstanding a psychological wellness reaction is urgent to counteract self-destructive conduct in India.

Soltaninejad et al. (2014) directed an investigation on 1659 Iranian military youth. Results uncovered that there was a noteworthy constructive connection among's neuroticism and suicide ideation; in any case, huge antagonistic relationships existed between three other identity qualities - extraversion, pleasantness, and uprightness and self-destructive ideation. In contrast to neuroticism, extraversion and good faith identity components could lessen altogether dimensions of self-destructive ideation.

Gong et al. (2011) dissected hazard factors for extreme self-destructive ideation of provincial China. Consequences of the examination uncovered discouragement, financial status and negative life occasions effectsly affected SSI. Financial status and negative life occasions effectsly affected SSI by means of sorrow. The most compelling component of the immediate impacts was discouragement, and the most persuasive factor of the aberrant impacts was financial status.

Nock et al. (2008) investigated government information on suicide and self-destructive conduct and led a methodical audit of concentrates on the study of disease transmission of suicide distributed from 1997 to 2007. Fundamental points were to look at the pervasiveness of, patterns in, and hazard and defensive components for self-destructive conduct in the United States and cross-broadly. The information uncovered huge cross-national fluctuation in the commonness of self-destructive conduct however consistency in period of beginning, change probabilities, and key hazard factors. Suicide is more predominant among men, though nonfatal self-destructive practices are more pervasive among ladies and people who are youthful, are unmarried, or have a mental issue. Regardless of an expansion in the treatment of self-destructive people over the previous decade, occurrence rates of self-destructive conduct have remained to a great extent unaltered. Most epidemiologic research on self-destructive conduct has concentrated on examples and associates of predominance.

Sareen et al. (2005) directed a longitudinal investigation of grown-ups in regards to information originate from the Netherlands Mental Health Survey and Incidence Study, an imminent populace based overview with a benchmark and 2 follow-up appraisals over a 3-year time span. The Composite International Diagnostic Interview was utilized to survey DSM-III-R mental disarranges. Lifetime findings of tension issue (social fear, basic fear, summed up nervousness issue, freeze issue, agoraphobia, over the top urgent confusion) were evaluated at benchmark. Different calculated relapse examinations were utilized to inspect whether nervousness issue were related with self-destructive ideation and endeavors at benchmark (n = 7076) and whether tension issue were hazard factors for ensuing beginning of self-destructive ideation and endeavors (n = 4796). Subsequent to altering for socio-statistic components and all other mental clutters evaluated in the review, gauge nearness of any nervousness issue was essentially connected with self-destructive ideation and suicide endeavors in both the cross-sectional investigation and longitudinal examination (balanced chances proportion for self-destructive ideation, balanced chances proportion for suicide endeavors, 3.64; 95% certainty interim, 1.70-7.83). Further investigations shown that the nearness of any uneasiness issue in mix with an inclination issue was related with a higher probability of suicide endeavors in examination with a disposition issue alone. This is the principal concentrate to show that a prior tension issue is an autonomous hazard factor for ensuing beginning of self-destructive ideation and endeavors. Additionally, the information unmistakably show that comorbid uneasiness issue intensify the danger of suicide endeavors in people with temperament issue. Clinicians and policymakers should know about these discoveries, and further research is required to portray whether treatment of tension issue diminishes the danger of ensuing self-destructive conduct.

De Shong et al. (2015) led an investigation to experimentally inspect the relationship of the Five Factor Model of identity with current, past and no suicide ideation, and with the two relational hazard components of suicide: obstructed belongingness and seen troublesomeness (Joiner, T., 2005. Why individuals pass on by suicide. Cambridge, MA, US: Harvard University Press). Results demonstrate that high neuroticism was related with both current ideation and a past filled with suicide ideation and extraversion was related with current ideation. Neuroticism was emphatically identified with frustrated belongingness and seen difficulty, while extraversion was adversely identified with these relational indicators of suicide. Pleasantness was adversely identified with ruined belongingness yet not seen difficulty, showing separated examples of connections between this identity area and the two suicide develops. Moreover, these identity spaces anticipated 23.82% of change for frustrated belongingness and 15.07% of the difference for seen troublesomeness, well beyond statistic factors related with suicide ideation. This examination, which was directed with a school test, shows the potential advantage of recognizing pre-dispositional hazard factors for suicide ideation and relational indicators of suicide.

Shakeri et al. (2015) led an examination on danger of redundancy of endeavored suicide among Iranian ladies with mental scatters. Members admitted to the Hospital following fizzled suicide endeavors. Mental disarranges were analyzed dependent on the Diagnostic and Statistical Manual of Mental Disorders (DSM-IV) manifestation agenda. Danger of redundancy was assessed utilizing the Suicide Behaviors Questionnaire-Revised (SBQ-R). The variables related with redundancy of endeavored suicide are ineffectively ordered in the Iranian populace. In this investigation, the commonness of various mental clutters among ladies who endeavored suicide and the danger of reiteration were surveyed. Mental clutters were analyzed dependent on the Diagnostic and Statistical Manual of Mental Disorders (DSM-IV) manifestation agenda. Danger of reiteration was assessed utilizing the Suicide Behaviors Questionnaire-Revised (SBQ-R).The factors related with redundancy of endeavored suicide are inadequately arranged in the Iranian populace. In this investigation, the commonness of various mental scatters among ladies who endeavored suicide and the danger of reiteration were surveyed. It was discovered that modification issue were the most widely recognized mental disarranges. In any case, the kind of mental issue was not related with the danger of redundancy. Conjugal status, instructive dimension, business, substance utilize, history of suicide among relatives, and inspiration were not determinant factors for reiteration of suicide endeavor. More youthful ladies were related with brutal strategies for endeavored suicide, for example, self-cutting, while more established people favored utilization of toxin. Medication overdose was more typical among single and hitched ladies though widows or divorced people favored self-consuming. About 72% of patients with fizzled suicide endeavors were at high hazard for rehashed endeavors. Age, conjugal status, and kind of mental issue were the main determinants of suicide strategy. Modification issue were the most well-known mental clutters among Iranian ladies. Be that as it may, this did not foresee the danger of further endeavors.

Yen et al. (2009) directed an examination to look at higher request identity components of pessimistic affectivity (NA) and dis-restraint (DIS), and also bring down request features of impulsivity, as forthcoming indicators of suicide endeavors in an overwhelmingly identity scattered example. Information were examined from 701 members of the Collaborative Longitudinal Personality Disorders Study with accessible follow-up information for up to 7 years. Cox corresponding risks relapse investigations was utilized to inspect NA and DIS, and aspects of impulsivity e.g. earnestness, absence of constancy, absence of intention and sensation chasing, as imminent indicators of suicide endeavors. Results shown that NA, DIS and all aspects of impulsivity aside from sensation looking for were huge in uni-variate examinations. In multivariate models which included sex, youth sexual maltreatment, course of real burdensome confusion and substance utilize clutters, just NA and absence of intention stayed noteworthy in anticipating suicide endeavors. DIS and the rest of the impulsivity features were not critical. NA developed as a more grounded and more hearty indicator of suicide endeavors than DIS and impulsivity, and warrants more noteworthy consideration in suicide chance evaluation. Recognizing aspects of impulsivity is vital for clinical hazard appraisal.

Auerbach, Stewart and Johnson (2016) directed an exploration on Impulsivity and Suicidality in Adolescent Inpatients. The present examination tried whether unmistakable spaces of impulsivity are differentially connected with suicide ideation, plans, and endeavors. Teenagers (n = 381; young men = 106, young ladies = 275) matured 13-19 years were enrolled from an intense, private treatment program. Inside 48 hours of admission to the doctor's facility, members were directed organized clinical meetings surveying emotional wellness issue and suicidality. Following these meetings, members finished self-report surveys evaluating indication seriousness and impulsivity. Predictable with past research, an exploratory factor investigation of our 90-thing impulsivity instrument brought about a three-factor arrangement: Pervasive Influence of Feelings, Feelings Trigger Action, and

Lack of Follow-Through. Simultaneous investigation of these components affirmed theories of exceptional relationship with suicide ideation and endeavors in the previous month. In particular, while Pervasive Influence of Feelings (i.e., propensity for feelings to shape considerations about oneself and what's to come) is exceptionally connected with more prominent self-destructive ideation, Feelings Trigger Action (i.e., indiscreet social reactivity to feelings) is remarkably connected with the event of suicide endeavors, even subsequent to controlling for current mental determinations and indications. Exploratory sexual orientation investigations uncovered that these impacts were huge in female however not male young people. These discoveries give new understanding about how particular spaces of impulsivity differentially increment hazard for suicide ideation and endeavors. Suggestions for early distinguishing proof and counteractive action of youth suicide are examined.

The examination by Cheung et al. (2013) researched the examples, co-event, and associates of NSSI and other self-destructive practices among an agent network test of in-school youths. A cross-sectional study of 2,317 young people was directed. Members were asked to self-report NSSI, self-destructive ideation, suicide endeavor, and psychosocial conditions in the course of recent months. Strategic relapse and combined logit displaying examinations were led to research the extraordinary and comparative associates among these self-hurt practices. The age-institutionalized pervasiveness rates of NSSI among male and female young people were assessed to be 13.4 and 19.7 %, individually, contrasted and 11.1 and 10.1 % for male and female suicide endeavor. Just a little extent occupied with NSSI only in the previous year. NSSI by consuming or foolhardy and unsafe practices, visit drinking, and sexual experience were related with expanding seriousness dimension of self-destructive practices among people with NSSI. NSSI is pervasive among in-school young people in Hong Kong. Be that as it may, it co-happens with self-destructive ideation and suicide endeavor. High lethality of NSSI, visit drinking propensity, and lifetime sexual experience are proposed to be pointers for screening potential suicide attempters among those having NSSI.

Krysinska et al. (2015) contemplated on model of causal impacts among appreciation, religiosity, and purpose behind living, adapting, and social help as indicators of self-destructive ideation, suicide dangers, and suicide endeavors in the wake of controlling for discouragement and distressing life occasions. An example of 165 understudies were regulated proportions of appreciation, religiosity, purposes behind living, social help, adapting abilities, stress, and sorrow. The examination evaluated lifetime and current self-destructive ideation and lifetime suicide risk and endeavor. Both appreciation and religiosity, alongside social help, adapting aptitudes, and explanations behind living, corresponded adversely with earlier self-destructive ideation, yet not with earlier endeavored suicide. Subsequent to controlling for hazard factor (wretchedness and stress), the effect of appreciation and religiosity was not any more factually critical.

Sokero et al. (2003) As a feature of the Vantaa Depression Study in Vantaa, Finland, 269 patients with DSM-IV real burdensome confusion (MDD), analyzed by meeting utilizing semi-organized World Health Organization Schedules for Clinical Assessment in Neuropsychiatry, variant 2.0, and Structured Clinical Interview for DSM-III-R Personality Disorders, were completely researched. Data was accumulated on patients' dimensions of despondency, uneasiness, misery, seen social help, social and word related working, and liquor utilize. Self-destructive conduct was evaluated by meetings, including the Scale for Suicidal Ideation, and by data from mental records. Results uncovered that amid the current MDD scene, 58% of all patients had encountered self-destructive ideation; among the 15% of the aggregate who had endeavored suicide, all (95%) had additionally had self-destructive ideation. In ostensible relapse models foreseeing self-destructive ideation, misery, liquor reliance or misuse, low dimension of social and word related working, and poor seen social help were observed to be critical free hazard factors. High seriousness of discouragement and current liquor reliance or maltreatment specifically, yet in addition more youthful age and low dimension 67 of social and word related working, anticipated suicide endeavor. It is reasoned that self-destructive ideation is predominant and gives off an impression of being a precondition for suicide endeavors among mental patients with MDD. The hazard factors for self-destructive ideation and endeavors situate in a few clinical and psychosocial spaces. While these hazard factors generally cover, the general dimension of psychopathology of suicide attempters is higher contrasted and that in patients with ideation, and substance utilize disarranges and seriousness of wretchedness might be of specific significance in foreseeing suicide endeavors.

2.4 Studies related to Emotional Intelligence:

Salovey and Mayer (1990) contend that the build of alexithymia ignores positive sentiments, blended feelings or nonpartisan states and rather centers around negative feelings.

Salovey and Mayer (1993) composed that a sincerely savvy individual is gifted in four regions distinguishing, utilizing, comprehension and controlling feelings.

Goleman (1995) focused on that passionate knowledge comprises of five parts knowing one's feelings, overseeing them, spurring self, perceiving feelings in others and taking care of connections.

Koifman, (1998), in his examination including 140 under alumni understudies, discoveries recommend that the capacity to precisely foresee enthusiastic substance in visual upgrades relies on how well the member can comprehend diverse passionate signs. The higher the EQ level, the more noteworthy their capacity to comprehend and foresee feelings identified with visual improvements.

Mayer, Caruso and salovey (1999) declared that all together for passionate knowledge to be viewed as a standard insight, it should increment with age and experience. They analyzed youths and grown-ups execution on the Multifactor Emotional Intelligence scale. Results demonstrated that the grown-up gathering worked at a fundamentally more elevated amount of passionate knowledge than the immature gathering.

Greenstein (2001) directed an investigation that took a gander at the triumphs and disappointments of eleven American presidents. They were evaluated on six characteristics association correspondence, vision, political expertise, subjective style and enthusiastic insight. The outcome demonstrated that enthusiastic knowledge was the key quality that recognized the effectively (e.g. Roosevelt) from the unsuccessful (e.g. Carter).

Derksen and Kramer (2002), in an examination discovered that the capacity to see feelings in others outward appearances and get subte motions about individuals' feelings anticipated evaluations of how important these individuals were to their association.

Dileep Kumar (2006) clarified that Emotional Intelligence is a set execution at work. The passionate competency is the capacity of the person to control and oversee dispositions and driving forces, which add to situational results, enthusiastic development and enthusiastic affectability that decide the achievement of flexibility and alteration with the changed situation. In a work circumstance, since it includes gathering of individuals with various thoughts, recommendations, and assessments, successful mixture of all these decide the best result.

Lokeswaran (2010) expressed that Emotional Intelligence is frequently alluded additionally as Emotional Quotient which is the capacity of a person to ability and expects apparatuses to survey this ability. Enthusiastic Intelligence has four principle parts in particular: 1. see feelings. 2. use these enthusiastic discernments to achieve different exercises or assignments; 3. comprehend enthusiastic varieties: and 4. oversee feelings to accomplish objectives. Hence, EI is an ability. Creating EI expects one to unlearn old propensities for thought, feeling, and activity that are profoundly instilled, and become new ones. Such a procedure takes inspiration, exertion, time, bolster, and supported practice.

Dalip Singh (2006) clarified that individuals with high Emotional Intelligence are generally mindful, on the grounds that mindfulness is the most vital piece of Emotional Intelligence. This is maybe the second-most vital component of Emotional Intelligence and other imperative components are inspiration, self control, compassion and social aptitudes. EI can be a key to progressive profession. The capacity to oversee individuals and connections is vital in all pioneers, so creating and utilizing EI can be a decent method to build up the activity execution. EI incorporates such factors as compassion, relational connections, inspiration, managing pressure and weight and adjusting one's close to home and expert life.

Geeta Ranga and Santhosh Ranganekar (2009) said that, EI is the response that comes to pass, when there is a poor match between occupation requests and capabilities, or workers assets, to oversee work weight. At the point when representatives confront troubles and change in their every day working daily schedule, such condition makes nervousness, tears, stresses, strain, and so forth., EI enables the person to think about the sentiments of the people, who are required to be influenced by his or her choices. EI causes the people to understand the way that, their choices will influence others in a constructive or a pessimistic way, and in this manner, they ought to think about the outcomes of their choices. At long last, social abilities enable the people to approach their subordinates and comprehend their passionate needs.

Nobleman (2002) said that, as opposed to the capacity demonstrate, blended model of Emotional Intelligence consolidates mental capacity with identity qualities, for example, good faith and well-Emotional Intelligence identifies with the potential for execution and achievement, and is viewed as process-situated as opposed to result arranged. It plots five segments of Emotional Intelligence to be specific intrapersonal, relational, flexibility, stretch administration, and general state of mind. Enthusiastic Intelligence creates after some time and that it very well may be enhanced through preparing, programming and treatment. Enthusiastic Intelligence can mean an absence of achievement and presence of a passionate issue.

Daniel Goleman (2008) presented enthusiastic skills inside each build of EI, passionate abilities are not natural gifts, yet rather learned capacities that must be taken a shot at and can be created to accomplish that are mindfulness, self administration, social mindfulness and relationship administration. EI decides their potential for learning enthusiastic capabilities, zone of psychological capacity including characteristics and social abilities that encourage relational conduct and spotlights on the parts of insight that oversee self information and social adjustment.

Jerrell Cassady (2008) expressed that pressure is an unavoidable normal forever and work. It is a summed up non-particular reaction of the body to any request set on it. Occupation stress can be physical, mental and enthusiastic. The parts of Emotional Intelligence were found to affect mental wellbeing and the capacity to oversee feeling and adapt to pressure, the drive to achieve individual objectives with the end goal to oversee and lead a more significant life.

Chapter - 3
Methodology

Chapter - 3
Methodology

3.1. Introduction:

In every field there is evolution of knowledge and in this field of knowledge research plays a very important role of knowledge. Any research starts with curiosities and questions about a given phenomenon or a set of phenomena. Systematic attempt are made to explore, analyze and understand the issues under question through suitable conceptual and methodological tools. The process of inquiry and the analytical tools are to a great extent relative to the specific domain of concern, and the conceptual, methodological, heuristic and pragmatic goals of the research. Research is common parlance which refers to search knowledge (Khothari, 1990). Today nothing is possible without planning and if you do our work with proper planning it can be done fast and easily. In a scientific language it called research methods or research methodology.

Research is systematic and refined technique of thinking, employing specialized tools, instruments, and procedures in order to obtain a more adequate solution of a problem than would be possible under ordinary means. It starts with a problem, collects data or facts, analyses them critically, and reaches decisions based on the actual evidence.

- Crawford, C.C. (2011)

According to **F.N. Kerlinger** (1986) research means "A systematic controlled experienced and minuet observation which does the study of natural incidence and their relation with hypothesis by logic."

In present research, as such has focus on certain dimensions of **mental health, suicidal tendency and emotional intelligence of higher secondary school students with reference to faculty, gender and area differences.**

This chapter gives the details about the methodology followed in this study. The method of research adopted, the description of tools and techniques used, the sample, the procedure of data collection and the outline of statistical techniques utilized in the analysis of data are described under appropriate heads and presented below.

3.2. Research Problem:

There are so many things & ideas on which we can research but as a researcher we must have decide one topic which we want to study, after that we formulate this general topic into a specific research problem (khothari, 1990). In the present study there is emphatic on **mental health, suicidal tendency and emotional intelligence of higher secondary school students.** Modern age is considered as the age of tension, competition and speed to human requirements are also increasing. When there is some interruption, problem to satisfy their need of there is some late human beings or few to satisfy their need or they can not satisfied it completely because of different reason. In the teenage, if they feel dissatisfied, stressed and unhappy these have greater negative impact on their personal and social life as well as it can affect to their academic performance too.

The study aims at identifying the mental health, suicidal tendency and emotional intelligence of higher secondary school students. Hence the problem under investigation is entitled as **"A comparative study of the Mental Health, Suicidal Tendency and Emotional Intelligence of Higher secondary School Students with reference to Faculty, Gender and Area differences".**

3.3. Objectives of Research:

The Purpose of research is to discover answer to questions though the application of scientific procedures. The main aim of research to find out the truth which is hidden and which has not been discovered as yet. Though each research study has its own specific purpose, we may think of research objectives as falling into a number of following broad groupings; (Slesinger, D. and Stephenson, 1930)

1. To gain familiarity with a phenomenon or to achieve new insights into it.
2. To portray accurately the characteristics of a particular individual, situation or a group.
3. To determine the frequency with which something occurs or with which it is associated with something else.
4. To test a hypothesis of a causal relationship between variables.

Where researchers make planning for research they are following scientific attitude. They are follow scientific process or the study of problems and they maintain objectivity, reliability, propriety, purity and ability to make hypothesis or prediction.

There are many factors responsible for research. Research without objectives can't be considered a research. So this research can be taken to do study of **mental health, emotional intelligence and suicidal tendency among higher secondary school students**.

The major objectives of the study are:

1. To know the level of mental health, suicidal tendency and emotional intelligence of Arts faculty higher secondary school students.
2. To know the level of mental health, suicidal tendency and emotional intelligence of commerce faculty higher secondary school students.
3. To know the level of mental health, suicidal tendency and emotional intelligence of science faculty higher secondary school students.
4. To compare the level of mental health, suicidal tendency and emotional intelligence of arts, commerce and science faculty higher secondary school students.
5. To know the level of mental health, suicidal tendency and emotional intelligence of male students of higher secondary school.
6. To know the level of mental health, suicidal tendency and emotional intelligence of female students of higher secondary school.
7. To know the level of mental health, suicidal tendency and emotional intelligence of male and female students of higher secondary school.
8. To know the level of mental health, suicidal tendency and emotional intelligence of higher secondary school student of urban area.
9. To know the level of mental health, suicidal tendency and emotional intelligence of higher secondary school student of rural area

10. To compare the level of mental health, suicidal tendency and emotional intelligence of higher secondary school student of urban and rural area

11. To check the interaction effect of mental health, suicidal tendency and emotional intelligence in reference to faculty and gender.

12. To check the interaction effect of mental health, suicidal tendency and emotional intelligence in reference to faculty and area.

13. To check the interaction effect of mental health, suicidal tendency and emotional intelligence in reference to gender and area.

14. To check the interaction effect of mental health, suicidal tendency and emotional intelligence in reference to faculty, gender and area.

3.4. Hypothesis:

Hypothesis is considered as the principal instrument in research (Khothari, 1990). Any research starts with hypothesis. So hypothesis is such a factor that its reliability remains to be checked.

The present study was undertaken with the following hypotheses:

1) There will be no significant difference among higher secondary school students of arts, commerce and science faculty with regards to their emotional stability.

2) There will be no significant difference among male and female higher secondary school students with regards to their emotional stability.

3) There will be no significant difference among higher secondary school students of urban and rural area with regards to their emotional stability.

4) There will be no significant interaction effect among faculty and gender of higher secondary school students with regards to their emotional stability.

5) There will be no significant interaction effect among faculty and area of higher secondary school students with regards to their emotional stability.

6) There will be no significant interaction effect among gender and area of higher secondary school students with regards to their emotional stability.

7) There will be no significant interaction effect among faculty, gender and area of higher secondary school students with regards to their emotional stability.

8) There will be no significant difference among higher secondary school students of arts, commerce and science faculty with regards to their overall adjustment.

9) There will be no significant difference among male and female higher secondary school students with regards to their overall adjustment.

10) There will be no significant difference among higher secondary school students of urban and rural area with regards to their overall adjustment.

11) There will be no significant interaction effect among faculty and gender of higher secondary school students with regards to their overall adjustment.

12) There will be no significant interaction effect among faculty and area of higher secondary school students with regards to their overall adjustment.

13) There will be no significant interaction effect among gender and area of higher secondary school students with regards to their overall adjustment.

14) There will be no significant interaction effect among faculty, gender and area of higher secondary school students with regards to their overall adjustment.

15) There will be no significant difference among higher secondary school students of arts, commerce and science faculty with regards to their autonomy.

16) There will be no significant difference among male and female higher secondary school students with regards to their autonomy.

17) There will be no significant difference among higher secondary school students of urban and rural area with regards to their autonomy.

18) There will be no significant interaction effect among faculty and gender of higher secondary school students with regards to their autonomy.

19) There will be no significant interaction effect among faculty and area of higher secondary school students with regards to their autonomy.

20) There will be no significant interaction effect among gender and area of higher secondary school students with regards to their autonomy.

21) There will be no significant interaction effect among faculty, gender and area of higher secondary school students with regards to their autonomy.

22) There will be no significant difference among higher secondary school students of arts, commerce and science faculty with regards to their security-insecurity.

23) There will be no significant difference among male and female higher secondary school students with regards to their security-insecurity.

24) There will be no significant difference among higher secondary school students of urban and rural area with regards to their security-insecurity.

25) There will be no significant interaction effect among faculty and gender of higher secondary school students with regards to their security-insecurity.

26) There will be no significant interaction effect among faculty and area of higher secondary school students with regards to their security-insecurity.

27) There will be no significant interaction effect among gender and area of higher secondary school students with regards to their security-insecurity.

28) There will be no significant interaction effect among faculty, gender and area of higher secondary school students with regards to their security-insecurity.

29) There will be no significant difference among higher secondary school students of arts, commerce and science faculty with regards to their self-concept.

30) There will be no significant difference among male and female higher secondary school students with regards to their self-concept.

31) There will be no significant difference among higher secondary school students of urban and rural area with regards to their self-concept.

32) There will be no significant interaction effect among faculty and gender of higher secondary school students with regards to their self-concept.

33) There will be no significant interaction effect among faculty and area of higher secondary school students with regards to their self-concept.

34) There will be no significant interaction effect among gender and area of higher secondary school students with regards to their self-concept.

35) There will be no significant interaction effect among faculty, gender and area of higher secondary school students with regards to their self-concept.

36) There will be no significant difference among higher secondary school students of arts, commerce and science faculty with regards to their intelligence.

37) There will be no significant difference among male and female higher secondary school students with regards to their intelligence.

38) There will be no significant difference among higher secondary school students of urban and rural area with regards to their intelligence.

39) There will be no significant interaction effect among faculty and gender of higher secondary school students with regards to their intelligence.

40) There will be no significant interaction effect among faculty and area of higher secondary school students with regards to their intelligence.

41) There will be no significant interaction effect among gender and area of higher secondary school students with regards to their intelligence.

42) There will be no significant interaction effect among faculty, gender and area of higher secondary school students with regards to their intelligence.

43) There will be no significant difference among higher secondary school students of arts, commerce and science faculty with regards to their mental health.

44) There will be no significant difference among male and female higher secondary school students with regards to their mental health.

45) There will be no significant difference among higher secondary school students of urban and rural area with regards to their mental health

46) There will be no significant interaction effect among faculty and gender of higher secondary school students with regards to their mental health.

47) There will be no significant interaction effect among faculty and area of higher secondary school students with regards to their mental health.

48) There will be no significant interaction effect among gender and area of higher secondary school students with regards to their mental health.

49) There will be no significant interaction effect among faculty, gender and area of higher secondary school students with regards to their mental health.

50) There will be no significant difference among higher secondary school students of arts, commerce and science faculty with regards to their personality trait.

51) There will be no significant difference among male and female higher secondary school students with regards to their personality trait.

52) There will be no significant difference among higher secondary school students of urban and rural area with regards to their personality trait.

53) There will be no significant interaction effect among faculty and gender of higher secondary school students with regards to their personality trait.

54) There will be no significant interaction effect among faculty and area of higher secondary school students with regards to their personality trait.

55) There will be no significant interaction effect among gender and area of higher secondary school students with regards to their personality trait.

56) There will be no significant interaction effect among faculty, gender and area of higher secondary school students with regards to their personality trait.

57) There will be no significant difference among higher secondary school students of arts, commerce and science faculty with regards to their emotional disturbances.

58) There will be no significant difference among male and female higher secondary school students with regards to their emotional disturbances.

59) There will be no significant difference among higher secondary school students of urban and rural area with regards to their emotional disturbances.

60) There will be no significant interaction effect among faculty and gender of higher secondary school students with regards to their emotional disturbances.

61) There will be no significant interaction effect among faculty and area of higher secondary school students with regards to their emotional disturbances.

62) There will be no significant interaction effect among gender and area of higher secondary school students with regards to their emotional disturbances.

63) There will be no significant interaction effect among faculty, gender and area of higher secondary school students with regards to their emotional disturbances.

64) There will be no significant difference among higher secondary school students of arts, commerce and science faculty with regards to their conflictive thoughts.

65) There will be no significant difference among male and female higher secondary school students with regards to their conflictive thoughts.

66) There will be no significant difference among higher secondary school students of urban and rural area with regards to their conflictive thoughts.

67) There will be no significant interaction effect among faculty and gender of higher secondary school students with regards to their conflictive thoughts.

68) There will be no significant interaction effect among faculty and area of higher secondary school students with regards to their conflictive thoughts.

69) There will be no significant interaction effect among gender and area of higher secondary school students with regards to their conflictive thoughts.

70) There will be no significant interaction effect among faculty, gender and area of higher secondary school students with regards to their conflictive thoughts.

71) There will be no significant difference among higher secondary school students of arts, commerce and science faculty with regards to their self-harm tendency.

72) There will be no significant difference among male and female higher secondary school students with regards to their self-harm tendency.

73) There will be no significant difference among higher secondary school students of urban and rural area with regards to their self-harm tendency.

74) There will be no significant interaction effect among faculty and gender of higher secondary school students with regards to their self-harm tendency.

75) There will be no significant interaction effect among faculty and area of higher secondary school students with regards to their self-harm tendency.

76) There will be no significant interaction effect among gender and area of higher secondary school students with regards to their self-harm tendency.

77) There will be no significant interaction effect among faculty, gender and area of higher secondary school students with regards to their self-harm tendency.

78) There will be no significant difference among higher secondary school students of arts, commerce and science faculty with regards to their suicidal tendency.

79) There will be no significant difference among male and female higher secondary school students with regards to their suicidal tendency.

80) There will be no significant difference among higher secondary school students of urban and rural area with regards to their suicidal tendency.

81) There will be no significant interaction effect among faculty and gender of higher secondary school students with regards to their suicidal tendency.

82) There will be no significant interaction effect among faculty and area of higher secondary school students with regards to their suicidal tendency.

83) There will be no significant interaction effect among gender and area of higher secondary school students with regards to their suicidal tendency.

84) There will be no significant interaction effect among faculty, gender and area of higher secondary school students with regards to their suicidal tendency.

85) There will be no significant difference among higher secondary school students of arts, commerce and science faculty with regards to their intra-personal awareness.

86) There will be no significant difference among male and female higher secondary school students with regards to their intra-personal awareness.

87) There will be no significant difference among higher secondary school students of urban and rural area with regards to their intra-personal awareness.

88) There will be no significant interaction effect among faculty and gender of higher secondary school students with regards to their intra-personal awareness.

89) There will be no significant interaction effect among faculty and area of higher secondary school students with regards to their intra-personal awareness.

90) There will be no significant interaction effect among gender and area of higher secondary school students with regards to their intra-personal awareness.

91) There will be no significant interaction effect among faculty, gender and area of higher secondary school students with regards to their intra-personal awareness.

92) There will be no significant difference among higher secondary school students of arts, commerce and science faculty with regards to their inter-personal awareness.

93) There will be no significant difference among male and female higher secondary school students with regards to their inter-personal awareness.

94) There will be no significant difference among higher secondary school students of urban and rural area with regards to their inter-personal awareness.

95) There will be no significant interaction effect among faculty and gender of higher secondary school students with regards to their inter-personal awareness.

96) There will be no significant interaction effect among faculty and area of higher secondary school students with regards to their inter-personal awareness.

97) There will be no significant interaction effect among gender and area of higher secondary school students with regards to their inter-personal awareness.

98) There will be no significant interaction effect among faculty, gender and area of higher secondary school students with regards to their inter-personal awareness.

99) There will be no significant difference among higher secondary school students of arts, commerce and science faculty with regards to their intra-personal management.

100) There will be no significant difference among male and female higher secondary school students with regards to their intra-personal management.

101) There will be no significant difference among higher secondary school students of urban and rural area with regards to their intra-personal management.

102) There will be no significant interaction effect among faculty and gender of higher secondary school students with regards to their intra-personal management.

103) There will be no significant interaction effect among faculty and area of higher secondary school students with regards to their intra-personal management.

104) There will be no significant interaction effect among gender and area of higher secondary school students with regards to their intra-personal management.

105) There will be no significant interaction effect among faculty, gender and area of higher secondary school students with regards to their intra-personal management.

106) There will be no significant difference among higher secondary school students of arts, commerce and science faculty with regards to their inter-personal management.

107) There will be no significant difference among male and female higher secondary school students with regards to their inter-personal management.

108) There will be no significant difference among higher secondary school students of urban and rural area with regards to their inter-personal management.

109) There will be no significant interaction effect among faculty and gender of higher secondary school students with regards to their inter-personal management.

110) There will be no significant interaction effect among faculty and area of higher secondary school students with regards to their inter-personal management.

111) There will be no significant interaction effect among gender and area of higher secondary school students with regards to their inter-personal management.

112) There will be no significant interaction effect among faculty, gender and area of higher secondary school students with regards to their inter-personal management.

113) There will be no significant difference among higher secondary school students of arts, commerce and science faculty with regards to their emotional intelligence.

114) There will be no significant difference among male and female higher secondary school students with regards to their emotional intelligence.

115) There will be no significant difference among higher secondary school students of urban and rural area with regards to their emotional intelligence.

116) There will be no significant interaction effect among faculty and gender of higher secondary school students with regards to their emotional intelligence.

117) There will be no significant interaction effect among faculty and area of higher secondary school students with regards to their emotional intelligence.

118) There will be no significant interaction effect among gender and area of higher secondary school students with regards to their emotional intelligence.

119) There will be no significant interaction effect among faculty, gender and area of higher secondary school students with regards to their emotional intelligence.

120) There is no significant relationship among mental health and suicidal tendency of higher secondary school students.

121) There is no significant relationship among mental health and emotional intelligence of higher secondary school students.

122) There is no significant relationship among suicidal tendency and emotional intelligence of higher secondary school students.

3.5. Operational Definitions of the Terms used in Present Study:

Mental Health:

Person's behaviors, perceptions and feelings that determine a person's overall level of personal effectiveness, success, happiness and excellence of functioning as person. (Kornhauser , 1965)

Suicidal Tendency:

A suicidal tendency is the propensity for a person to have suicidal ideation or to make suicide attempts.

Emotional Intelligence:

Emotional Intelligence is the capacity to distinguish and deal with your very own feelings and the feelings of others.

Higher secondary school students:

A student who have completed 10th std as per norms of Gujarat board or CBSE board and studying in 11th or 12th std with main stream of arts, commerce or science.

3.6. Research Method:

The investigation was led however descriptive method for research. The Descriptive strategy has been most generally utilized research technique in brain science and instruction. The technique requires test and certain apparatus for the lead consider. The portrayal of instruments, testing and variable is given hereunder.

3.6.1. Variables:

Variables have an important place in research. In research some variables are independent and their effects are searched on dependent variable. **D'Amato** explains variables in experimental psychology:

"Features of animals, situation and anything which are changeable and which can be measured these type of factor are called variable"

Table 3.1. Showing the Nature, Types, Level and Name of Variables;

No.	Name of Variable	Variable	Level	Name of Level
1	Faculty	Independent	3	1. Arts 2. Commerce 3. Science
2	Gender	Independent	2	1. Male 2. Female
3	Area	Independent	2	1. Urban 2. Rural
4	Mental Health	Dependent	7	1. Emotional Stability (ES) 2. Over- all Adjustment (OA) 3. Autonomy (AY) 4. Security-Insecurity (SI) 5. Self Concept(SC) 6. Intelligence (IG) 7. Mental Health (Overall)
5	Suicidal Tendency	Dependent	5	1. Personality Trait 2. Emotional Disturbance 3. Conflictive Thoughts 4. Self-harm Tendency 5. Suicidal Tendency
6.	Emotional Intelligence	Dependent	5	1. Intra-personal Awareness 2. Inter-personal Awareness 3. Intra-personal Management 4. Inter-personal Management 5. Emotional Intelligence

3.6.2. Sample:

The whole sample comprised of total 720 higher secondary school students. The randomized sampling technique was employed to constitute the sample. These subjects were equally selected from higher secondary students male and female (n=360) of high schools. Both groups comprised of equal number of students belonging to Urban (n=360) and rural (n=360) area difference. Further all three groups were constituted with equal number of Faculty Arts (n=240), commerce (n=240) and Science (n=240) students. Hence all experimental groups consist of 60 numbers of subjects. The sample distribution is depicted as follows;

	Gender (B)				
	Male (B1)		Female (B2)		
Faculty (A)	Area (C)				**TOTAL**
	Urban (C1)	Rural (C2)	Urban (C1)	Rural (C2)	
Arts (A1)	60	60	60	60	**240**
Commerce (A2)	60	60	60	60	**240**
Science (A3)	60	60	60	60	**240**
Total	**180**	**180**	**180**	**180**	**720**

3.6.3. Research Design:

Research configuration is such a plan from which we come to know what number of free factors have been taken, how might we measure subordinate variable, which sort of tests have been chosen.

"A research design is the arrangement of conditions for collection and analysis of data in a manner that aims to combine relevance to the research purpose with economy procedure"

- Claire selltiz and others (2000)

For the present research variables like mental health, suicidal tendency and emotional intelligence have been taken as depend variable. And many variables of high school students have been taken as independent variable and hypothesis has been made keeping these variables in mind, this research design have been prepared to know the effect of different variables. Technically known as 3 x 2 x 2 factorial design:

	Gender (B)			
	Male (B1)		Female (B2)	
Faculty (A)	Area (C)			
	Urban (C1)	Rural (C2)	Urban (C1)	Rural (C2)
Arts (A1)	A1B1C1	A1B1C2	A1B2C1	A1B2C2
Commerce (A2)	A2B1C1	A2B1C2	A2B2C1	A2B2C2
Science (A3)	A3B1C1	A3B1C2	A3B2C1	A3B2C2

3.7. Research Tool:

For gathering information one may utilize different research gadgets. For every last research we require certain device to accumulate or to investigate new fields, which go about as means and called inquire about instruments. The achievement of any examination attempt is to a great extent subordinate upon the devices which are utilized for the information gathering. The accompanying instruments were chosen and utilized by me in the present examination.

3.7.1. Mental Health Battery:

Areas of the Scale/ Basic information about scale:

The Mental Health Battery by A. K. Singh & Alpana Sengupta (2000) takes a 'gestalt' view of the individual with regards mental health. The test authors view mental health as an attitudinal concept towards self and others; and thereby also present a humanistic approach towards the understanding and assessment of the self, positive feeling, attitudes towards self and others. The battery is intended to measure mental health using 6 popular indices; emotional stability (Part I), over-all adjustment (Part II), autonomy (Part III), security-insecurity (Part IV), self-concept (Part V) and intelligence (Part VI).

Reliability:

Both temporal stability reliability and inter consistency reliability of MHB were computed. The details are as under

	N	Test-retest reliability	Odd-even (Whole length) reliability
Part I – Emotional Stability	102	0.876	0.725
Part II – Over All Adjustment		0.821	0.871
Part III – Autonomy		0.767	0.812
Part IV – Security – Insecurity		0.826	0.829
Part V – Self Concept		0.786	0.861
Part VI – Intelligence		0.823	0.792

Validity:

Mental Health Battery was validity against the different tests developed earlier, with all validity coefficients significant ay 0.01 level. Part I, Emotional Stability was validated against Emotional Stability Test developed earlier by Sen Gupta and Singh

(1985). Part II, Overall Adjustment was validated against High School Adjustment Inventory (HSAI) developed earlier by Singh and Sen Gupta (1987) and Hindi Version of Bell's Adjustment Inventory by Mohsin, Shamshad and Jehan (1967). Construct Validity was computed for Part III, Autonomy and Part V, Self Concept. Part IV, Security – Insecurity was validated against Neuroticism Scale of MPI, as adapted by Jalota and Kapoor (1975), Likewise Part VI was validated against Jalota Group Genereal Mental Ability Test (1976). Only relevant parts of MHB, with suitable criteria were given to the random sample of 102. The standard instructions of the test and the criteria were followed. validity coefficients of Mental Health Battery are as under

	Concurrent Validity	Construct Validity
Part I – Emotional Stability	0.673	--
Part II – Over All Adjustment	0.704	--
Part III – Autonomy	--	0.681
Part IV – Security – Insecurity	0.821	--
Part V – Self Concept	--	0.601
Part VI – Intelligence	0.823	--

Scoring:

The answers of those items (in each of the parts I - VI) which tally with the answers given in the scoring key would be given a score of +1, if they don't tally; they will be given a score of zero.

Test Components	Item Numbers	Scoring Key
Part I– Emotional Stability	1,2,3,5,7,8,9,10,12,14,15 6,11,13	No Yes
Part II – Over All Adjustment	16,19,22,26,27,30,35,37,40,41,42,43,47,49,50,52,53 17,18,20,21,23,24,25,28,29,31,32,33,34,36,38,39,44,45, 46,48,51,54,55	Yes No No
Part III – Autonomy	58,60,61,62,63,65,66 56,57,59,64,67,68,69,70	(A) (B)
Part IV – Security – Insecurity	71,72,73,74,75,77,79,80,82 76,78,81,83,84,85	Yes No
Part V – Self Concept	86,87,88,89,91,92,93,94,95,96,97,100 90,98,99	Correct Wrong

3.7.2. Suicide Tendency Scale:

Areas of the Scale/ Basic information about scale:

The Suicide Tendency Scale developed and standardized by Rasik Meghnathi and Dilip Bhatt (2002). The items of the scale have been selected on the base of literature and judgment of experts all the items of the scale are presented in simple and brisk style. On the basis of available literature review and related existing tools, the preliminary scale of suicidal tendency was prepared which consist 80 items. The present scale is based on the book "Abnormal Psychology" 8th Edition, by Irwin, Barbara Sarson.

These items are related with four modes of suicidal tendency, each mode has 10 items. STS modes and items described as under:

A. Personality Trait: The items of this mode is related to feeling of restlessness, boredom, general lack of interest, vague fears and anxieties, disturbed sleep, self-hate etc.

B. Emotional Disturbances: This mode is related to hopelessness, weakness, lake of interest, deprivation to intimate relationship, loneliness, short temperedness, disability to express feeling, disturbance in work etc.

C. Conflictive thoughts: It is concern with disappointed past experiences, insecurity, anxiety, avoiding responsibility, inferiority, complex, meaninglessness, guilt feeling, mental instability etc.

D. Self-harm tendency: These items are connected with death wishing behavior viz. carelessness, self-inflicted act, injury unnecessary risk making, verbalized threat of self-harm, feelings of despair, and depression.

Reliability:

For the established the reliability co-efficient, the scale was administered to 160 subjects both males and females belonging to Urban and Rural area of Surendranagar (Age range 16 to 30 years) the split-half reliability has been calculated by odd-even method. The correlation coefficient was 0.92 which indicated the S.T.S. is highly reliable. (Index of reliability was found 0.96).

The test-retest reliability of this scale has also been calculated by administration twice of this scale on a sample of 80 subjects the reliability coefficient was r. 0.83 (index of reliability was 0.91).

Validity:

The validity of the scale has been calculated for the criterion validity. The scale was administrated to two groups Normal (N=40) and Abnormal (N=40) in Abnormal group has been comprised the patients of depression, suicidal attempters, schizophrenia and other Neurosis diagnosed by psychiatrics the abnormal group was indicated high scores of suicidal tendency than normal group on the scale.

The t-test was applied for calculation of differences between above both groups there is significant differences between above both groups. The abnormal group was significantly higher than normal group in their Suicidal tendency.

Norms are remained to be established. The scale is prepared in Gujarati version for Gujarati speaking population.

Scoring:

All the 40 items of the scale are presented in simple and brisk style. Each of the 40 items has four alternate like as under bellow:

	Strongly Agree	**Agree**	**Disagree**	**Strongly Disagree**
Score	4	3	2	1

3.7.3. Mangal Emotional Intelligence Inventory:

Areas of the Scale/ Basic information about scale:

Emotional intelligence Mangal Emotional intelligence Inventory (MEII) constructed by Dr.S.K.Mangal and Dr.Shubhra Mangal in 1971 was used. It has been designed for use with Hindi knowing above 16th years age of School, College and University Students for the measurement of their emotional intelligence. Inventory Consist of 100 statements, which identifies four areas of emotional intelligence as follows:-

1. Intra-personal Awareness (Own Emotions)
2. Inter-personal Awareness (Others Emotions)
3. Intra-personal Management (Own Emotions)
4. Inter-personal Management (Other Emotions)

Reliability:

Reliability of the inventory was examined through three different methods and found to be in range of 0.89 to 0.92.

Validity:

The validity for the inventory has been established by adopting two different approaches namely factorial and criterion related approach. It was found adequate for both the approaches.

Scoring:

'Yes' indicates of presence of emotional intelligence and 'No' indicates lack of emotional intelligence. Higher score shows higher emotional intelligence criteria.

3.8. Data Collation:

For assembling information specialist has actually visited the chosen instructive organization and directed the tests in the wake of taking consent from the school co-ordinator and guideline. Prior to controlling the test, clear guidelines were given to the instructors and questions were elucidated. Tests were managed in perfect conditions. Along these lines, information was gathered from the aggregate example, scoring was done and results were allotted to instructors who were intrigued to know.

3.9. Statistical Analysis:

For the elucidation or the investigation of gathered information in the exploration, factual techniques are utilized. With the assistance of measurable strategies flawless and logical outcome can be acquired. To check contrast and connection between mean score three way analysis of variance – "ANOVA" and Pearson correlation methods will be used. Statistical analysis will be done by SPSS (v16.0) computer program.

In chapter three the exploration strategy, examining technique, test, theory, targets of present investigation, factual examination are planned. The peruser is currently alluded to section four with examination and elucidation of consequences of the present investigation.

Chapter - 4
Analysis and Interpretation of Data

Chapter - 4
Analysis and Interpretation of Data

4.1. Introduction:

In the wake of regulating the instruments and accumulation of information, the information must be prepared and examined as per the layout set down for the reason at the season of building up the exploration plan. After the information has been gathered, it is fundamental to put the sloppy data in a methodical way with the end goal to acquire the coveted outcomes and their translations experimentally. Along these lines it is crucial that the information ought to be exhibited in a very much organized way with the goal that the reason for the investigation can be presented by it. Henceforth, the measurement plays an interesting and imperative job in each examination work. That is the reason, now daily's insights is as a rule unavoidably utilized for getting clear outcomes in an exploration work, in light of the fact that the outcomes are justifiable based on factual computations and they can be given a particular significance moreover.

Actually, preparing infers altering, coding, grouping and classification of gathered information with the goal that they are anything but difficult to complete examination. The term investigation alludes to the calculation of specific measures alongside a scan for examples of relationship that exists among information gatherings. When strategies for gathering information have been resolved utilizing study or some other strategies, the following stage is the decision of suitable systems and methodology for information examination.

4.2. Statistical Procedure:

For proper analysis, there should be a familiarity with the background of survey and with all its stages. Then the hypotheses should be formulated and tested. The ANOVA, and correlation analysis were included in this investigation. It is a pre requisite of any successful research, for it enables researchers to get rid of vague approaches and meaningless interpretations.

4.3. Level of Significance:

This is a very important concept in the context of hypothesis testing. It is always some percentage (usually 5%) which should be chosen with great care, thought and reason. In case, we take implies that the null hypotheses will be rejected when the sampling result has less than 0.05 probability of occurring if the null hypotheses is true. (C.R.Kothari, 2008)

4.4. Presentation and Postulation of the Structural Model of independent variables:

A = Faculty	A1 = Arts
	A2 = Commerce
	A3 = Science
B = Gender	B1 = Male
	B2 = Female
C = Area	C1 = Urban
	C2 = Rural

4.5. Result and Discussion:

4.5.1 Result and Discussion of Mental Health:

The results and discussion of scores of seven areas of mental health are described as under.

4.5.1.1 Result and Discussion on Emotional Stability:

Table A: Showing Results of ANOVA of Emotional stability of high school Students:

Source of Variation	Sum of Square	Df	Mean sum of Square	F	Level of Significant
A (Faculty)	4.69	2	2.34	0.64	NS
B (Gender)	37.36	1	37.36	10.24	0.01
C (Area)	15.61	1	15.61	4.28	0.05
A x B	2.60	2	1.30	0.36	NS
A x C	0.37	2	0.19	0.05	NS
B x C	5.34	1	5.34	1.46	NS
A x B x C	9.39	2	4.69	1.29	NS
Error	2583.63	708	3.65		
Total	44734.00	720			

Significant level of 'F' value: 0.05 level 3.85 (df=1), 0.01 level 6.67 (df=1)
0.05 level 3.01 (df=2), 0.01 level 4.63 (df=2)

Table No: 4.1
Showing Means Scores of Emotional stability of high school Students - Variable-A (Faculty)

	A1	A2	A3
Mean	7.62	7.56	7.75
N	240	240	240

Results of ANOVA main and interaction group on emotional stability of high school Students scores, Table A - consulted and it is found that the f ratio for Ass (faculty) is 0.64, which is not significant. It means higher secondary school Students from arts, commerce and science faculty do not significantly differ on score of emotional stability. By the same point of view Table 4.1 show mean score of arts faculty Students is 7.62, mean score of commerce faculty Students is 7.56 and mean score of science faculty Students is 7.75, it can be said there is no significant difference is existed among arts, commerce and science faculty on emotional stability. It can be seen in figure 4.1.There is no difference found in the scores of emotional stability. It means Students of arts, commerce and science faculty have similar level of emotional stability. So, the result is that Ho_1 is accepted.

Figure No: 4.1
Showing Bar Graph with Means Scores of Emotional stability of high school Students - Variable-A (Faculty)

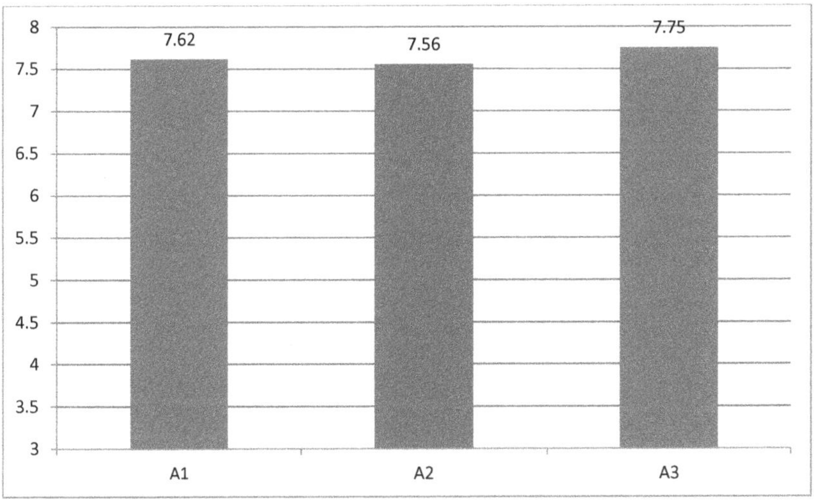

Table No: 4.2
Showing Means Scores of Emotional stability of high school Students - Variable-B (Gender)

	B1	**B2**
Mean	7.87	7.42
N	360	360

F ratio for Bss (Gender) is 10.24, which is significant at 0.01 level. It means male and female Students of high school significantly differ on emotional stability. By the same point of view Table 4.2 show mean score of male Students is 7.87, and mean score of female

Students is 7.42, it can be clearly said that significant difference is existed between male and female Students of high school on emotional stability. It can be seen in figure 4.2. Male and female Students of high school have different level of emotional stability; mean score of result indicates that male Students have higher emotional stability in compare to female Students. This may be because of male persons thinking more logically and comparatively strong in emotionally. So, the result is that Ho_2 is rejected. Normally girl students of high school have lots many responsibilities and even hormonal changes affects so emotional stability is higher in boys in compare to girls.

Figure No: 4.2
Showing Bar graph of Means Scores of Emotional stability of high school Students - Variable-B (Gender)

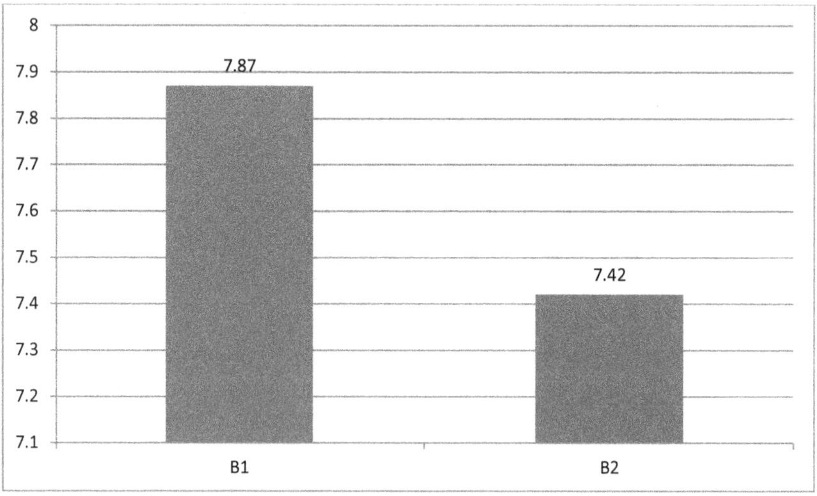

Table No: 4.3
Showing Means Scores of Emotional stability of high school Students - Variable-C (Area)

	C1	C2
Mean	7.79	7.50
N	360	360

F ratio for Css (Area) is 4.28, which is significant at 0.05 level. It means high school Students of urban area and rural area significantly differ on emotional stability. By the same point of view Table 4.3 show the mean score of urban area Students is 7.79, mean score of rural area Students is 7.50. It can be clearly said that significant difference is existed among urban and rural area high school Students on emotional stability; mean score of result indicates that Students of urban area have more emotional stability in compare to rural area Students. It can be seen in figure 4.3. Students of urban area have more challenges in compare to Students of rural area, may be just because that urban area Students scored more. So, the result is that Ho_3 is rejected. A student of urban area gets more various type of exposure so that affects on indirect way to emotional stability.

Figure No: 4.3
Showing Bar Graph of Means Scores of Emotional stability of high school Students - Variable-C (Area)

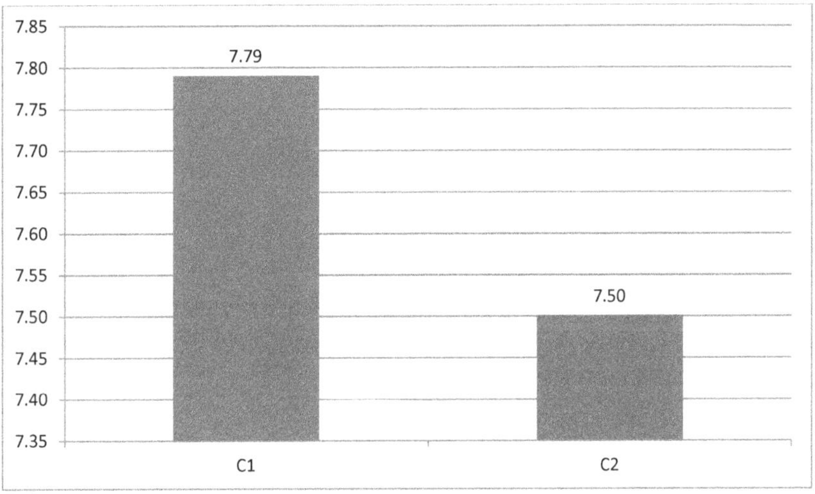

Table No: 4.4
Showing Means Scores of Emotional stability of high school Students - Variable-A x B (Faculty x Gender)

		A1	A2	A3
B1	**Mean**	7.81	7.88	7.93
	N	120	120	120
B2	**Mean**	7.43	7.25	7.58
	N	120	120	120

F ratio for A x Bss (Faculty x Gender) is 0.36, which is not significant. It means faculty and gender of high school Students do not interact each other significantly on emotional stability. By the same point of view Table 4.4 show the mean score of male Students of arts faculty is 7.81, mean score of male Students of commerce faculty is 7.88, mean score of male Students of science faculty is 7.93, mean score of female Students of arts faculty is 7.43, mean score of female Students of commerce faculty is 7.25, and mean score of female Students of science faculty is 7.58; which are not interacting each other significantly on emotional stability of high school Students. It can be seen in figure 4.4. So, the result is that Ho_4 is accepted.

Figure No: 4.4
Showing Bar Graph of Mean Scores of Emotional stability of high school Students - Variable-A x B (Faculty x Gender)

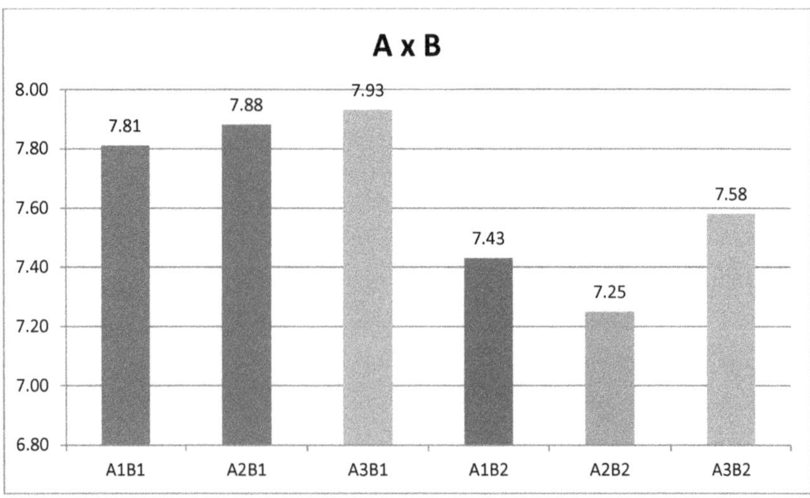

Table No: 4.5
Showing Means Scores of Emotional stability of high school Students - Variable-A x C (Faculty x Area)

		A1	A2	A3
C1	**Mean**	7.75	7.69	7.93
	N	120	120	120
C2	**Mean**	7.48	7.43	7.58
	N	120	120	120

F ratio for A x Css (Faculty x Area) is 0.05, which is not significant. It means faculty and gender do not differ on emotional stability of high school Students. By the same point of view Table 4.5 show the mean score of arts Students of urban area is 7.75, mean score of commerce Students of urban area is 7.69, mean score of science Students of urban area is 7.93, mean score of arts Students of rural area is 7.48, mean score of commerce Students of rural area is 7.43, mean score of science Students of rural area is 7.58; which are not interacting each other significantly on emotional stability of high school Students. It means all group of faculty and gender have similar level of emotional stability. It can be seen in figure 4.5. So, the result is that Ho_5 is accepted.

Figure No: 4.5
Showing Bar Graph of Mean Scores of Emotional stability of high school Students - Variable-A x C (Faculty x Area)

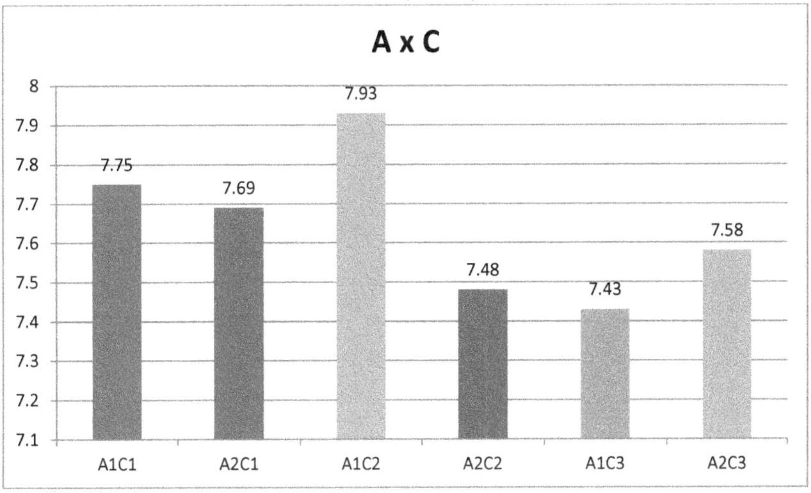

Table No: 4.6
Showing Means Scores of Emotional stability of high school Students - Variable-B x C (Gender x Area)

		B1	B2
C1	Mean	8.10	7.48
	N	180	180
C2	Mean	7.64	7.36
	N	180	180

F ratio for B x Css (Gender x Area) is 1.46, which is not significant. It means gender and area do not interact each other on emotional stability of high school Students. By the same point of view Table 4.6 shows the mean score of male Students of urban area is 8.10, mean score of female Students of urban area is 7.48, mean score of male Students of rural area is 7.64, mean score of female Students of rural area is 7.36, which are not differently interacting each other significantly on emotional stability of high school Students. It can be seen in figure 4.6. It means all group of gender and area have similar level of emotional stability. So, the result is that Ho_6 is accepted.

Figure No: 4.6
Showing Bar Graph of Mean Scores of Emotional stability of high school Students - Variable-B x C (Gender x Area)

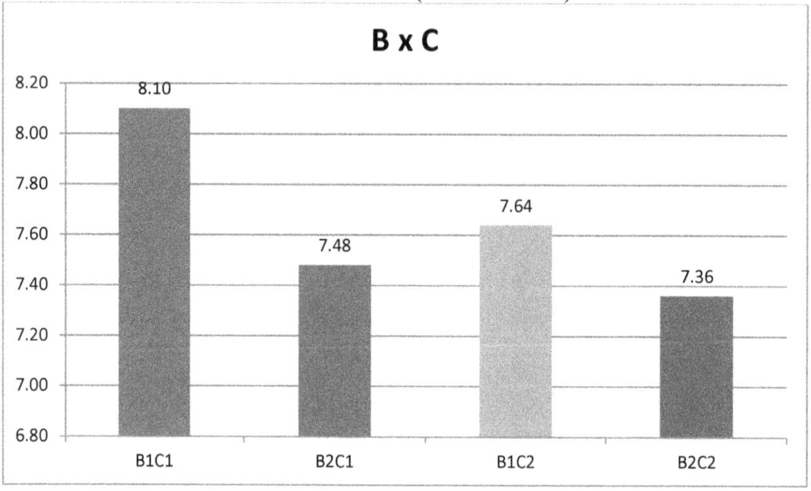

Table No: 4.7
Showing Means Scores of Emotional stability of high school Students - Variable-A x B x C (Faculty x Gender x Area)

		A1		A2		A3	
		B1	**B2**	**B1**	**B2**	**B1**	**B2**
C1	**Mean**	7.88	7.61	8.101	7.28	8.33	7.53
	N	60	60	60	60	60	60
C2	**Mean**	7.73	7.23	7.65	7.22	7.53	7.61
	N	60	60	60	60	60	60

F ratio for A x B x Css (Faculty x Gender x Area) is 1.29, which is not significant. It means faculty, gender and area do not interact significantly each other on scores of emotional stability of high school Students. By the same point of view, table 4.7 shows the mean scores of male Students of urban area with arts faculty is 7.88, mean scores of female Students of urban area with arts faculty is 7.61, mean scores of male Students of urban area with commerce faculty is 8.10, mean scores of female Students of urban area with commerce faculty is 7.28, mean scores of male Students of urban area with science faculty is 8.33, mean scores of female Students of urban area with science faculty is 7.53, mean scores of male Students of rural area with arts faculty is 7.73, mean scores of female Students of rural area with arts faculty is 7.23, mean scores of male Students of rural area with commerce faculty is 7.65, mean scores of female Students of rural area with commerce faculty is 7.22, mean scores of male Students of rural area with science faculty is 7.53, mean scores of female Students of rural area with science faculty is 7.61, which do not differently interacting each other significantly on emotional stability of high school Students. It can be seen in figure 4.7. It means that all the groups of faculty, gender and area have similar level of emotional stability. So, the result is that Ho_7 is accepted.

Figure No: 4.7
Showing Bar Graph of Means Scores of Emotional stability of high school Students - Variable-A x B x C (Faculty x Gender x Area)

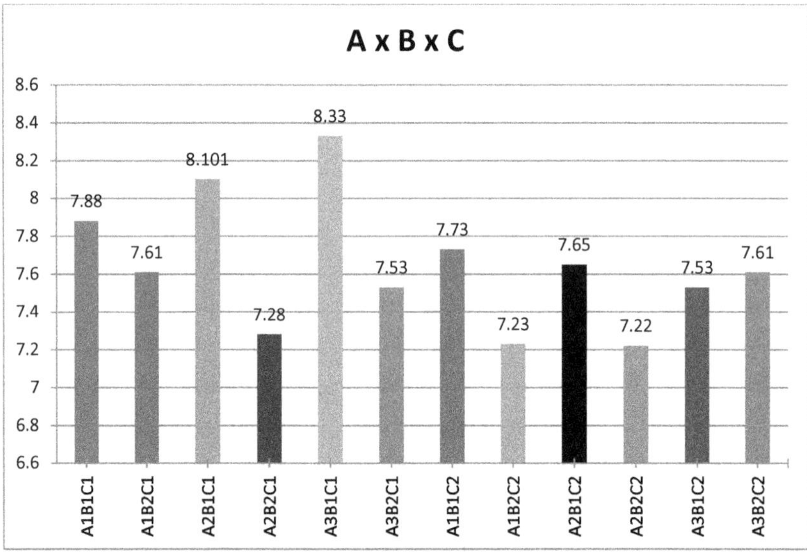

4.5.1.2 Result and Discussion on Overall adjustment:

Table B: Showing Results of ANOVA of Overall adjustment of high school Students:

Source of Variation	Sum of Square	df	Mean sum of Square	F	Level of Significant
A (Faculty)	18.81	2	9.40	0.72	NS
B (Gender)	32.51	1	32.51	2.47	NS
C (Area)	35.11	1	35.11	2.67	NS
A x B	4.73	2	2.36	0.18	NS
A x C	2.73	2	1.36	0.10	NS
B x C	1.70	1	1.70	0.13	NS
A x B x C	34.02	2	17.01	1.29	NS
Error	9312.88	708	13.15		
Total	300933.00	720			

Significant level of 'F' value: 0.05 level 3.85 (df=1), 0.01 level 6.67 (df=1)
0.05 level 3.01 (df=2), 0.01 level 4.63 (df=2)

Table No: 4.8
Showing Means Scores of Overall adjustment of high school Students - Variable-A (Faculty)

	A1	A2	A3
Mean	20.30	19.91	20.15
N	240	240	240

Results of ANOVA main and interaction group on overall adjustment of high school Students scores, Table B - consulted and it is found that the f ratio for Ass (faculty) is 0.72, which is not significant. It means higher secondary school Students from arts, commerce and science faculty do not significantly differ on score of overall adjustment. By the same point of view Table 4.8 show mean score of arts faculty Students is 20.30, mean score of commerce faculty Students is 19.91 and mean score of science faculty Students is 20.15, it can be said there is no significant difference is existed among arts, commerce and science faculty on overall adjustment. It can be seen in figure 4.8. There is no difference found in the scores of overall adjustment. It means Students of arts, commerce and science faculty have similar level of overall adjustment. So, the result is that Ho_8 is accepted.

Figure No: 4.8
Showing Bar Graph with Means Scores of Overall adjustment of high school Students - Variable-A (Faculty)

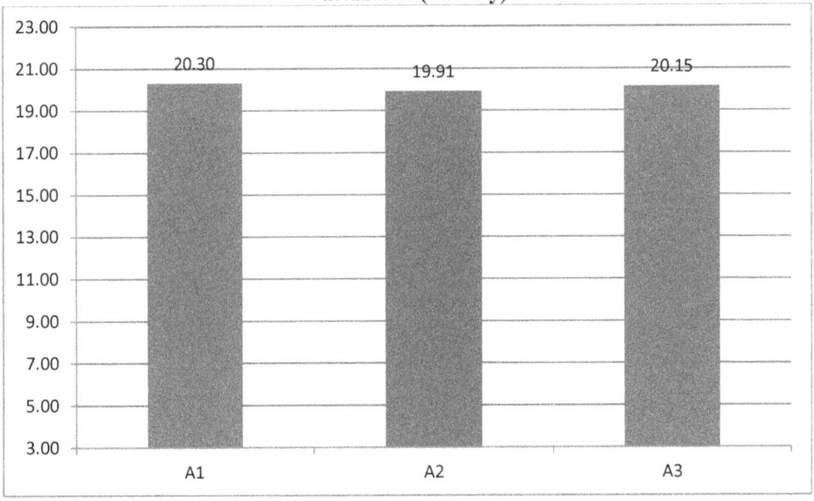

Table No: 4.9
Showing Means Scores of Overall adjustment of high school Students - Variable-B (Gender)

	B1	B2
Mean	19.91	20.33
N	360	360

F ratio for Bss (Gender) is 2.47, which is not significant. It means male and female Students of high school do not differ significantly on overall adjustment. By the same point of view Table 4.9 show mean score of male Students is 19.91, and mean score of female Students is 20.33, it can be clearly said that no significant difference is existed between male and female Students of high school on overall adjustment. It can be seen in figure 4.9. Male and female Students of high school have similar level of overall adjustment. So, the result is that Ho_9 is accepted.

Figure No: 4.9
Showing Bar graph of Means Scores of Overall adjustment of high school Students - Variable-B (Gender)

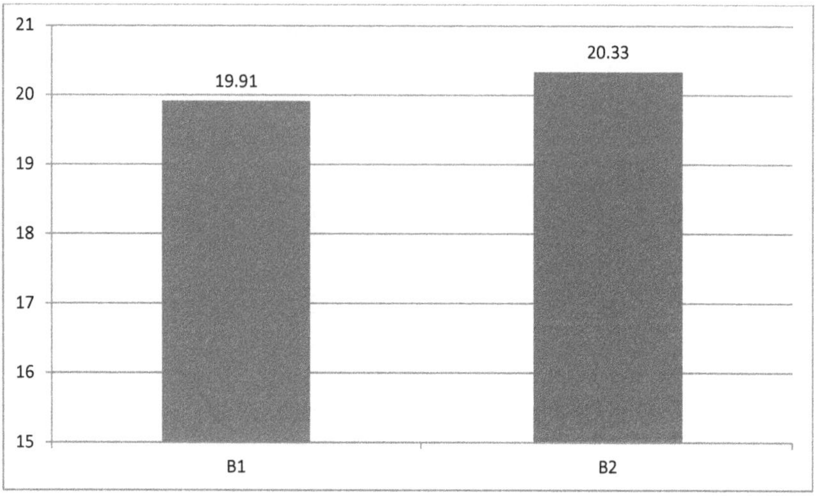

Table No: 4.10
Showing Means Scores of Overall adjustment of high school Students - Variable-C (Area)

	C1	C2
Mean	19.90	20.34
N	360	360

F ratio for Css (Area) is 2.67, which is not significant. It means high school Students of urban area and rural area do not differ significantly on overall adjustment. By the same point of view Table 4.10 show the mean score of urban area Students is 19.90, mean score of rural area Students is 20.34. It can be clearly said that no significant difference is existed among urban and rural area high school Students on overall adjustment. It can be seen in figure 4.10. So, the result is that Ho_{10} is accepted.

Figure No: 4.10
Showing Bar Graph of Means Scores of Overall adjustment of high school Students - Variable-C (Area)

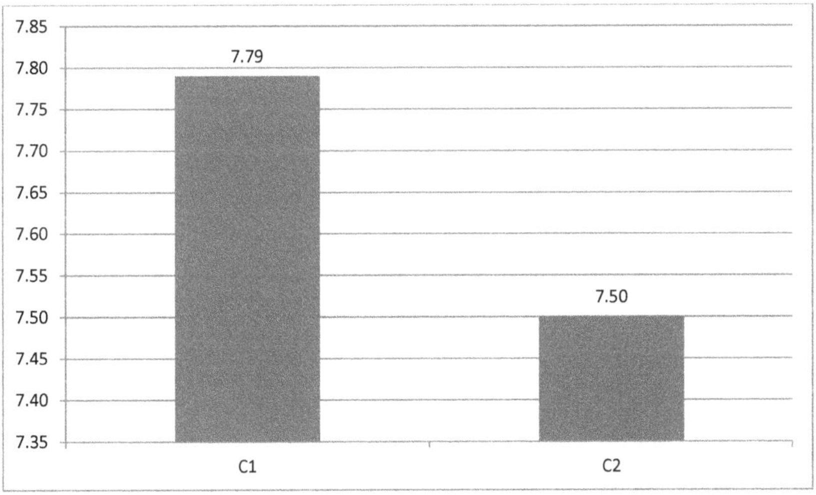

Table No: 4.11

Showing Means Scores of Overall adjustment of high school Students - Variable-A x B (Faculty x Gender)

		A1	A2	A3
B1	**Mean**	20.20	19.66	19.87
	N	120	120	120
B2	**Mean**	20.40	20.16	20.44
	N	120	120	120

F ratio for A x Bss (Faculty x Gender) is 0.18, which is not significant. It means faculty and gender of high school Students do not interact each other significantly on overall adjustment. By the same point of view Table 4.11 show the mean score of male Students of arts faculty is 20.20, mean score of male Students of commerce faculty is 19.66, mean score of male Students of science faculty is 19.87, mean score of female Students of arts faculty is 20.40, mean score of female Students of commerce faculty is 20.16, and mean score of female Students of science faculty is 20.44; which are not interacting each other significantly on overall adjustment of high school Students. It can be seen in figure 4.11. So, the result is that Ho_{11} is accepted.

Figure No: 4.11

Showing Bar Graph of Mean Scores of Overall adjustment of high school Students - Variable-A x B (Faculty x Gender)

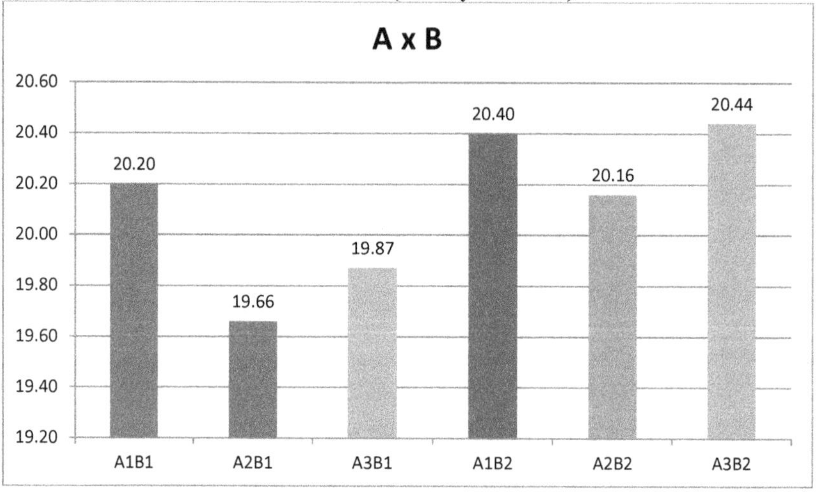

Table No: 4.12

Showing Means Scores of Overall adjustment of high school Students - Variable-A x C (Faculty x Area)

		A1	A2	A3
C1	**Mean**	20.16	19.62	19.93
	N	120	120	120
C2	**Mean**	20.44	20.20	20.38
	N	120	120	120

F ratio for A x Css (Faculty x Area) is 0.10, which is not significant. It means faculty and gender do not differ on overall adjustment of high school Students. By the same point of view Table 4.12 show the mean score of arts Students of urban area is 20.16, mean score of commerce Students of urban area is 19.62, mean score of science Students of urban area is 19.93, mean score of arts Students of rural area is 20.44, mean score of commerce Students of rural area is 20.20, mean score of science Students of rural area is 20.38; which are not interacting each other significantly on overall adjustment of high school Students. It means all group of faculty and gender have similar level of overall adjustment. It can be seen in figure 4.12. So, the result is that Ho_{12} is accepted.

Figure No: 4.12

Showing Bar Graph of Mean Scores of Overall adjustment of high school Students - Variable-A x C (Faculty x Area)

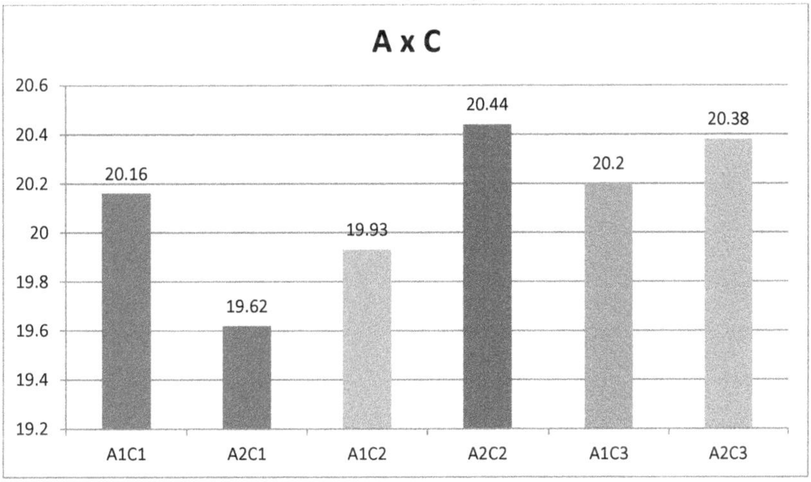

Table No: 4.13
Showing Means Scores of Overall adjustment of high school Students - Variable-B x C (Gender x Area)

		B1	B2
C1	Mean	19.64	20.16
	N	180	180
C2	Mean	20.18	20.51
	N	180	180

F ratio for B x Css (Gender x Area) is 0.13, which is not significant. It means gender and area do not interact each other on overall adjustment of high school Students. By the same point of view Table 4.13 shows the mean score of male Students of urban area is 19.64, mean score of female Students of urban area is 20.16, mean score of male Students of rural area is 20.18, mean score of female Students of rural area is 20.51, which are not differently interacting each other significantly on overall adjustment of high school Students. It can be seen in figure 4.13. It means all group of gender and area have similar level of overall adjustment. So, the result is that Ho_{13} is accepted.

Figure No: 4.13
Showing Bar Graph of Mean Scores of Overall adjustment of high school Students - Variable-B x C (Gender x Area)

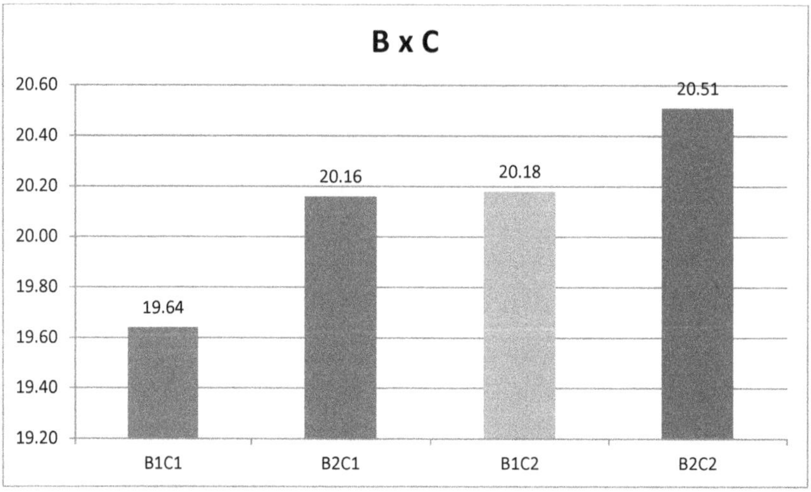

Table No: 4.14

Showing Means Scores of Overall adjustment of high school Students - Variable-A x B x C (Faculty x Gender x Area)

		A1		A2		A3	
		B1	**B2**	**B1**	**B2**	**B1**	**B2**
C1	**Mean**	20.32	20.00	19.15	20.08	19.45	20.40
	N	60	60	60	60	60	60
C2	**Mean**	20.08	20.80	20.17	20.23	20.28	20.48
	N	60	60	60	60	60	60

F ratio for A x B x Css (Faculty x Gender x Area) is 1.29, which is not significant. It means faculty, gender and area do not interact significantly each other on scores of overall adjustment of high school Students. By the same point of view, table 4.14 shows the mean scores of male Students of urban area with arts faculty is 20.32, mean scores of female Students of urban area with arts faculty is 20.00, mean scores of male Students of urban area with commerce faculty is 19.15, mean scores of female Students of urban area with commerce faculty is 20.08, mean scores of male Students of urban area with science faculty is 19.45, mean scores of female Students of urban area with science faculty is 2.040, mean scores of male Students of rural area with arts faculty is 20.08, mean scores of female Students of rural area with arts faculty is 20.80, mean scores of male Students of rural area with commerce faculty is 20.17, mean scores of female Students of rural area with commerce faculty is 20.23, mean scores of male Students of rural area with science faculty is 20.28, mean scores of female Students of rural area with science faculty is 20.48, which do not differently interacting each other significantly on overall adjustment of high school Students. It can be seen in figure 4.14. It means that all the groups of faculty, gender and area have similar level of overall adjustment. So, the result is that Ho_{14} is accepted.

Figure No: 4.14
Showing Bar Graph of Means Scores of Overall adjustment of high school Students - Variable-A x B x C (Faculty x Gender x Area)

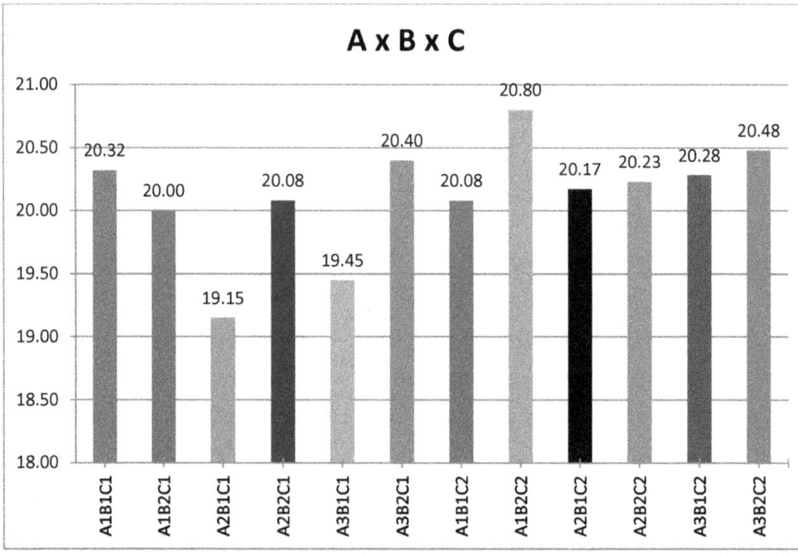

4.5.1.3 Result and Discussion on Autonomy:

Table C: Showing Results of ANOVA of Autonomy of high school Students:

Source of Variation	Sum of Square	Df	Mean sum of Square	F	Level of Significant
A (Faculty)	4.59	2	2.29	0.59	NS
B (Gender)	4.84	1	4.84	1.25	NS
C (Area)	0.17	1	0.17	0.04	NS
A x B	1.20	2	0.60	0.16	NS
A x C	6.32	2	3.16	0.82	NS
B x C	1.51	1	1.51	0.39	NS
A x B x C	3.36	2	1.68	0.43	NS
Error	2740.98	708	3.87		
Total	37973.00	720			

Significant level of 'F' value: 0.05 level 3.85 (df=1), 0.01 level 6.67 (df=1)
0.05 level 3.01 (df=2), 0.01 level 4.63 (df=2)

Table No: 4.15
Showing Means Scores of Autonomy of high school Students - Variable-A (Faculty)

	A1	A2	A3
Mean	7.07	7.03	6.88
N	240	240	240

Results of ANOVA main and interaction group on Autonomy of high school Students scores, Table C - consulted and it is found that the f ratio for Ass (faculty) is 0.59, which is not significant. It means higher secondary school Students from arts, commerce and science faculty do not significantly differ on score of Autonomy. By the same point of view Table 4.15 show mean score of arts faculty Students is 7.07, mean score of commerce faculty Students is 7.03 and mean score of science faculty Students is 6.88, it can be said there is no significant difference is existed among arts, commerce and science faculty on Autonomy. It can be seen in figure 4.15. There is no difference found in the scores of Autonomy. It means Students of arts, commerce and science faculty have similar level of Autonomy. So, the result is that Ho_{15} is accepted.

Figure No: 4.15
Showing Bar Graph with Means Scores of Autonomy of high school Students - Variable-A (Faculty)

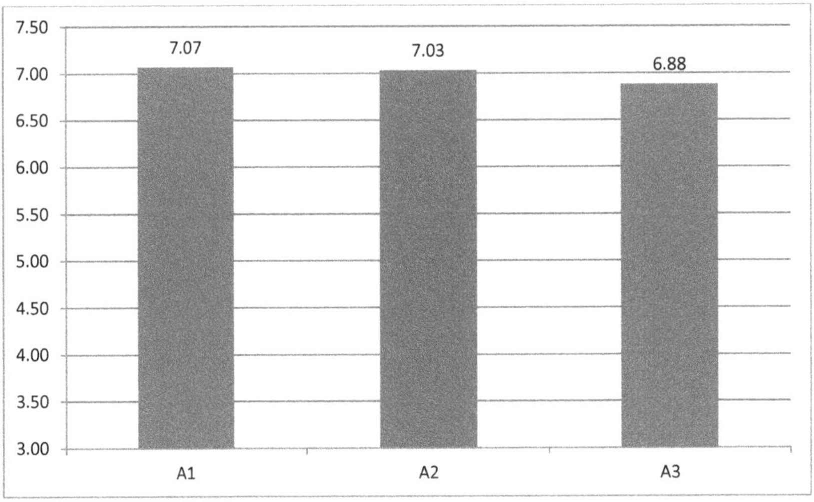

Table No: 4.16
Showing Means Scores of Autonomy of high school Students - Variable-B (Gender)

	B1	B2
Mean	7.08	6.91
N	360	360

F ratio for Bss (Gender) is 1.25, which is not significant. It means male and female Students of high school do not differ significantly on Autonomy. By the same point of view Table 4.16 show mean score of male Students is 7.08, and mean score of female Students is 6.91, it can be clearly said that no significant difference is existed between male and female Students of high school on Autonomy. It can be seen in figure 4.16. Male and female Students of high school have similar level of Autonomy. So, the result is that Ho_{16} is accepted.

Figure No: 4.16
Showing Bar graph of Means Scores of Autonomy of high school Students - Variable-B (Gender)

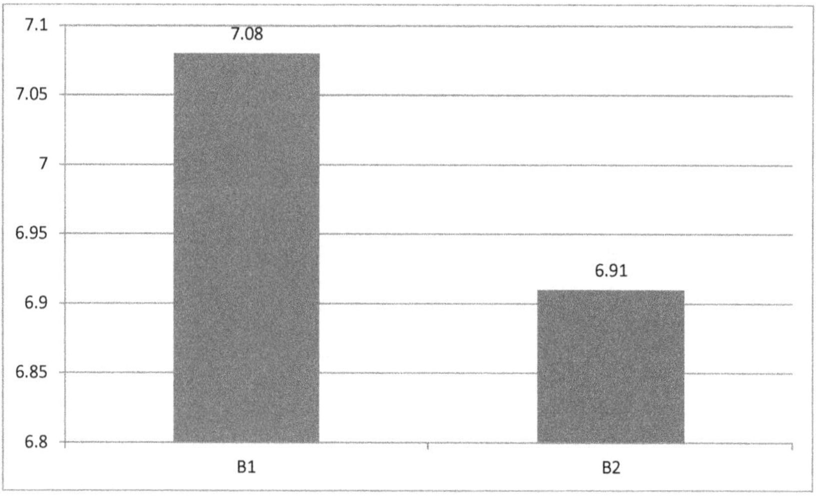

Table No: 4.17
Showing Means Scores of Autonomy of high school Students - Variable-C (Area)

	C1	C2
Mean	7.01	6.98
N	360	360

F ratio for Css (Area) is 0.04, which is not significant. It means high school Students of urban area and rural area do not differ significantly on Autonomy. By the same point of view Table 4.17 show the mean score of urban area Students is 7.01, mean score of rural area Students is 6.98. It can be clearly said that no significant difference is existed among urban and rural area high school Students on Autonomy. It can be seen in figure 4.17. So, the result is that Ho_{17} is accepted.

Figure No: 4.17
Showing Bar Graph of Means Scores of Autonomy of high school Students - Variable-C (Area)

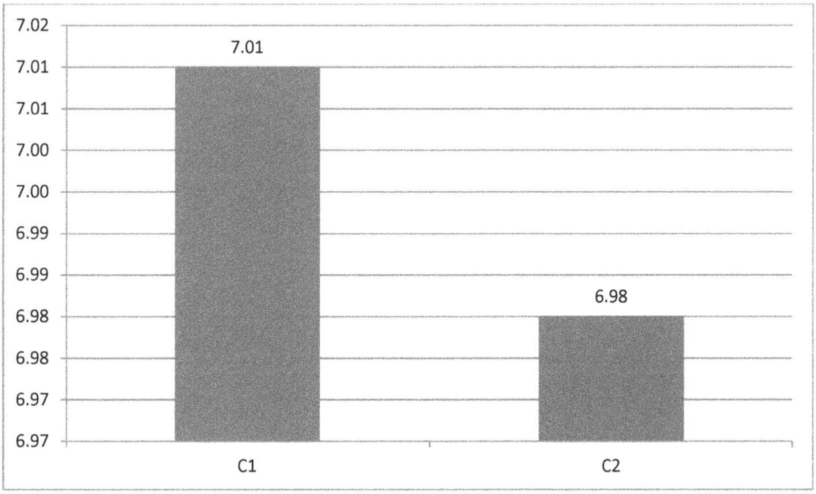

Table No: 4.18
Showing Means Scores of Autonomy of high school Students - Variable-A x B (Faculty x Gender)

		A1	A2	A3
B1	**Mean**	7.15	7.06	7.02
	N	120	120	120
B2	**Mean**	6.99	6.99	6.75
	N	120	120	120

F ratio for A x Bss (Faculty x Gender) is 0.16, which is not significant. It means faculty and gender of high school Students do not interact each other significantly on Autonomy. By the same point of view Table 4.18 show the mean score of male Students of arts faculty is 7.15, mean score of male Students of commerce faculty is 7.06, mean score of male Students of science faculty is 7.02, mean score of female Students of arts faculty is 6.99, mean score of female Students of commerce faculty is 6.99, and mean score of female Students of science faculty is 6.75; which are not interacting each other significantly on Autonomy of high school Students. It can be seen in figure 4.18. So, the result is that Ho_{18} is accepted.

Figure No: 4.18
Showing Bar Graph of Mean Scores of Autonomy of high school Students - Variable-A x B (Faculty x Gender)

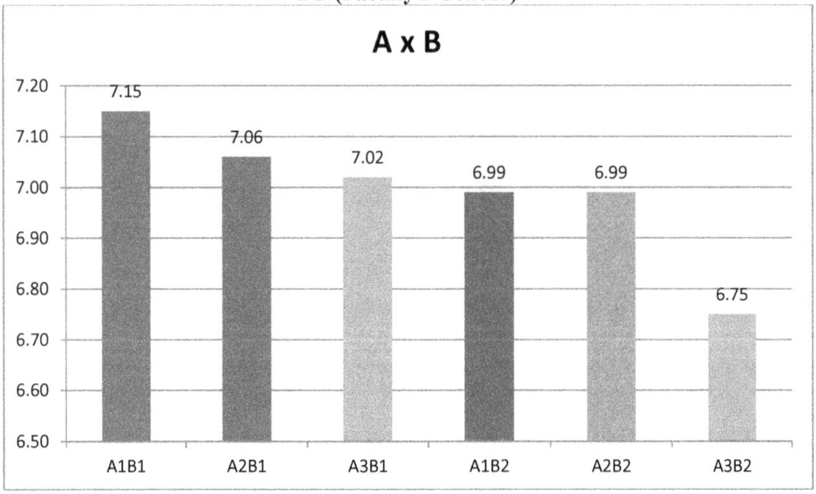

Table No: 4.19

Showing Means Scores of Autonomy of high school Students - Variable-A x C (Faculty x Area)

		A1	A2	A3
C1	**Mean**	6.98	7.03	7.02
	N	120	120	120
C2	**Mean**	7.17	7.02	6.75
	N	120	120	120

F ratio for A x Css (Faculty x Area) is 0.82, which is not significant. It means faculty and gender do not differ on Autonomy of high school Students. By the same point of view Table 4.19 show the mean score of arts Students of urban area is 6.98, mean score of commerce Students of urban area is 7.03, mean score of science Students of urban area is 7.02, mean score of arts Students of rural area is 7.17, mean score of commerce Students of rural area is 7.02, mean score of science Students of rural area is 6.75; which are not interacting each other significantly on Autonomy of high school Students. It means all group of faculty and gender have similar level of Autonomy. It can be seen in figure 4.19. So, the result is that Ho_{19} is accepted.

Figure No: 4.19

Showing Bar Graph of Mean Scores of Autonomy of high school Students - Variable-A x C (Faculty x Area)

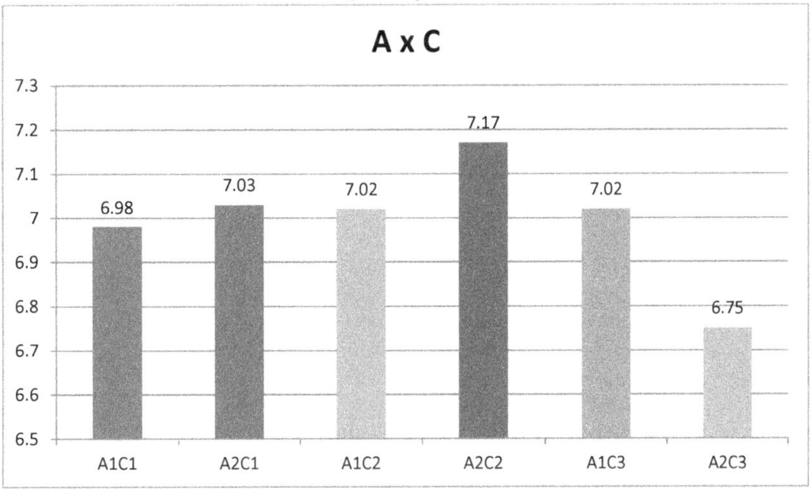

Table No: 4.20
Showing Means Scores of Autonomy of high school Students - Variable-B x C (Gender x Area)

		B1	B2
C1	**Mean**	7.04	6.97
	N	180	180
C2	**Mean**	7.11	6.85
	N	180	180

F ratio for B x Css (Gender x Area) is 0.39, which is not significant. It means gender and area do not interact each other on Autonomy of high school Students. By the same point of view Table 4.20 shows the mean score of male Students of urban area is 7.04, mean score of female Students of urban area is 6.97, mean score of male Students of rural area is 7.11, mean score of female Students of rural area is 6.85, which are not differently interacting each other significantly on Autonomy of high school Students. It can be seen in figure 4.20. It means all group of gender and area have similar level of Autonomy. So, the result is that Ho_{20} is accepted.

Figure No: 4.20
Showing Bar Graph of Mean Scores of Autonomy of high school Students - Variable-B x C (Gender x Area)

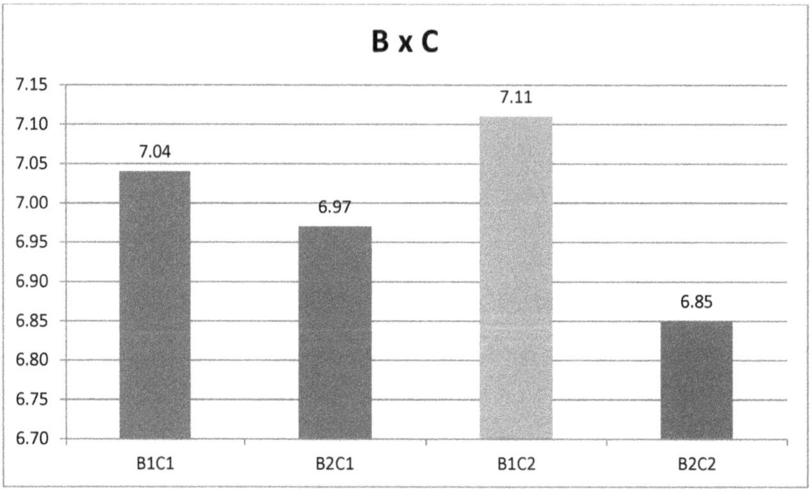

Table No: 4.21
Showing Means Scores of Autonomy of high school Students - Variable-A x B x C (Faculty x Gender x Area)

		A1		A2		A3	
		B1	**B2**	**B1**	**B2**	**B1**	**B2**
C1	**Mean**	7.02	6.93	7.10	6.97	7.02	7.02
	N	60	60	60	60	60	60
C2	**Mean**	7.28	7.05	7.02	7.02	7.02	6.48
	N	60	60	60	60	60	60

F ratio for A x B x Css (Faculty x Gender x Area) is 0.43, which is not significant. It means faculty, gender and area do not interact significantly each other on scores of Autonomy of high school Students. By the same point of view, table 4.21 shows the mean scores of male Students of urban area with arts faculty is 7.02, mean scores of female Students of urban area with arts faculty is 6.93, mean scores of male Students of urban area with commerce faculty is 7.10, mean scores of female Students of urban area with commerce faculty is 6.97, mean scores of male Students of urban area with science faculty is 7.02, mean scores of female Students of urban area with science faculty is 7.02, mean scores of male Students of rural area with arts faculty is 7.25, mean scores of female Students of rural area with arts faculty is 7.05, mean scores of male Students of rural area with commerce faculty is 7.02, mean scores of female Students of rural area with commerce faculty is 7.02, mean scores of male Students of rural area with science faculty is 7.02, mean scores of female Students of rural area with science faculty is 6.48, which do not differently interacting each other significantly on Autonomy of high school Students. It can be seen in figure 4.21. It means that all the groups of faculty, gender and area have similar level of Autonomy. So, the result is that Ho_{21} is accepted.

Figure No: 4.21
Showing Bar Graph of Means Scores of Autonomy of high school Students - Variable- A x B x C (Faculty x Gender x Area)

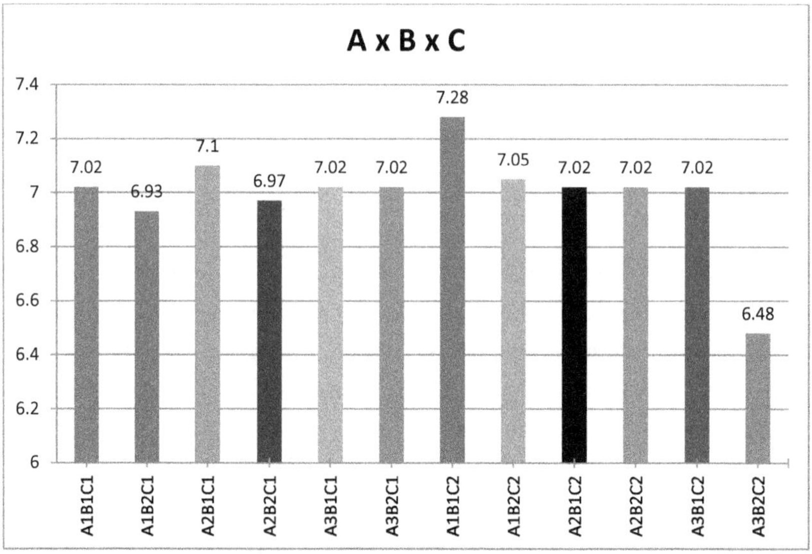

4.5.1.4 Result and Discussion on Security-insecurity:

Table D: Showing Results of ANOVA of Security-insecurity of high school Students:

Source of Variation	Sum of Square	Df	Mean sum of Square	F	Level of Significant
A (Faculty)	1.41	2	0.70	0.16	NS
B (Gender)	0.20	1	0.20	0.05	NS
C (Area)	0.67	1	0.67	0.15	NS
A x B	1.23	2	0.61	0.14	NS
A x C	2.45	2	1.23	0.28	NS
B x C	0.00	1	0.00	0.00	NS
A x B x C	2.76	2	1.38	0.31	NS
Error	3124.83	708	4.41		
Total	38666.00	720			

Significant level of 'F' value: 0.05 level 3.85 (df=1), 0.01 level 6.67 (df=1)
0.05 level 3.01 (df=2), 0.01 level 4.63 (df=2)

Table No: 4.22
Showing Means Scores of Security-insecurity of high school Students - Variable-A (Faculty)

	A1	A2	A3
Mean	6.96	7.05	7.06
N	240	240	240

Results of ANOVA main and interaction group on Security-insecurity of high school Students scores, Table D - consulted and it is found that the f ratio for Ass (faculty) is 0.16, which is not significant. It means higher secondary school Students from arts, commerce and science faculty do not significantly differ on score of Security-insecurity. By the same point of view Table 4.22 show mean score of arts faculty Students is 6.96, mean score of commerce faculty Students is 7.05 and mean score of science faculty Students is 7.06, it can be said there is no significant difference is existed among arts, commerce and science faculty on Security-insecurity. It can be seen in figure 4.22. There is no difference found in the scores of Security-insecurity. It means Students of arts, commerce and science faculty have similar level of Security-insecurity. So, the result is that Ho_{22} is accepted.

Figure No: 4.22
Showing Bar Graph with Means Scores of Security-insecurity of high school Students - Variable-A (Faculty)

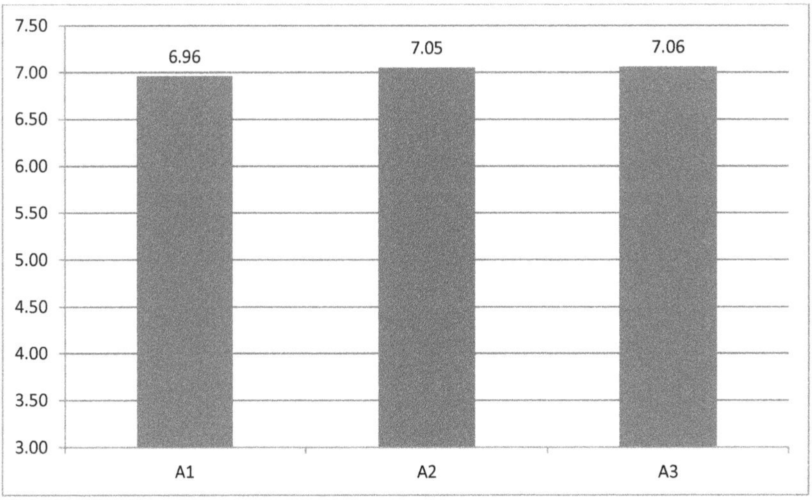

Table No: 4.23
Showing Means Scores of Security-insecurity of high school Students - Variable-B (Gender)

	B1	B2
Mean	7.01	7.04
N	360	360

F ratio for Bss (Gender) is 0.05, which is not significant. It means male and female Students of high school do not differ significantly on Security-insecurity. By the same point of view Table 4.23 show mean score of male Students is 7.01, and mean score of female Students is 7.04, it can be clearly said that no significant difference is existed between male and female Students of high school on Security-insecurity. It can be seen in figure 4.23. Male and female Students of high school have similar level of Security-insecurity. So, the result is that Ho_{23} is accepted.

Figure No: 4.23
Showing Bar graph of Means Scores of Security-insecurity of high school Students - Variable-B (Gender)

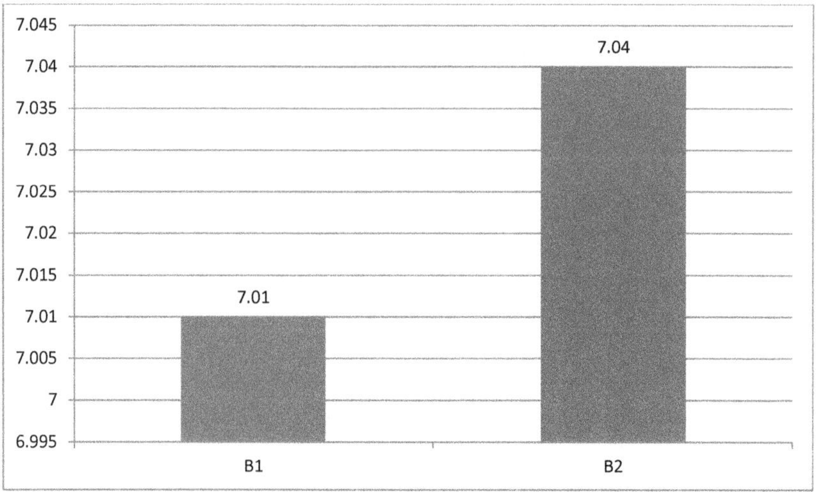

Table No: 4.24

Showing Means Scores of Security-insecurity of high school Students - Variable-C (Area)

	C1	C2
Mean	7.06	6.99
N	360	360

F ratio for Css (Area) is 0.15, which is not significant. It means high school Students of urban area and rural area do not differ significantly on Security-insecurity. By the same point of view Table 4.24 show the mean score of urban area Students is 7.06, mean score of rural area Students is 6.99. It can be clearly said that no significant difference is existed among urban and rural area high school Students on Security-insecurity. It can be seen in figure 4.24. So, the result is that Ho_{24} is accepted.

Figure No: 4.24

Showing Bar Graph of Means Scores of Security-insecurity of high school Students - Variable-C (Area)

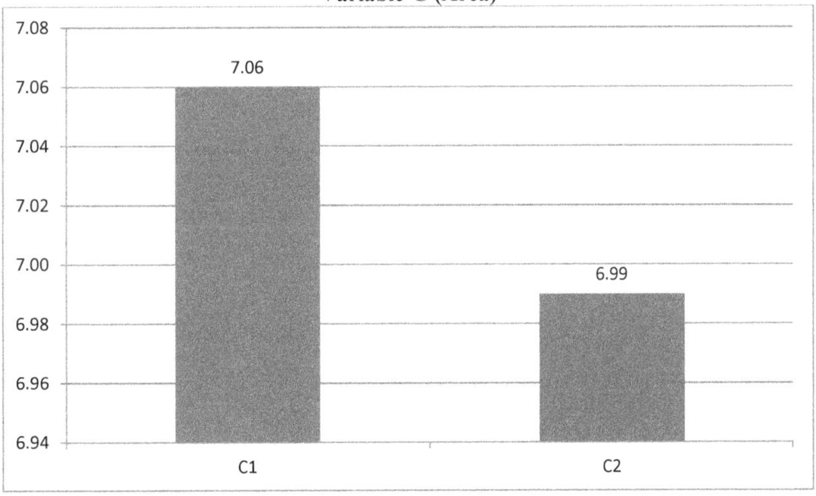

Table No: 4.25
Showing Means Scores of Security-insecurity of high school Students - Variable-A x B (Faculty x Gender)

		A1	A2	A3
B1	**Mean**	6.92	7.01	7.10
	N	120	120	120
B2	**Mean**	7.01	7.10	7.02
	N	120	120	120

F ratio for A x Bss (Faculty x Gender) is 0.14, which is not significant. It means faculty and gender of high school Students do not interact each other significantly on Security-insecurity. By the same point of view Table 4.25 show the mean score of male Students of arts faculty is 6.92, mean score of male Students of commerce faculty is 7.01, mean score of male Students of science faculty is 7.10, mean score of female Students of arts faculty is 7.01, mean score of female Students of commerce faculty is 7.10, and mean score of female Students of science faculty is 7.02; which are not interacting each other significantly on Security-insecurity of high school Students. It can be seen in figure 4.25. So, the result is that Ho_{25} is accepted.

Figure No: 4.25
Showing Bar Graph of Mean Scores of Security-insecurity of high school Students - Variable-A x B (Faculty x Gender)

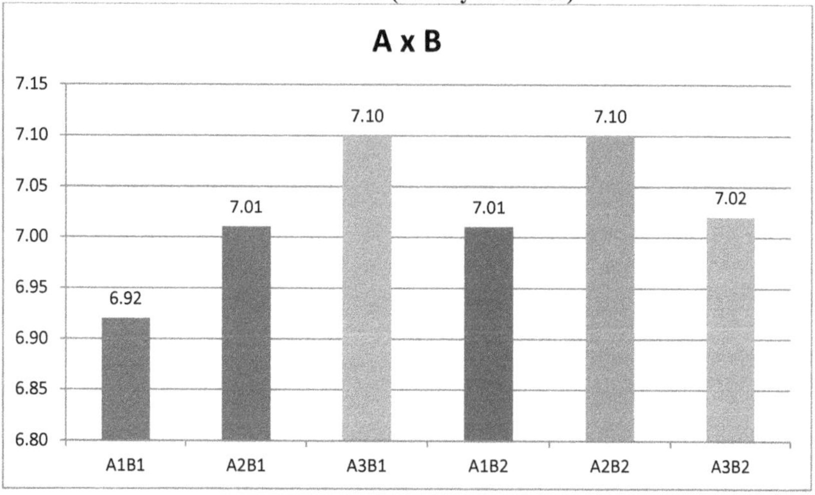

Table No: 4.26

Showing Means Scores of Security-insecurity of high school Students - Variable-A x C (Faculty x Area)

		A1	A2	A3
C1	**Mean**	7.06	7.01	7.10
	N	120	120	120
C2	**Mean**	6.87	7.10	7.02
	N	120	120	120

F ratio for A x Css (Faculty x Area) is 0.28, which is not significant. It means faculty and gender do not differ on Security-insecurity of high school Students. By the same point of view Table 4.26 show the mean score of arts Students of urban area is 7.06, mean score of commerce Students of urban area is 7.01, mean score of science Students of urban area is 7.10, mean score of arts Students of rural area is 6.87, mean score of commerce Students of rural area is 7.10, mean score of science Students of rural area is 7.02; which are not interacting each other significantly on Security-insecurity of high school Students. It means all group of faculty and gender have similar level of Security-insecurity. It can be seen in figure 4.26. So, the result is that Ho_{26} is accepted.

Figure No: 4.26

Showing Bar Graph of Mean Scores of Security-insecurity of high school Students - Variable-A x C (Faculty x Area)

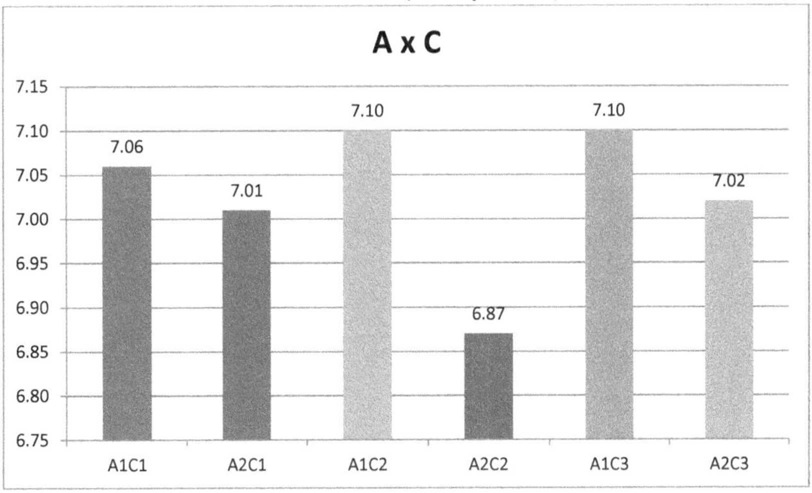

Table No: 4.27
Showing Means Scores of Security-insecurity of high school Students - Variable-B x C (Gender x Area)

		B1	B2
C1	Mean	7.04	7.07
	N	180	180
C2	Mean	6.98	7.01
	N	180	180

F ratio for B x Css (Gender x Area) is 0.00, which is not significant. It means gender and area do not interact each other on Security-insecurity of high school Students. By the same point of view Table 4.27 shows the mean score of male Students of urban area is 7.04, mean score of female Students of urban area is 7.07, mean score of male Students of rural area is 6.98, mean score of female Students of rural area is 7.01, which are not differently interacting each other significantly on Security-insecurity of high school Students. It can be seen in figure 4.27. It means all group of gender and area have similar level of Security-insecurity. So, the result is that Ho_{27} is accepted.

Figure No: 4.27
Showing Bar Graph of Mean Scores of Security-insecurity of high school Students - Variable-B x C (Gender x Area)

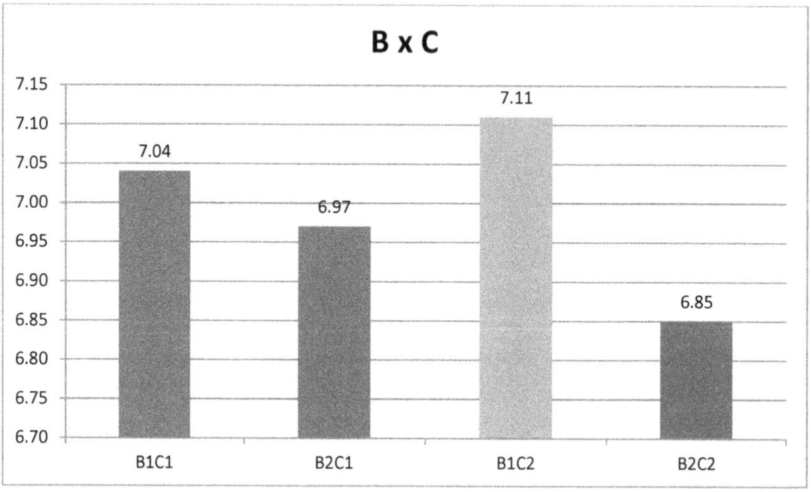

Table No: 4.28
Showing Means Scores of Security-insecurity of high school Students - Variable-A x B x C (Faculty x Gender x Area)

		A1		A2		A3	
		B1	**B2**	**B1**	**B2**	**B1**	**B2**
C1	**Mean**	7.10	7.02	6.92	7.10	7.10	7.10
	N	60	60	60	60	60	60
C2	**Mean**	6.73	7.00	7.10	7.10	7.10	6.93
	N	60	60	60	60	60	60

F ratio for A x B x Css (Faculty x Gender x Area) is 0.31, which is not significant. It means faculty, gender and area do not interact significantly each other on scores of Security-insecurity of high school Students. By the same point of view, table 4.28 shows the mean scores of male Students of urban area with arts faculty is 7.10, mean scores of female Students of urban area with arts faculty is 7.02, mean scores of male Students of urban area with commerce faculty is 6.92, mean scores of female Students of urban area with commerce faculty is 7.10, mean scores of male Students of urban area with science faculty is 7.10, mean scores of female Students of urban area with science faculty is 7.10, mean scores of male Students of rural area with arts faculty is 6.73, mean scores of female Students of rural area with arts faculty is 7.00, mean scores of male Students of rural area with commerce faculty is 7.10, mean scores of female Students of rural area with commerce faculty is 7.10, mean scores of male Students of rural area with science faculty is 7.10, mean scores of female Students of rural area with science faculty is 6.93, which do not differently interacting each other significantly on Security-insecurity of high school Students. It can be seen in figure 4.28. It means that all the groups of faculty, gender and area have similar level of Security-insecurity. So, the result is that Ho_{28} is accepted.

Figure No: 4.28
Showing Bar Graph of Means Scores of Security-insecurity of high school Students - Variable-A x B x C (Faculty x Gender x Area)

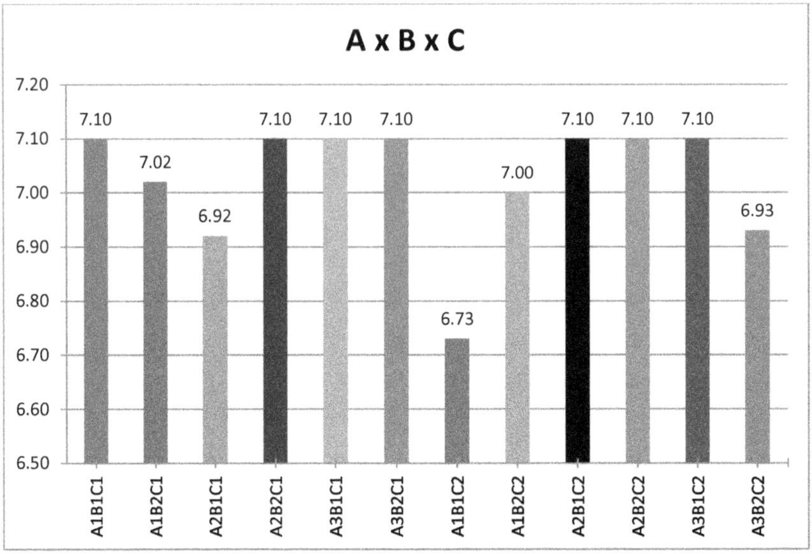

4.5.1.5 Result and Discussion on Self concept:

Table E: **Showing Results of ANOVA of Self concept of high school Students:**

Source of Variation	Sum of Square	Df	Mean sum of Square	F	Level of Significant
A (Faculty)	1.54	2	0.77	0.06	NS
B (Gender)	27.22	1	27.22	2.18	NS
C (Area)	57.80	1	57.80	4.63	0.05
A x B	1.41	2	0.71	0.06	NS
A x C	3.90	2	1.95	0.16	NS
B x C	32.09	1	32.09	2.57	NS
A x B x C	0.58	2	0.29	0.02	NS
Error	8839.03	708	12.49		
Total	52706.00	720			

Significant level of 'F' value: 0.05 level 3.85 (df=1), 0.01 level 6.67 (df=1)
0.05 level 3.01 (df=2), 0.01 level 4.63 (df=2)

Table No: 4.29
Showing Means Scores of Self concept of high school Students - Variable-A (Faculty)

	A1	A2	A3
Mean	7.78	7.75	7.86
N	240	240	240

Results of ANOVA main and interaction group on Self concept of high school Students scores, Table E - consulted and it is found that the f ratio for Ass (faculty) is 0.06, which is not significant. It means higher secondary school Students from arts, commerce and science faculty do not significantly differ on score of Self concept. By the same point of view Table 4.29 show mean score of arts faculty Students is 7.78, mean score of commerce faculty Students is 7.75 and mean score of science faculty Students is 7.86, it can be said there is no significant difference is existed among arts, commerce and science faculty on Self concept. It can be seen in figure 4.29. There is no difference found in the scores of Self concept. It means Students of arts, commerce and science faculty have similar level of Self concept. So, the result is that Ho_{29} is accepted.

Figure No: 4.29
Showing Bar Graph with Means Scores of Self concept of high school Students - Variable-A (Faculty)

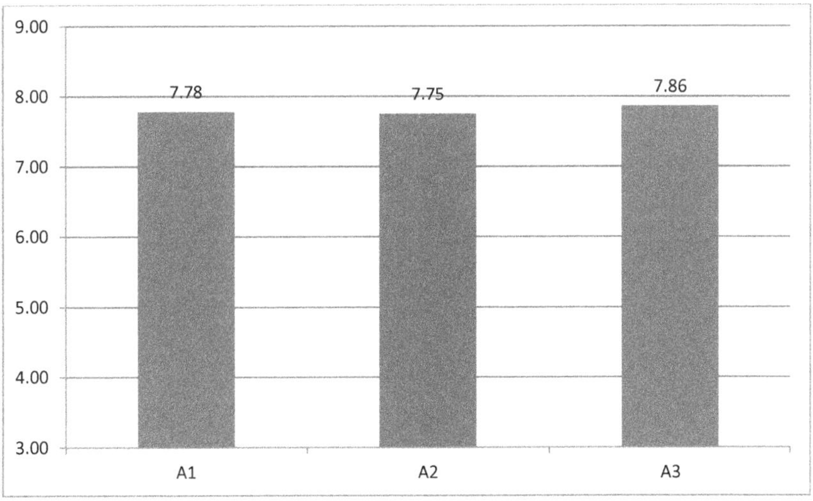

Table No: 4.30
Showing Means Scores of Self concept of high school Students - Variable-B (Gender)

	B1	B2
Mean	7.60	7.99
N	360	360

F ratio for Bss (Gender) is 2.18, which is not significant. It means male and female Students of high school do not differ significantly on Self concept. By the same point of view Table 4.30 show mean score of male Students is 7.60, and mean score of female Students is 7.99, it can be clearly said that no significant difference is existed between male and female Students of high school on Self concept. It can be seen in figure 4.30. Male and female Students of high school have similar level of Self concept. So, the result is that Ho_{30} is accepted.

Figure No: 4.30
Showing Bar graph of Means Scores of Self concept of high school Students - Variable-B (Gender)

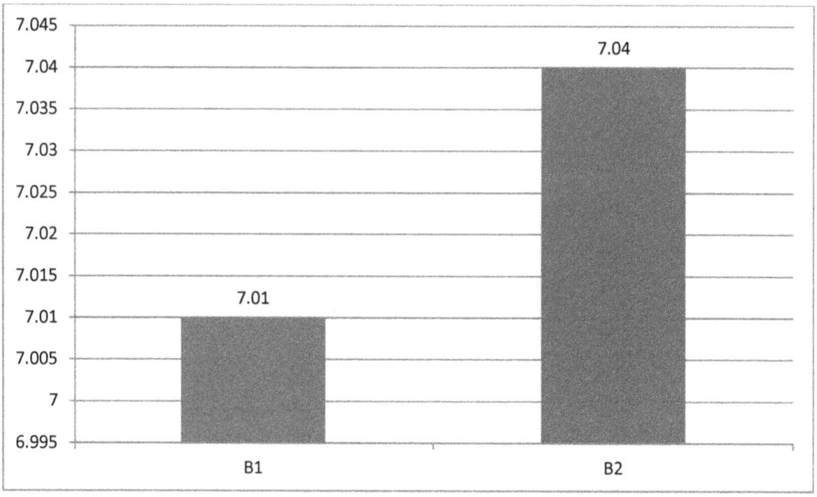

Table No: 4.31
Showing Means Scores of Self concept of high school Students - Variable-C (Area)

	C1	C2
Mean	7.51	8.08
N	360	360

F ratio for Css (Area) is 4.63, which is significant at 0.05 level. It means high school Students of urban area and rural area significantly differ on Self concept. By the same point of view Table 4.31 show the mean score of urban area Students is 7.51, mean score of rural area Students is 8.08. It can be clearly said that significant difference is existed among urban and rural area high school Students on Self concept; mean score shows that Students of rural area have high self concept in compare to urban area Students. It can be seen in figure 4.31. Students of rural area spend more time with self and having more social intelligence so it could be the reason of high self concept. So, the result is that Ho_{31} is rejected. Students of total area have high need of achievement and seriousness towards education, this could be the reason of high self concept in rural area.

Figure No: 4.31
Showing Bar Graph of Means Scores of Self concept of high school Students - Variable-C (Area)

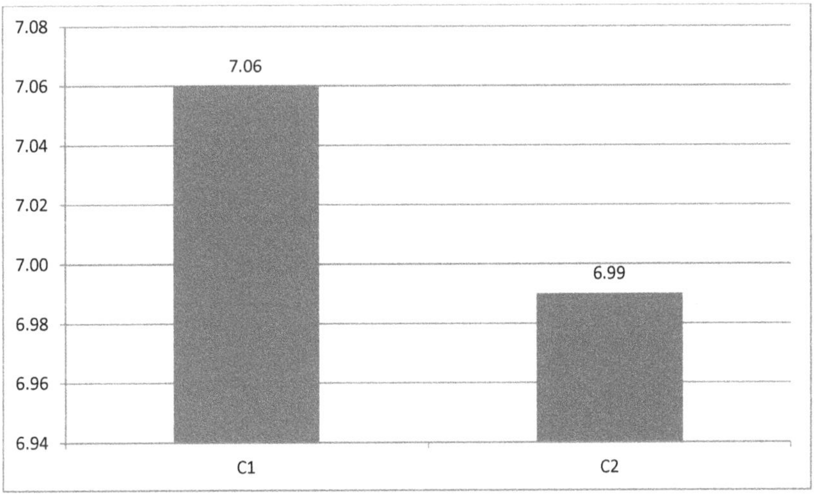

Table No: 4.32
Showing Means Scores of Self concept of high school Students - Variable-A x B (Faculty x Gender)

		A1	A2	A3
B1	**Mean**	7.53	7.61	7.67
	N	120	120	120
B2	**Mean**	8.03	7.89	8.05
	N	120	120	120

F ratio for A x Bss (Faculty x Gender) is 0.14, which is not significant. It means faculty and gender of high school Students do not interact each other significantly on Self concept. By the same point of view Table 4.32 show the mean score of male Students of arts faculty is 7.53, mean score of male Students of commerce faculty is 7.61, mean score of male Students of science faculty is 7.67, mean score of female Students of arts faculty is 8.03, mean score of female Students of commerce faculty is 7.89, and mean score of female Students of science faculty is 8.05; which are not interacting each other significantly on Self concept of high school Students. It can be seen in figure 4.32. So, the result is that Ho_{32} is accepted.

Figure No: 4.32
Showing Bar Graph of Mean Scores of Self concept of high school Students - Variable-A x B (Faculty x Gender)

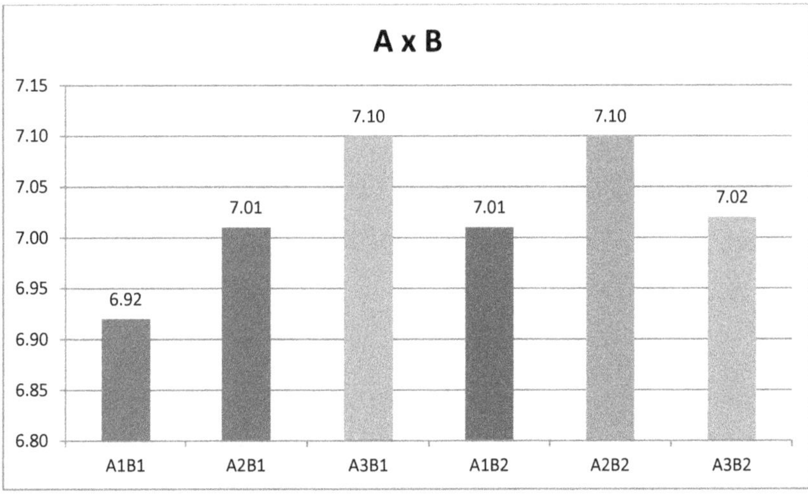

Table No: 4.33

Showing Means Scores of Self concept of high school Students - Variable-A x C (Faculty x Area)

		A1	A2	A3
C1	**Mean**	7.57	7.49	7.48
	N	120	120	120
C2	**Mean**	7.98	8.01	8.24
	N	120	120	120

F ratio for A x Css (Faculty x Area) is 0.16, which is not significant. It means faculty and gender do not differ on Self concept of high school Students. By the same point of view Table 4.33 show the mean score of arts Students of urban area is 7.57, mean score of commerce Students of urban area is 7.49, mean score of science Students of urban area is 7.48, mean score of arts Students of rural area is 7.98, mean score of commerce Students of rural area is 8.01, mean score of science Students of rural area is 8.24; which are not interacting each other significantly on Self concept of high school Students. It means all group of faculty and gender have similar level of Self concept. It can be seen in figure 4.33. So, the result is that Ho_{33} is accepted.

Figure No: 4.33

Showing Bar Graph of Mean Scores of Self concept of high school Students - Variable-A x C (Faculty x Area)

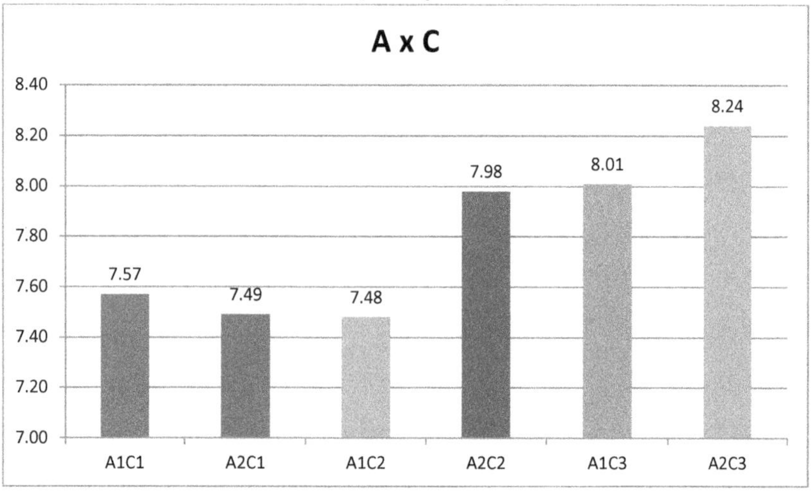

Table No: 4.34

Showing Means Scores of Self concept of high school Students - Variable-B x C (Gender x Area)

		B1	B2
C1	Mean	7.11	7.92
	N	180	180
C2	Mean	8.09	8.06
	N	180	180

F ratio for B x Css (Gender x Area) is 2.57, which is not significant. It means gender and area do not interact each other on Self concept of high school Students. By the same point of view Table 4.34 shows the mean score of male Students of urban area is 7.11, mean score of female Students of urban area is 7.92, mean score of male Students of rural area is 8.09, mean score of female Students of rural area is 8.06, which are not differently interacting each other significantly on Self concept of high school Students. It can be seen in figure 4.34. It means all group of gender and area have similar level of Self concept. So, the result is that Ho_{34} is accepted.

Figure No: 4.34

Showing Bar Graph of Mean Scores of Self concept of high school Students - Variable-B x C (Gender x Area)

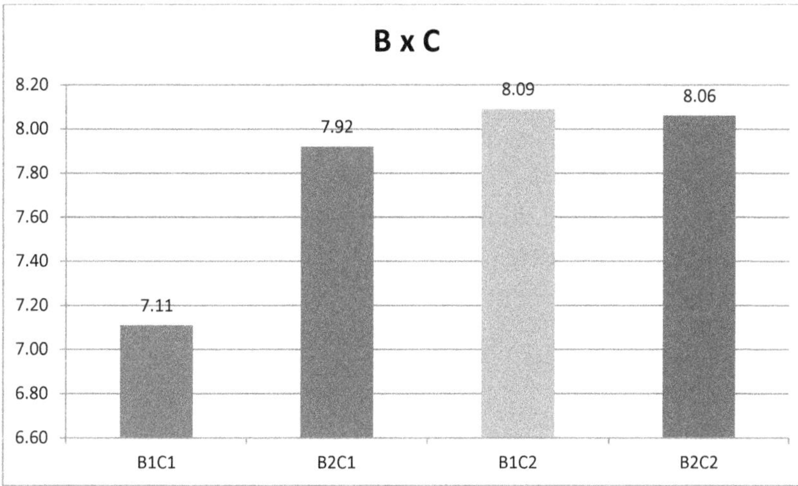

Table No: 4.35
Showing Means Scores of Self concept of high school Students - Variable-A x B x C (Faculty x Gender x Area)

		A1		A2		A3	
		B1	**B2**	**B1**	**B2**	**B1**	**B2**
C1	**Mean**	7.13	8.00	7.10	7.88	7.08	7.87
	N	60	60	60	60	60	60
C2	**Mean**	7.92	8.05	8.12	7.90	8.25	8.23
	N	60	60	60	60	60	60

F ratio for A x B x Css (Faculty x Gender x Area) is 0.02, which is not significant. It means faculty, gender and area do not interact significantly each other on scores of Self concept of high school Students. By the same point of view, table 4.35 shows the mean scores of male Students of urban area with arts faculty is 7.13, mean scores of female Students of urban area with arts faculty is 8.00, mean scores of male Students of urban area with commerce faculty is 7.10, mean scores of female Students of urban area with commerce faculty is 7.88, mean scores of male Students of urban area with science faculty is

7.08, mean scores of female Students of urban area with science faculty is 7.86, mean scores of male Students of rural area with arts faculty is 7.92, mean scores of female Students of rural area with arts faculty is 8.05, mean scores of male Students of rural area with commerce faculty is 8.12, mean scores of female Students of rural area with commerce faculty is 7.90, mean scores of male Students of rural area with science faculty is 8.25, mean scores of female Students of rural area with science faculty is 8.23, which do not differently interacting each other significantly on Self concept of high school Students. It can be seen in figure 4.35. It means that all the groups of faculty, gender and area have similar level of Self concept. So, the result is that Ho_{35} is accepted.

Figure No: 4.35
Showing Bar Graph of Means Scores of Self concept of high school Students - Variable-A x B x C (Faculty x Gender x Area)

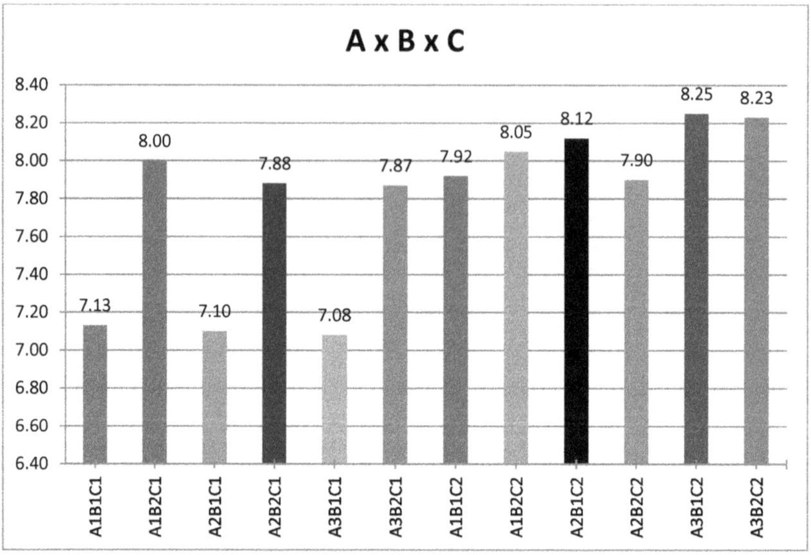

4.5.1.6 Result and Discussion on Intelligence:

Table F: **Showing Results of ANOVA of Intelligence of high school Students:**

Source of Variation	Sum of Square	Df	Mean sum of Square	F	Level of Significant
A (Faculty)	1.68	2	0.84	0.05	NS
B (Gender)	0.31	1	0.31	0.02	NS
C (Area)	15.90	1	15.90	0.86	NS
A x B	36.53	2	18.26	0.99	NS
A x C	4.24	2	2.12	0.11	NS
B x C	0.03	1	0.04	0.01	NS
A x B x C	11.45	2	5.73	0.31	NS
Error	13114.75	708	18.52		
Total	135099.00	720			

Significant level of 'F' value: 0.05 level 3.85 (df=1), 0.01 level 6.67 (df=1)
0.05 level 3.01 (df=2), 0.01 level 4.63 (df=2)

Table No: 4.36
Showing Means Scores of Intelligence of high school Students - Variable-A (Faculty)

	A1	A2	A3
Mean	12.97	13.08	12.99
N	240	240	240

Results of ANOVA main and interaction group on Intelligence of high school Students scores, Table F - consulted and it is found that the f ratio for Ass (faculty) is 0.05, which is not significant. It means higher secondary school Students from arts, commerce and science faculty do not significantly differ on score of Intelligence. By the same point of view Table 4.36 show mean score of arts faculty Students is 12.97, mean score of commerce faculty Students is 13.08 and mean score of science faculty Students is 12.99, it can be said there is no significant difference is existed among arts, commerce and science faculty on Intelligence. It can be seen in figure 4.36. There is no difference found in the scores of Intelligence. It means Students of arts, commerce and science faculty have similar level of Intelligence. So, the result is that Ho_{36} is accepted.

Figure No: 4.36
Showing Bar Graph with Means Scores of Intelligence of high school Students - Variable-A (Faculty)

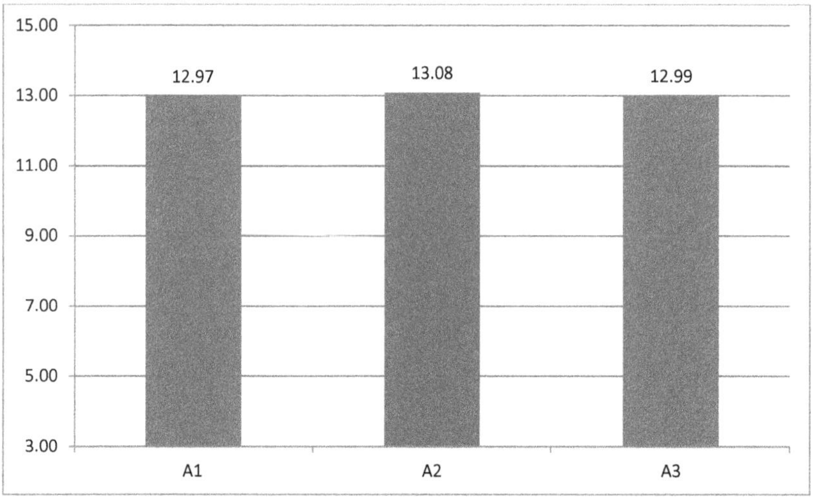

Table No: 4.37
Showing Means Scores of Intelligence of high school Students - Variable-B (Gender)

	B1	B2
Mean	12.99	13.03
N	360	360

F ratio for Bss (Gender) is 0.02, which is not significant. It means male and female Students of high school do not differ significantly on Intelligence. By the same point of view Table 4.37 show mean score of male Students is 12.99, and mean score of female Students is 13.03, it can be clearly said that no significant difference is existed between male and female Students of high school on Intelligence. It can be seen in figure 4.37. Male and female Students of high school have similar level of Intelligence. So, the result is that Ho_{37} is accepted.

Figure No: 4.37
Showing Bar graph of Means Scores of Intelligence of high school Students - Variable-B (Gender)

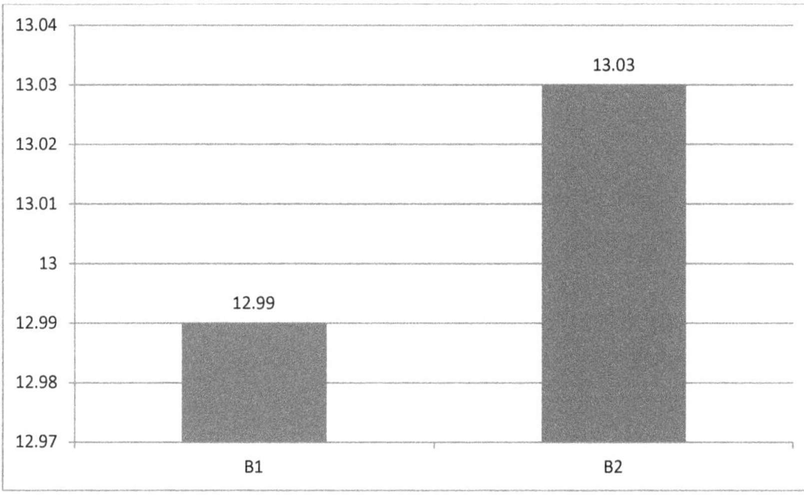

Table No: 4.38
Showing Means Scores of Intelligence of high school Students - Variable-C (Area)

	C1	C2
Mean	13.16	12.86
N	360	360

F ratio for Css (Area) is 0.86, which is not significant. It means high school Students of urban area and rural area do not differ significantly on Intelligence. By the same point of view Table 4.38 show the mean score of urban area Students is 13.16, mean score of rural area Students is 12.86. It can be clearly said that no significant difference is existed among urban and rural area high school Students on Intelligence. It can be seen in figure 4.38. So, the result is that Ho_{38} is accepted.

Figure No: 4.38
Showing Bar Graph of Means Scores of Intelligence of high school Students - Variable-C (Area)

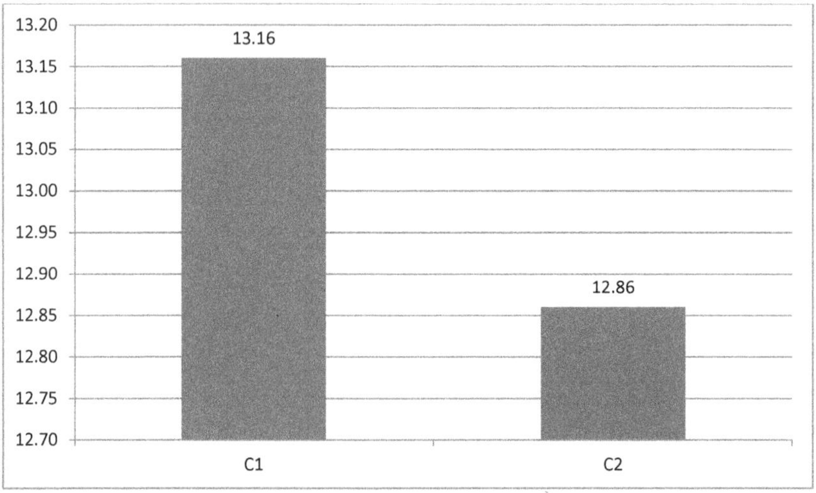

Table No: 4.39
Showing Means Scores of Intelligence of high school Students - Variable-A x B (Faculty x Gender)

		A1	A2	A3
B1	**Mean**	12.68	13.03	13.26
	N	120	120	120
B2	**Mean**	13.25	13.13	12.73
	N	120	120	120

F ratio for A x Bss (Faculty x Gender) is 0.99, which is not significant. It means faculty and gender of high school Students do not interact each other significantly on Intelligence. By the same point of view Table 4.39 show the mean score of male Students of arts faculty is 12.68, mean score of male Students of commerce faculty is 13.03, mean score of male Students of science faculty is 13.26, mean score of female Students of arts faculty is 13.25, mean score of female Students of commerce faculty is 13.13, and mean score of female Students of science faculty is 12.73; which are not interacting each other significantly on Intelligence of high school Students. It can be seen in figure 4.39. So, the result is that Ho_{39} is accepted.

Figure No: 4.39
Showing Bar Graph of Mean Scores of Intelligence of high school Students - Variable-A x B (Faculty x Gender)

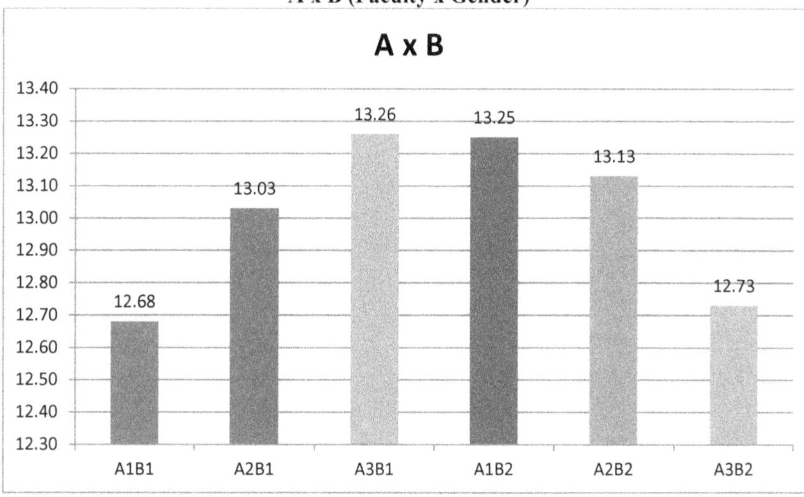

Table No: 4.40
Showing Means Scores of Intelligence of high school Students - Variable-A x C (Faculty x Area)

		A1	A2	A3
C1	**Mean**	13.03	13.33	13.13
	N	120	120	120
C2	**Mean**	12.91	12.83	12.85
	N	120	120	120

F ratio for A x Css (Faculty x Area) is 0.11, which is not significant. It means faculty and gender do not differ on Intelligence of high school Students. By the same point of view Table 4.40 show the mean score of arts Students of urban area is 13.03, mean score of commerce Students of urban area is 13.33, mean score of science Students of urban area is 13.13, mean score of arts Students of rural area is 12.91, mean score of commerce Students of rural area is 12.83, mean score of science Students of rural area is 12.85; which are not interacting each other significantly on Intelligence of high school Students. It means all group of faculty and gender have similar level of Intelligence. It can be seen in figure 4.40. So, the result is that Ho_{40} is accepted.

Figure No: 4.40

Showing Bar Graph of Mean Scores of Intelligence of high school Students - Variable-A x C (Faculty x Area)

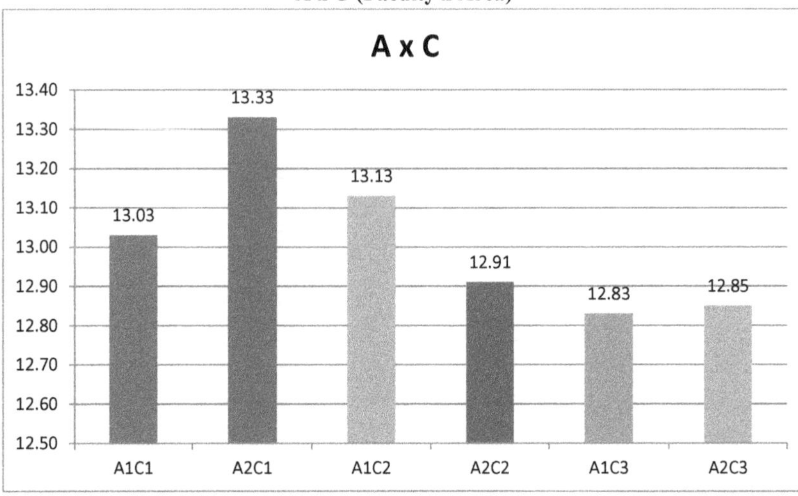

Table No: 4.41

Showing Means Scores of Intelligence of high school Students - Variable-B x C (Gender x Area)

		B1	B2
C1	Mean	13.13	13.19
	N	180	180
C2	Mean	12.85	12.88
	N	180	180

F ratio for B x Css (Gender x Area) is 0.01, which is not significant. It means gender and area do not interact each other on Intelligence of high school Students. By the same point of view Table 4.41 shows the mean score of male Students of urban area is 13.13, mean score of female Students of urban area is 13.19, mean score of male Students of rural area is 12.85, mean score of female Students of rural area is 12.88, which are not differently interacting each other significantly on Intelligence of high school Students. It can be seen in figure 4.41. It means all group of gender and area have similar level of Intelligence. So, the result is that Ho_{41} is accepted.

Figure No: 4.41
Showing Bar Graph of Mean Scores of Intelligence of high school Students - Variable-B x C (Gender x Area)

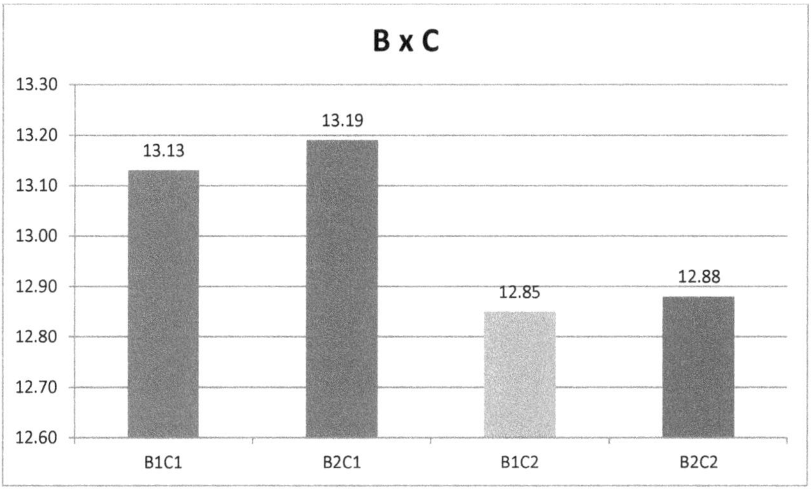

Table No: 4.42
Showing Means Scores of Intelligence of high school Students - Variable-A x B x C (Faculty x Gender x Area)

		A1		A2		A3	
		B1	**B2**	**B1**	**B2**	**B1**	**B2**
C1	**Mean**	12.63	13.42	13.45	13.20	13.32	12.95
	N	60	60	60	60	60	60
C2	**Mean**	12.73	13.08	12.62	13.05	13.20	12.50
	N	60	60	60	60	60	60

F ratio for A x B x Css (Faculty x Gender x Area) is 0.31, which is not significant. It means faculty, gender and area do not interact significantly each other on scores of Intelligence of high school Students. By the same point of view, table 4.42 shows the mean scores of male Students of urban area with arts faculty is 12.63, mean scores of female Students of urban area with arts faculty is 13.42, mean scores of male Students of urban area with commerce faculty is 13.45, mean scores of female Students of urban area with commerce faculty is 13.20, mean scores of male Students of urban area with science faculty is 13.32, mean scores of female Students of urban area with science faculty is 12.95, mean scores of male Students of rural area with arts faculty is 12.73, mean scores of female Students of rural area with arts faculty is 13.08, mean scores of male Students of rural area with commerce faculty is 12.62, mean scores of female Students of rural area with commerce faculty is 13.05, mean scores of male Students of rural area with science faculty is 13.20, mean scores of female Students of rural area with science faculty is 12.50, which do not differently interacting each other significantly on Intelligence of high school Students. It can be seen in figure 4.42. It means that all the groups of faculty, gender and area have similar level of Intelligence. So, the result is that Ho_{42} is accepted.

Figure No: 4.42
Showing Bar Graph of Means Scores of Intelligence of high school Students - Variable- A x B x C (Faculty x Gender x Area)

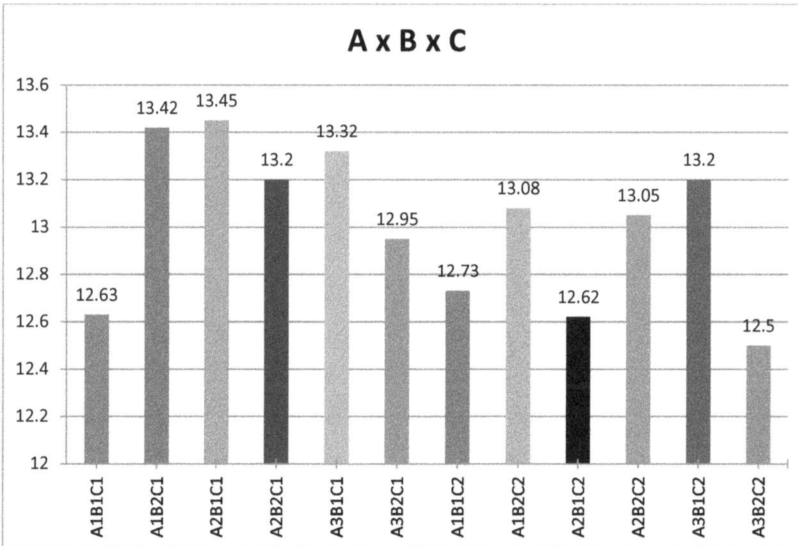

4.5.1.7 Result and Discussion on Mental health:

Table G: Showing Results of ANOVA of Mental health of high school Students:

Source of Variation	Sum of Square	Df	Mean sum of Square	F	Level of Significant
A (Faculty)	16.05	2	8.03	0.10	NS
B (Gender)	13.07	1	13.07	0.17	NS
C (Area)	19.01	1	19.01	0.24	NS
A x B	36.30	2	18.15	0.23	NS
A x C	1.11	2	0.55	0.01	NS
B x C	36.90	1	36.90	0.47	NS
A x B x C	17.70	2	8.85	0.11	NS
Error	55325.98	708	78.14		
Total	2876097.00	720			

Significant level of 'F' value: 0.05 level 3.85 (df=1), 0.01 level 6.67 (df=1)
0.05 level 3.01 (df=2), 0.01 level 4.63 (df=2)

Table No: 4.43
Showing Means Scores of Mental health of high school Students - Variable-A (Faculty)

	A1	A2	A3
Mean	62.69	62.38	62.70
N	240	240	240

Results of ANOVA main and interaction group on mental health of high school Students scores, Table G - consulted and it is found that the f ratio for Ass (faculty) is 0.10, which is not significant. It means higher secondary school Students from arts, commerce and science faculty do not significantly differ on score of mental health. By the same point of view Table 4.43 show mean score of arts faculty Students is 62.69, mean score of commerce faculty Students is 62.38 and mean score of science faculty Students is 62.70, it can be said there is no significant difference is existed among arts, commerce and science faculty on mental health. It can be seen in figure 4.43. There is no difference found in the scores of mental health. It means Students of arts, commerce and science faculty have similar level of mental health. So, the result is that Ho_{43} is accepted.

Figure No: 4.43
Showing Bar Graph with Means Scores of Mental health of high school Students - Variable-A (Faculty)

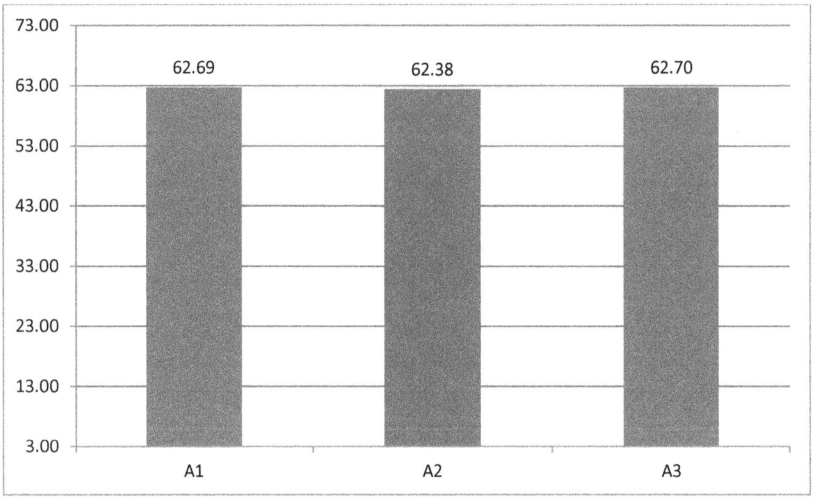

Table No: 4.44
Showing Means Scores of Mental health of high school Students - Variable-B (Gender)

	B1	B2
Mean	62.46	62.73
N	360	360

F ratio for Bss (Gender) is 0.17, which is not significant. It means male and female Students of high school do not differ significantly on mental health. By the same point of view Table 4.44 show mean score of male Students is 62.46, and mean score of female Students is 62.73, it can be clearly said that no significant difference is existed between male and female Students of high school on mental health. It can be seen in figure 4.44. Male and female Students of high school have similar level of mental health. So, the result is that Ho_{44} is accepted.

Figure No: 4.44
Showing Bar graph of Means Scores of Mental health of high school Students - Variable-B (Gender)

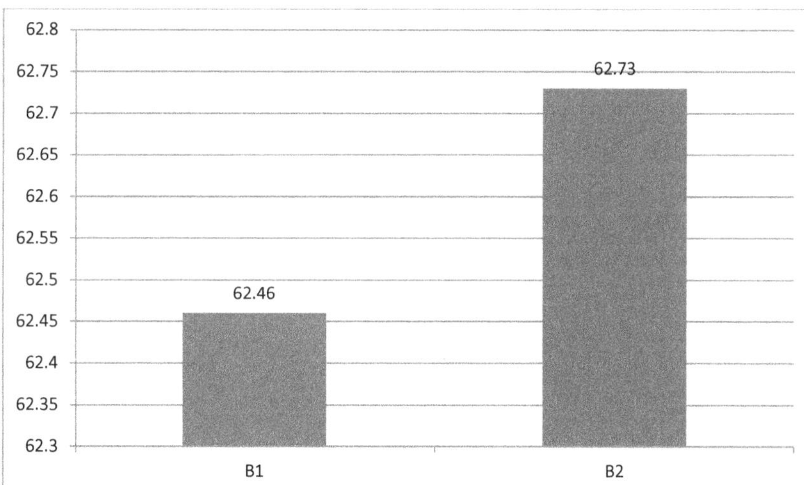

Table No: 4.45
Showing Means Scores of Mental health of high school Students - Variable-C (Area)

	C1	C2
Mean	62.43	62.75
N	360	360

F ratio for Css (Area) is 0.24, which is not significant. It means high school Students of urban area and rural area do not differ significantly on mental health. By the same point of view Table 4.45 show the mean score of urban area Students is 62.43, mean score of rural area Students is 62.75. It can be clearly said that no significant difference is existed among urban and rural area high school Students on mental health. It can be seen in figure 4.45. So, the result is that Ho_{45} is accepted.

Figure No: 4.45
Showing Bar Graph of Means Scores of Mental health of high school Students - Variable-C (Area)

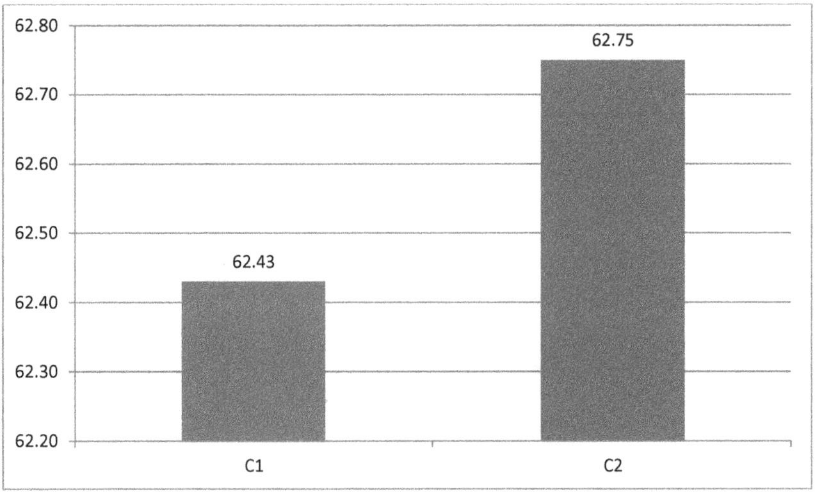

Table No: 4.46
Showing Means Scores of Mental health of high school Students - Variable-A x B (Faculty x Gender)

		A1	A2	A3
B1	**Mean**	62.28	62.24	62.84
	N	120	120	120
B2	**Mean**	63.10	62.52	62.56
	N	120	120	120

F ratio for A x Bss (Faculty x Gender) is 0.23, which is not significant. It means faculty and gender of high school Students do not interact each other significantly on Mental health. By the same point of view Table 4.46 show the mean score of male Students of arts faculty is 62.28, mean score of male Students of commerce faculty is 62.24, mean score of male Students of science faculty is 62.84, mean score of female Students of arts faculty is 63.10, mean score of female Students of commerce faculty is 62.52, and mean score of female Students of science faculty is 62.56; which are not interacting each other significantly on Mental health of high school Students. It can be seen in figure 4.46. So, the result is that Ho_{46} is accepted.

Figure No: 4.46
Showing Bar Graph of Mean Scores of Mental health of high school Students - Variable-A x B (Faculty x Gender)

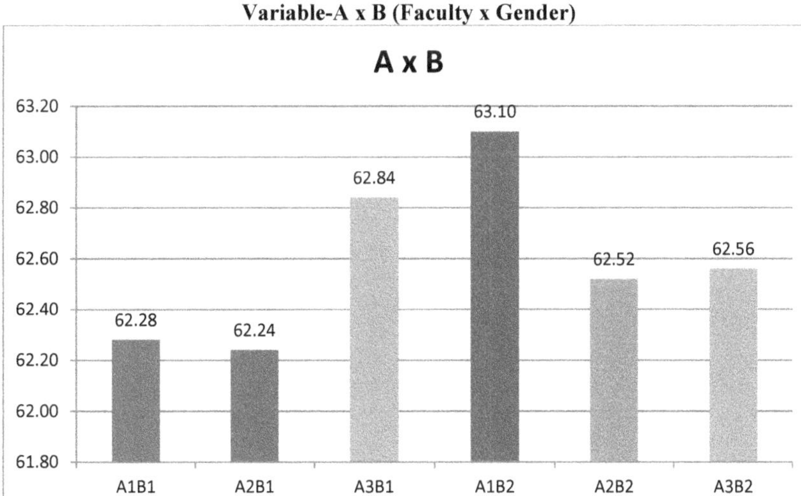

Table No: 4.47

Showing Means Scores of Mental health of high school Students - Variable-A x C (Faculty x Area)

		A1	A2	A3
C1	Mean	62.53	62.17	62.58
	N	120	120	120
C2	Mean	62.85	62.59	62.82
	N	120	120	120

F ratio for A x Css (Faculty x Area) is 0.01, which is not significant. It means faculty and gender do not differ on mental health of high school Students. By the same point of view Table 4.47 show the mean score of arts Students of urban area is 62.53, mean score of commerce Students of urban area is 62.17, mean score of science Students of urban area is 62.58, mean score of arts Students of rural area is 62.85, mean score of commerce Students of rural area is 62.59, mean score of science Students of rural area is 62.82; which are not interacting each other significantly on mental health of high school Students. It means all group of faculty and gender have similar level of mental health. It can be seen in figure 4.47. So, the result is that Ho_{47} is accepted.

Figure No: 4.47

Showing Bar Graph of Mean Scores of Mental health of high school Students - Variable-A x C (Faculty x Area)

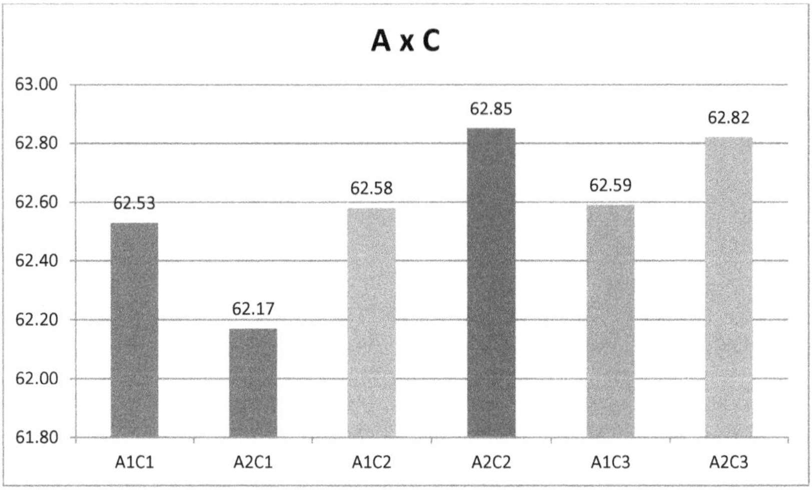

Table No: 4.48
Showing Means Scores of Mental health of high school Students - Variable-B x C (Gender x Area)

		B1	B2
C1	Mean	62.07	62.79
	N	180	180
C2	Mean	62.84	62.66
	N	180	180

F ratio for B x Css (Gender x Area) is 0.47, which is not significant. It means gender and area do not interact each other on mental health of high school Students. By the same point of view Table 4.48 shows the mean score of male Students of urban area is 62.07, mean score of female Students of urban area is 62.79, mean score of male Students of rural area is 62.84, mean score of female Students of rural area is 62.66, which are not differently interacting each other significantly on mental health of high school Students. It can be seen in figure 4.48. It means all group of gender and area have similar level of mental health. So, the result is that Ho_{48} is accepted.

Figure No: 4.48
Showing Bar Graph of Mean Scores of Mental health of high school Students - Variable-B x C (Gender x Area)

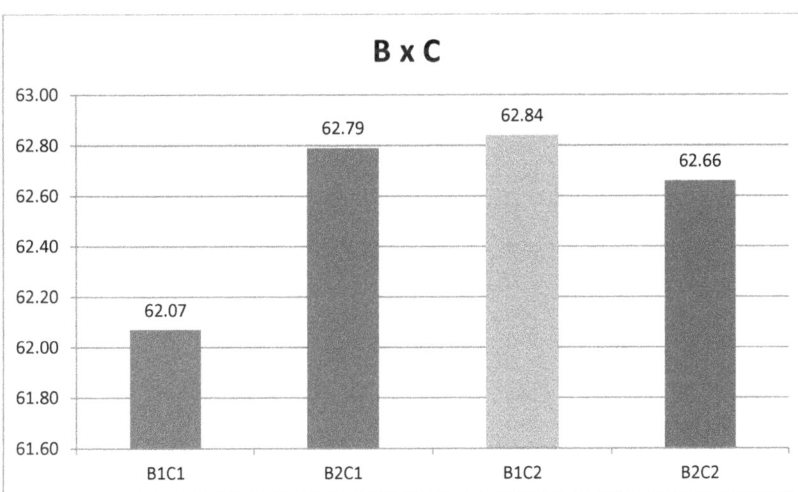

Table No: 4.49
Showing Means Scores of Mental health of high school Students - Variable-A x B x C (Faculty x Gender x Area)

		A1		A2		A3	
		B1	**B2**	**B1**	**B2**	**B1**	**B2**
C1	**Mean**	62.08	62.98	61.82	62.52	62.30	62.87
	N	60	60	60	60	60	60
C2	**Mean**	62.48	63.22	62.67	62.52	63.38	62.25
	N	60	60	60	60	60	60

F ratio for A x B x Css (Faculty x Gender x Area) is 0.11, which is not significant. It means faculty, gender and area do not interact significantly each other on scores of mental health of high school Students. By the same point of view, table 62.08 shows the mean scores of male Students of urban area with arts faculty is 62.98, mean scores of female Students of urban area with arts faculty is 61.82, mean scores of male Students of urban area with commerce faculty is 62.52, mean scores of female Students of urban area with commerce faculty is 62.30, mean scores of male Students of urban area with science faculty is 62.87, mean scores of female Students of urban area with science faculty is 62.48, mean scores of male Students of rural area with arts faculty is 62.48, mean scores of female Students of rural area with arts faculty is 63.23, mean scores of male Students of rural area with commerce faculty is 62.67, mean scores of female Students of rural area with commerce faculty is 62.52, mean scores of male Students of rural area with science faculty is 63.38, mean scores of female Students of rural area with science faculty is 62.25, which do not differently interacting each other significantly on mental health of high school Students. It can be seen in figure 4.49. It means that all the groups of faculty, gender and area have similar level of mental health. So, the result is that Ho_{49} is accepted.

Figure No: 4.49
Showing Bar Graph of Means Scores of Mental health of high school Students - Variable-A x B x C (Faculty x Gender x Area)

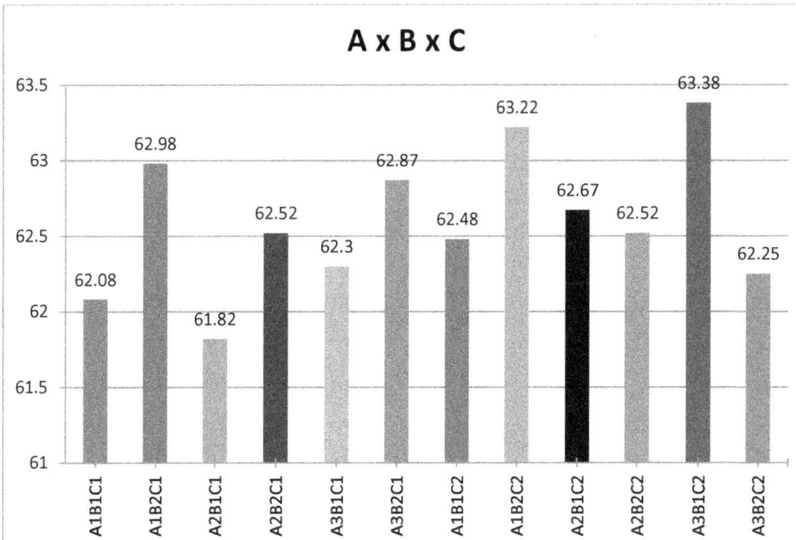

4.5.2 Result and Discussion of Suicidal Tendency:

The results and discussion of scores of five areas of suicidal tendency are described as under.

4.5.2.1 Result and Discussion on Personality trait:

Table H: Showing Results of ANOVA of Personality trait of high school Students:

Source of Variation	Sum of Square	Df	Mean sum of Square	F	Level of Significant
A (Faculty)	27.27	2	13.64	0.96	NS
B (Gender)	421.70	1	421.70	29.63	0.01
C (Area)	577.73	1	577.73	40.59	0.01
A x B	58.91	2	29.45	2.07	NS
A x C	3.50	2	1.75	0.12	NS
B x C	198.79	1	198.79	13.97	0.01
A x B x C	43.99	2	21.99	1.55	NS
Error	10062.22	707	14.23		
Total	289751.00	719			

Significant level of 'F' value: 0.05 level 3.85 (df=1), 0.01 level 6.67 (df=1)
0.05 level 3.01 (df=2), 0.01 level 4.63 (df=2)

Table No: 4.50
Showing Means Scores of Personality trait of high school Students - Variable-A(Gender)

	A1	A2	A3
Mean	19.42	19.90	19.71
N	240	240	240

Results of ANOVA main and interaction group on Personality trait of high school Students scores, Table H - consulted and it is found that the f ratio for Ass (faculty) is 0.96, which is not significant. It means higher secondary school Students from arts, commerce and science faculty do not significantly differ on score of Personality trait. By the same point of view Table 4.50 show mean score of arts faculty Students is 19.42, mean score of commerce faculty Students is 19.90 and mean score of science faculty Students is 19.71, it can be said there is no significant difference is existed among arts, commerce and science faculty on Personality trait. It can be seen in figure 4.50.There is no difference found in the scores of Personality trait. It means Students of arts, commerce and science faculty have similar level of Personality trait. So, the result is that Ho_{50} is accepted.

Figure No: 4.50
Showing Bar Graph with Means Scores of Personality trait of high school Students - Variable-A (Faculty)

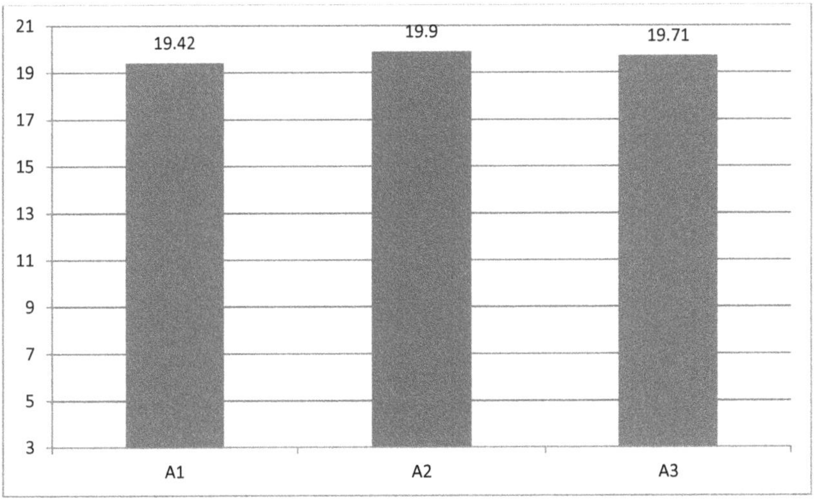

Table No: 4.51
Showing Means Scores of Personality trait of high school Students - Variable-B (Gender)

	B1	B2
Mean	18.91	20.44
N	360	360

F ratio for Bss (Gender) is 29.63, which is significant at 0.01 level. It means male and female Students of high school significantly differ on Personality trait. By the same point of view Table 4.51 show mean score of male Students is 18.91, and mean score of female Students is 20.44, it can be clearly said that significant difference is existed between male and female Students of high school on Personality trait. It can be seen in figure 4.51. Male and female Students of high school have different level of Personality trait; mean score of result indicates that female Students have higher Personality trait for suicidal tendency in compare to male Students. Female are more emotional and sensitive in compare to male, so female could have more personality trait to commit suicide. So, the result is that Ho_{51} is rejected. Female students may have high social control and that directly affects the personality trait of the person. So because of this female students have high personality trait.

Figure No: 4.51
Showing Bar graph of Means Scores of Personality trait of high school Students - Variable-B (Gender)

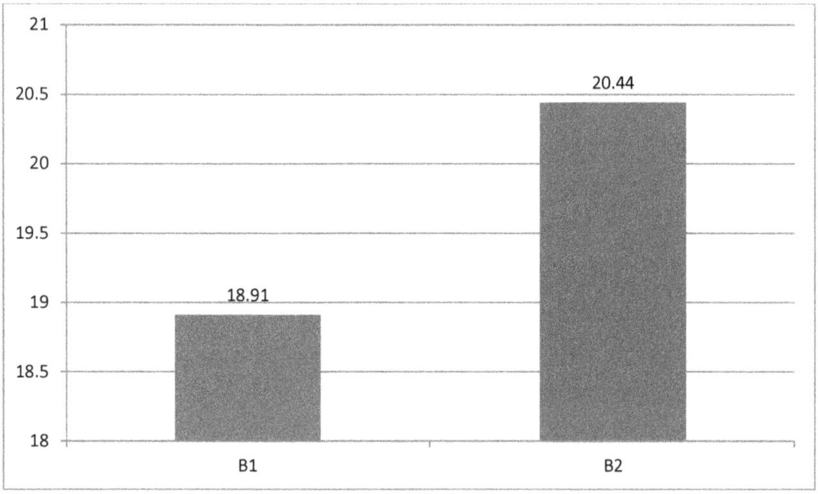

Table No: 4.52
Showing Means Scores of Personality trait of high school Students - Variable-C (Area)

	C1	C2
Mean	18.78	20.57
N	360	360

F ratio for Css (Area) is 40.59, which is significant at 0.01 level. It means high school Students of urban area and rural area significantly differ on Personality trait. By the same point of view Table 4.52 show the mean score of urban area Students is 18.78, mean score of rural area Students is 20.57. It can be clearly said that significant difference is existed among urban and rural area high school Students on Personality trait; mean score of result indicates that Students of rural area have more Personality trait in compare to urban area Students. It can be seen in figure 4.52. May Students of rural area unable to get proper guidance or help from mental health expert, so personality trait may be more in rural area in compare to urban area. So, the result is that Ho_{52} is rejected. Personality trait somewhere depends on moral and social value of the students of rural area have high values because of strong family bonding; this might be reason of high personality trait in students of rural area.

Figure No: 4.52
Showing Bar Graph of Means Scores of Personality trait of high school Students - Variable-C (Area)

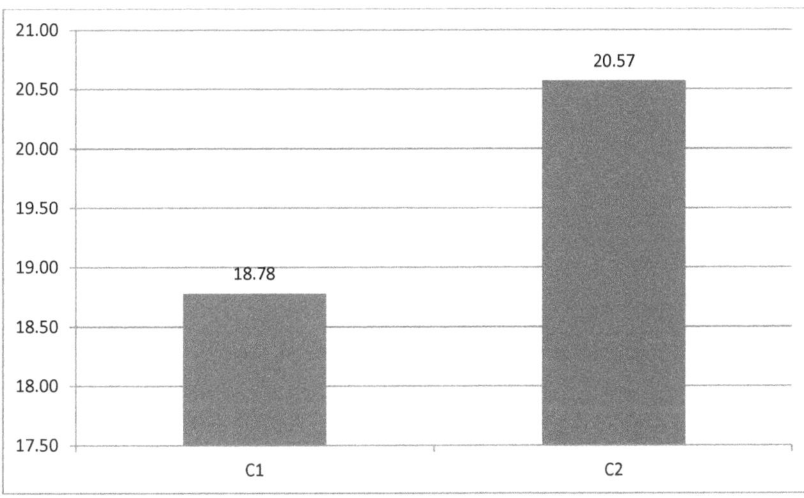

Table No: 4.53
Showing Means Scores of Personality trait of high school Students - Variable-A x B (Faculty x Gender)

		A1	A2	A3
B1	**Mean**	19.03	18.80	18.91
	N	120	120	120
B2	**Mean**	19.82	20.99	20.52
	N	120	120	120

F ratio for A x Bss (Faculty x Gender) is 2.07, which is not significant. It means faculty and gender of high school Students do not interact each other significantly on

Personality trait. By the same point of view Table 4.53 show the mean score of male Students of arts faculty is 19.03, mean score of male Students of commerce faculty is 18.80, mean score of male Students of science faculty is 18.91, mean score of female Students of arts faculty is 19.82, mean score of female Students of commerce faculty is 20.99, and mean score of female Students of science faculty is 20.52; which are not interacting each other significantly on Personality trait of high school Students. It can be seen in figure 4.53. So, the result is that Ho_{53} is accepted.

Figure No: 4.53
Showing Bar Graph of Mean Scores of Personality trait of high school Students - Variable-A x B (Faculty x Gender)

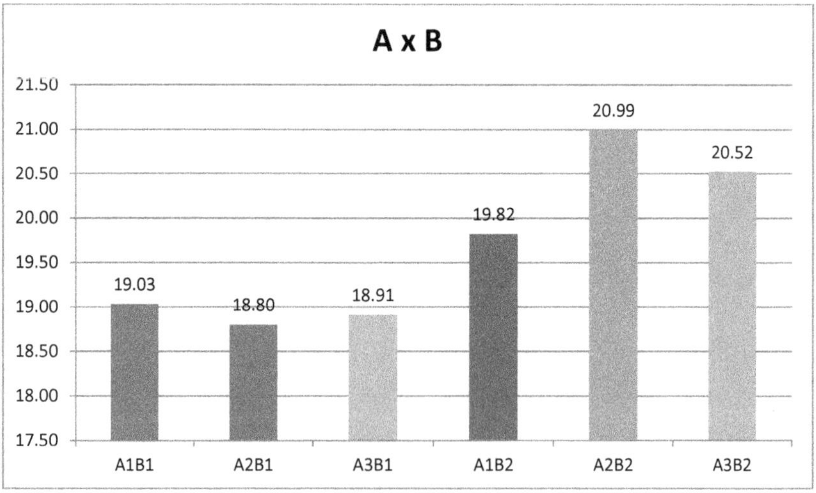

Table No: 4.54
Showing Means Scores of Personality trait of high school Students - Variable-A x C (Faculty x Area)

		A1	A2	A3
C1	Mean	18.43	19.02	18.89
	N	120	120	120
C2	Mean	20.41	20.78	20.53
	N	120	120	120

F ratio for A x Css (Faculty x Area) is 0.12, which is not significant. It means faculty and gender do not differ on Personality trait of high school Students. By the same point of view Table 4.54 show the mean score of arts Students of urban area is 18.43, mean score of commerce Students of urban area is 19.02, mean score of science Students of urban area is 18.89, mean score of arts Students of rural area is 20.41, mean score of commerce Students of rural area is 20.78, mean score of science Students of rural area is 20.53; which are not interacting each other significantly on Personality trait of high school Students. It means all group of faculty and gender have similar level of Personality trait. It can be seen in figure 4.54. So, the result is that Ho_{54} is accepted.

Figure No: 4.54

Showing Bar Graph of Mean Scores of Personality trait of high school Students - Variable-A x C (Faculty x Area)

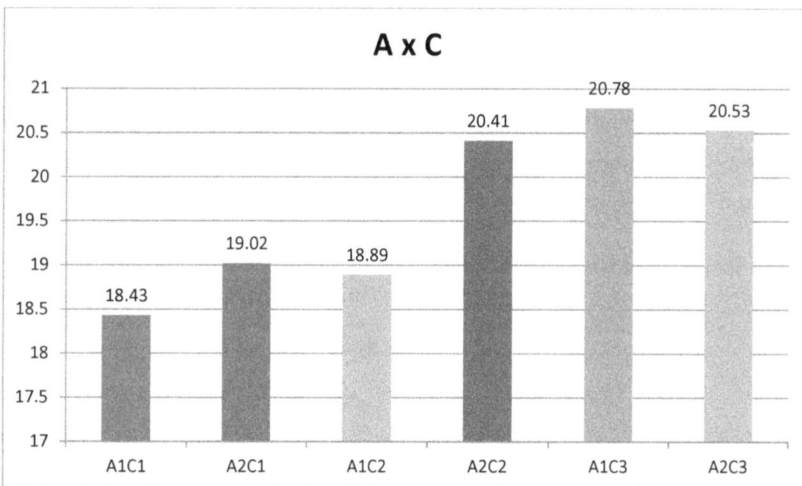

Table No: 4.55
Showing Means Scores of Personality trait of high school Students - Variable-B x C (Gender x Area)

		B1	B2
C1	Mean	17.49	20.07
	N	180	180
C2	Mean	20.33	20.81
	N	180	180

F ratio for B x Css (Gender x Area) is 13.97, which is significant at 0.01 level. It means gender and area interact significantly each other on Personality trait of high school Students. By the same point of view Table 4.55 shows the mean score of male Students of urban area is 17.49, mean score of female Students of urban area is 20.07, mean score of male Students of rural area is 20.33, mean score of female Students of rural area is 20.81, which are significantly interacting each other significantly on Personality trait of high school Students. It can be seen in figure 4.55. Mean score shows that female Students of rural area have higher level of Personality trait in compare to other group. So, the result is that Ho_{55} is rejected. Female students who lives in rural area have high social and family control so because of that personality trait is high in female students of rural area.

Figure No: 4.55
Showing Bar Graph of Mean Scores of Personality trait of high school Students - Variable-B x C (Gender x Area)

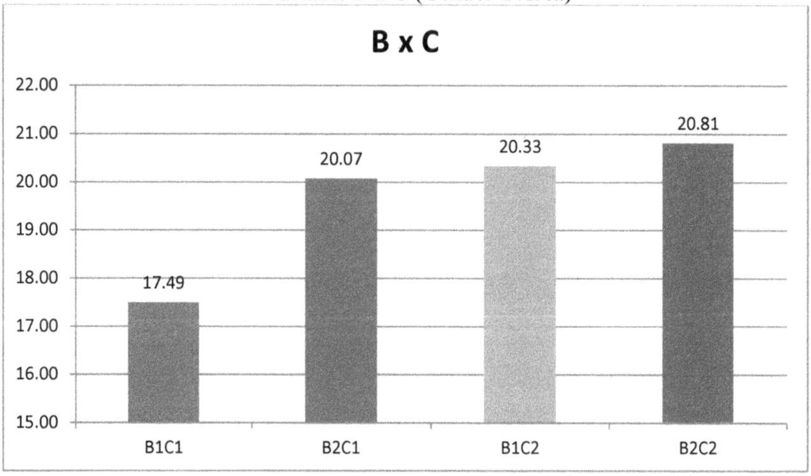

Table No: 4.56
Showing Means Scores of Personality trait of high school Students - Variable-A x B x C (Faculty x Gender x Area)

		A1		A2		A3	
		B1	**B2**	**B1**	**B2**	**B1**	**B2**
C1	**Mean**	17.63	19.23	17.05	20.98	17.78	20.00
	N	60	60	60	60	60	60
C2	**Mean**	20.42	20.41	20.55	21.00	20.03	21.03
	N	60	60	60	60	60	60

F ratio for A x B x Css (Faculty x Gender x Area) is 1.55, which is not significant. It means faculty, gender and area do not interact significantly each other on scores of Personality trait of high school Students. By the same point of view, table 4.56 shows the mean scores of male Students of urban area with arts faculty is 17.63, mean scores of female Students of urban area with arts faculty is 19.23, mean scores of male Students of urban area with commerce faculty is 17.05, mean scores of female Students of urban area with commerce faculty is 20.98, mean scores of male Students of urban area with science faculty is 17.78, mean scores of female Students of urban area with science faculty is 20.00, mean scores of male Students of rural area with arts faculty is 20.42, mean scores of female Students of rural area with arts faculty is 20.41, mean scores of male Students of rural area with commerce faculty is 20.55, mean scores of female Students of rural area with commerce faculty is 21.00, mean scores of male Students of rural area with science faculty is 20.03, mean scores of female Students of rural area with science faculty is 21.03, which do not differently interacting each other significantly on Personality trait of high school Students. It can be seen in figure 4.56. It means that all the groups of faculty, gender and area have similar level of Personality trait. So, the result is that Ho_{56} is accepted.

Figure No: 4.56

Showing Bar Graph of Means Scores of Personality trait of high school Students - Variable-A x B x C (Faculty x Gender x Area)

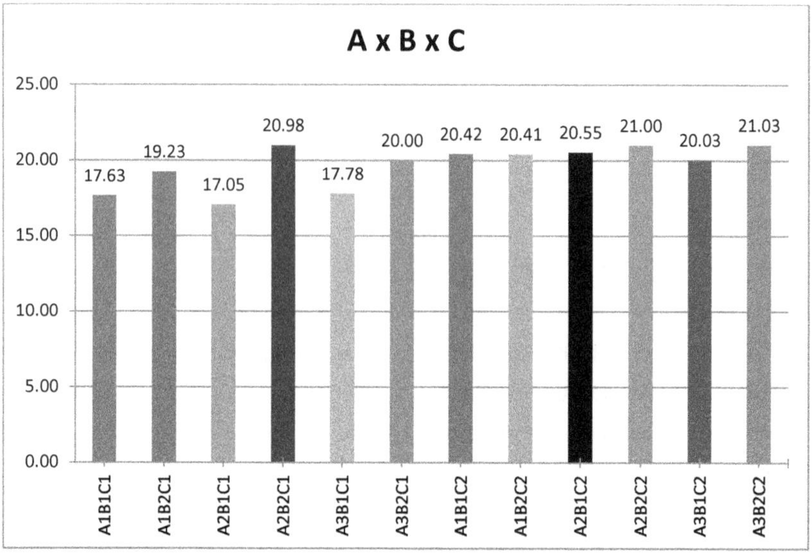

4.5.2.2 Result and Discussion on Emotional disturbance:

Table I: Showing Results of ANOVA of Emotional disturbance of high school:

Source of Variation	Sum of Square	Df	Mean sum of Square	F	Level of Significant
A (Faculty)	48.71	2	24.36	1.63	NS
B (Gender)	105.31	1	105.31	7.04	0.01
C (Area)	195.62	1	195.62	13.08	0.01
A x B	150.22	2	75.11	5.02	0.01
A x C	5.44	2	2.72	0.18	NS
B x C	166.46	1	166.46	11.13	0.01
A x B x C	42.51	2	21.25	1.42	NS
Error	10571.74	707	14.95		
Total	286464.00	719			

Significant level of 'F' value: 0.05 level 3.85 (df=1), 0.01 level 6.67 (df=1)
0.05 level 3.01 (df=2), 0.01 level 4.63 (df=2)

Table No: 4.57
Showing Means Scores of Emotional disturbance of high school Students - Variable-A (Faculty)

	A1	A2	A3
Mean	19.52	19.90	19.27
N	240	240	240

Results of ANOVA main and interaction group on Emotional disturbance of high school Students scores, Table I - consulted and it is found that the f ratio for Ass (faculty) is 1.63, which is not significant. It means higher secondary school Students from arts, commerce and science faculty do not significantly differ on score of Emotional disturbance. By the same point of view Table 4.57 show mean score of arts faculty Students is 19.52, mean score of commerce faculty Students is 19.90 and mean score of science faculty Students is 19.27, it can be said there is no significant difference is existed among arts, commerce and science faculty on Emotional disturbance. It can be seen in figure 4.57.There is no difference found in the scores of Emotional disturbance. It means Students of arts, commerce and science faculty have similar level of Emotional disturbance. So, the result is that Ho_{57} is accepted.

Figure No: 4.57
Showing Bar Graph with Means Scores of Emotional disturbance of high school Students - Variable-A (Faculty)

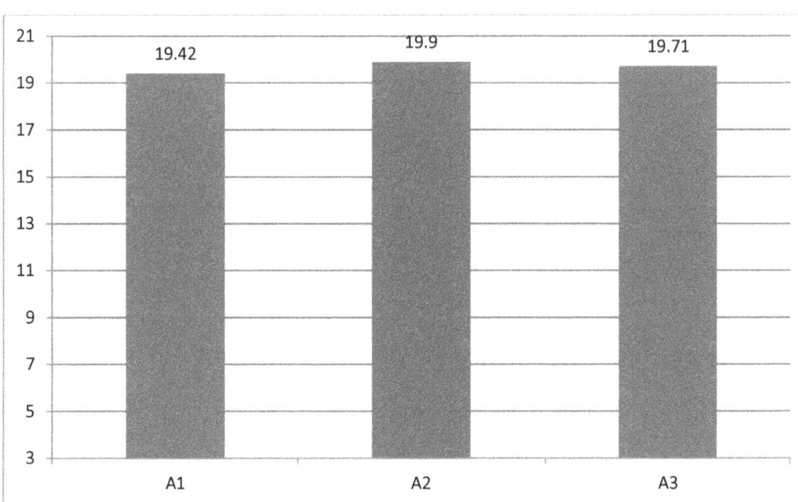

Table No: 4.58
Showing Means Scores of Emotional disturbance of high school Students - Variable-B (Gender)

	B1	B2
Mean	19.18	19.95
N	360	360

F ratio for Bss (Gender) is 7.04, which is significant at 0.01 level. It means male and female Students of high school significantly differ on Emotional disturbance. By the same point of view Table 4.58 show mean score of male Students is 19.18, and mean score of female Students is 19.95, it can be clearly said that significant difference is existed between male and female Students of high school on Emotional disturbance. It can be seen in figure 4.58. Male and female Students of high school have different level of Emotional disturbance; mean score of result indicates that female Students have higher Emotional disturbance for suicidal tendency in compare to male Students. Female have most likely involve with social and other responsibility including menstruation cycle can be the reason of emotional disturbance. So, the result is that Ho_{58} is rejected. Emotional disturbance high in female might because of hormonal changes.

Figure No: 4.58
Showing Bar graph of Means Scores of Emotional disturbance of high school Students - Variable-B (Gender)

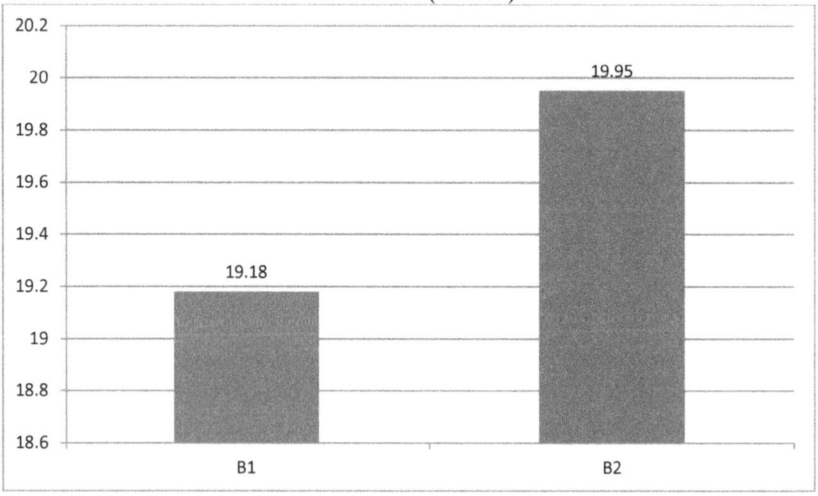

Table No: 4.59
Showing Means Scores of Emotional disturbance of high school Students - Variable-C (Area)

	C1	C2
Mean	19.04	20.09
N	360	360

F ratio for Css (Area) is 13.08, which is significant at 0.01 level. It means high school Students of urban area and rural area significantly differ on Emotional disturbance. By the same point of view Table 4.59 show the mean score of urban area Students is 19.04, mean score of rural area Students is 20.09. It can be clearly said that significant difference is existed among urban and rural area high school Students on Emotional disturbance; mean score of result indicates that Students of rural area have more Emotional disturbance in compare to urban area Students. It can be seen in figure 4.59. Students of rural area have more social involvement and have to follow social norms strongly, so this can also create emotional conflicts and also emotional disturbance. So, the result is that Ho_{59} is rejected. In rural area there are many social events and restriction so that can affects persons emotional disturbance.

Figure No: 4.59
Showing Bar Graph of Means Scores of Emotional disturbance of high school Students - Variable-C (Area)

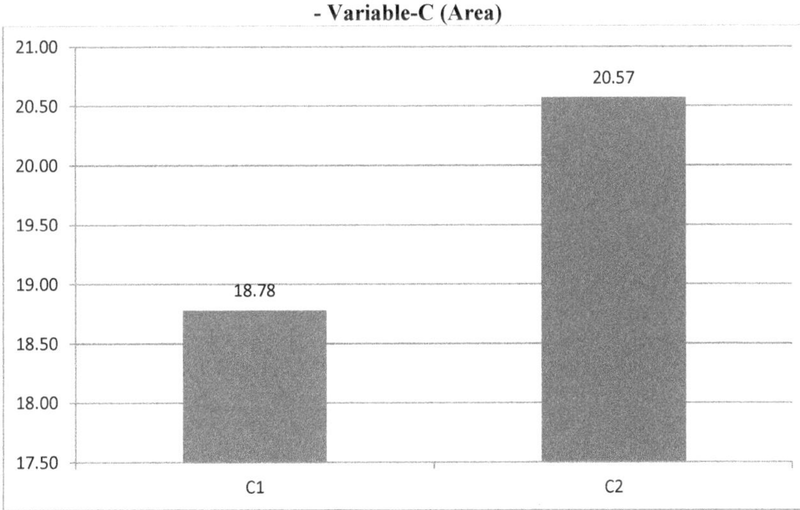

Table No: 4.60
Showing Means Scores of Emotional disturbance of high school Students - Variable-A x B (Faculty x Gender)

		A1	A2	A3
B1	**Mean**	19.57	18.88	19.09
	N	120	120	120
B2	**Mean**	19.48	20.92	19.44
	N	120	120	120

F ratio for A x Bss (Faculty x Gender) is 5.02, which is significant at 0.01 level. It means faculty and gender of high school Students interact significantly each other significantly on Emotional disturbance. By the same point of view Table 4.60 show the mean score of male Students of arts faculty is 19.57, mean score of male Students of commerce faculty is 18.88, mean score of male Students of science faculty is 19.09, mean score of female Students of arts faculty is 19.48, mean score of female Students of commerce faculty is 20.92, and mean score of female Students of science faculty is 19.44; which are not interacting each other significantly on Emotional disturbance of high school Students. Mean score shows that female Students of commerce faculty have high level of emotional disturbance in compare to all other groups. It can be seen in figure 4.60. So, the result is that Ho_{60} is rejected.

Figure No: 4.60
Showing Bar Graph of Mean Scores of Emotional disturbance of high school Students - Variable-A x B (Faculty x Gender)

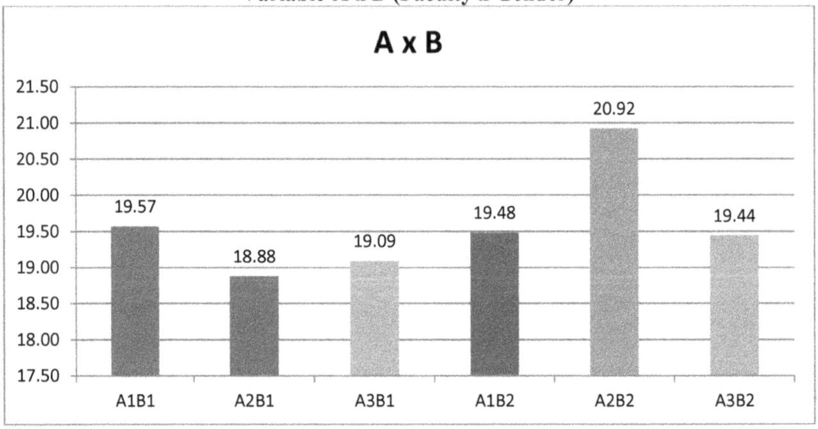

Table No: 4.61

Showing Means Scores of Emotional disturbance of high school Students - Variable-A x C (Faculty x Area)

		A1	A2	A3
C1	Mean	18.93	19.50	18.70
	N	120	120	120
C2	Mean	20.12	20.30	19.83
	N	120	120	120

F ratio for A x Css (Faculty x Area) is 0.18, which is not significant. It means faculty and gender do not differ on Emotional disturbance of high school Students. By the same point of view Table 4.61 show the mean score of arts Students of urban area is 18.93, mean score of commerce Students of urban area is 19.50, mean score of science Students of urban area is 18.70, mean score of arts Students of rural area is 20.12, mean score of commerce Students of rural area is 20.30, mean score of science Students of rural area is 19.83; which are not interacting each other significantly on Emotional disturbance of high school Students. It means all group of faculty and gender has similar level of Emotional disturbance. It can be seen in figure 4.61. So, the result is that Ho_{61} is accepted.

Figure No: 4.61

Showing Bar Graph of Mean Scores of Emotional disturbance of high school Students - Variable-A x C (Faculty x Area)

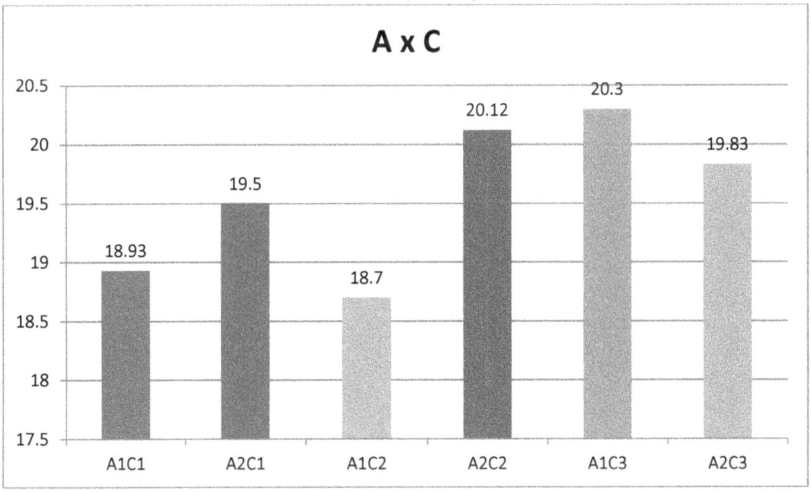

Table No: 4.62

Showing Means Scores of Emotional disturbance of high school Students - Variable-B x C (Gender x Area)

		B1	B2
C1	Mean	18.18	19.91
	N	180	180
C2	Mean	20.18	19.99
	N	180	180

F ratio for B x Css (Gender x Area) is 11.13, which is significant at 0.01 level. It means gender and area interact significantly each other on Emotional disturbance of high school Students. By the same point of view Table 4.62 shows the mean score of male Students of urban area is 18.18, mean score of female Students of urban area is 19.91, mean score of male Students of rural area is 20.18, mean score of female Students of rural area is 19.99, which are significantly interacting each other significantly on Emotional disturbance of high school Students. It can be seen in figure 4.62. Mean score shows that male Students of rural area have higher level of Emotional disturbance in compare to other group. So, the result is that Ho_{62} is rejected.

Figure No: 4.62

Showing Bar Graph of Mean Scores of Emotional disturbance of high school Students - Variable-B x C (Gender x Area)

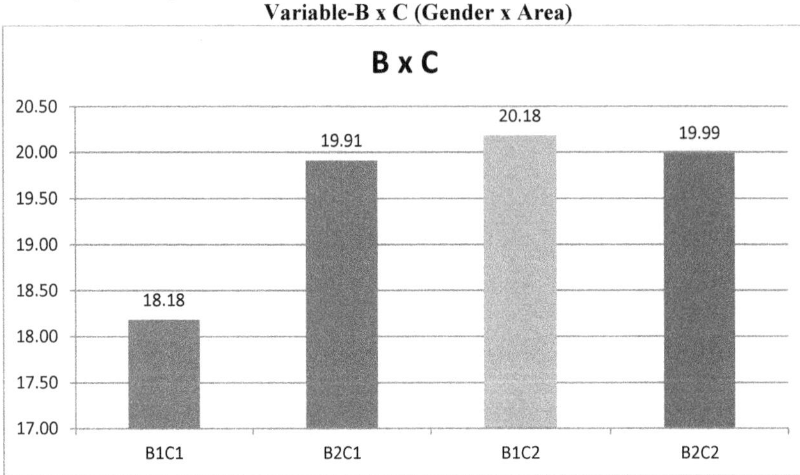

Table No: 4.63

Showing Means Scores of Emotional disturbance of high school Students - Variable-A x B x C (Faculty x Gender x Area)

		A1		A2		A3	
		B1	**B2**	**B1**	**B2**	**B1**	**B2**
C1	**Mean**	18.45	19.40	18.32	20.68	17.77	19.63
	N	60	60	60	60	60	60
C2	**Mean**	20.68	19.56	19.45	21.15	20.42	19.25
	N	60	60	60	60	60	60

F ratio for A x B x Css (Faculty x Gender x Area) is 1.42, which is not significant. It means faculty, gender and area do not interact significantly each other on scores of Emotional disturbance of high school Students. By the same point of view, table 4.63 shows the mean scores of male Students of urban area with arts faculty is 18.48, mean scores of female Students of urban area with arts faculty is 19.40, mean scores of male Students of urban area with commerce faculty is 18.32, mean scores of female Students of urban area with commerce faculty is 20.68, mean scores of male Students of urban area with science faculty is 17.77, mean scores of female Students of urban area with science faculty is 19.63, mean scores of male Students of rural area with arts faculty is 20.68, mean scores of female Students of rural area with arts faculty is 19.56, mean scores of male Students of rural area with commerce faculty is 19.45, mean scores of female Students of rural area with commerce faculty is 21.15, mean scores of male Students of rural area with science faculty is 20.42, mean scores of female Students of rural area with science faculty is 19.25, which do not differently interacting each other significantly on Emotional disturbance of high school Students. It can be seen in figure 4.63. It means that all the groups of faculty, gender and area have similar level of Emotional disturbance. So, the result is that Ho_{63} is accepted.

Figure No: 4.63

Showing Bar Graph of Means Scores of Emotional disturbance of high school Students - Variable-A x B x C (Faculty x Gender x Area)

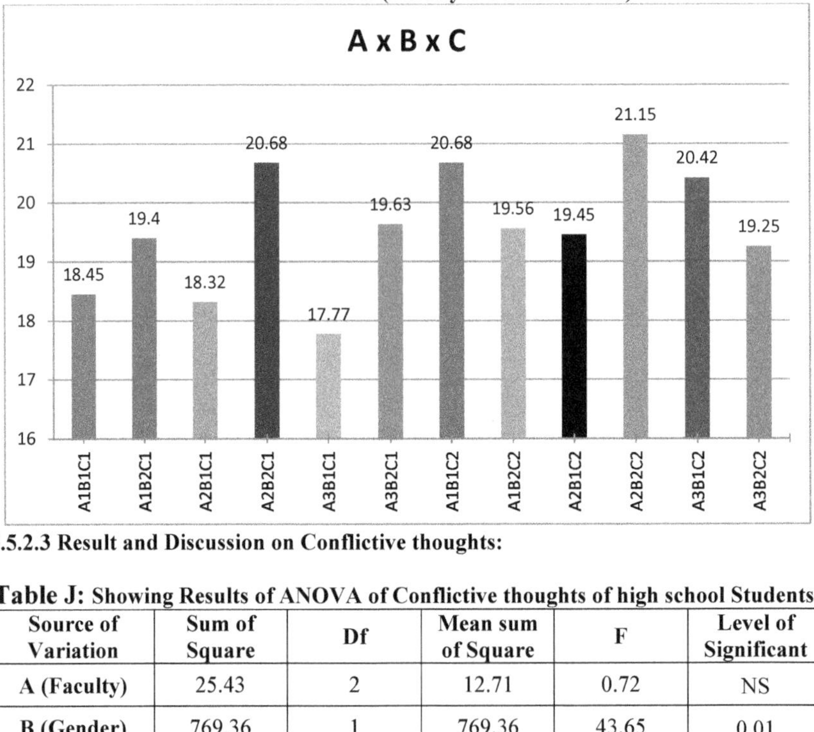

4.5.2.3 Result and Discussion on Conflictive thoughts:

Table J: Showing Results of ANOVA of Conflictive thoughts of high school Students:

Source of Variation	Sum of Square	Df	Mean sum of Square	F	Level of Significant
A (Faculty)	25.43	2	12.71	0.72	NS
B (Gender)	769.36	1	769.36	43.65	0.01
C (Area)	876.13	1	876.13	49.71	0.01
A x B	547.62	2	273.81	15.54	0.01
A x C	42.33	2	21.17	1.20	NS
B x C	545.59	1	545.59	30.96	0.01
A x B x C	63.34	2	31.67	1.79	NS
Error	12460.84	707	17.63		
Total	300341.00	719			

Significant level of 'F' value: 0.05 level 3.85 (df=1), 0.01 level 6.67 (df=1)
0.05 level 3.01 (df=2), 0.01 level 4.63 (df=2)

Table No: 4.64
Showing Means Scores of Conflictive thoughts of high school Students - Variable-A (Faculty)

	A1	A2	A3
Mean	19.69	19.88	20.15
N	240	240	240

Results of ANOVA main and interaction group on Conflictive thoughts of high school Students scores, Table J - consulted and it is found that the f ratio for Ass (faculty) is 0.72, which is not significant. It means higher secondary school Students from arts, commerce and science faculty do not significantly differ on score of Conflictive thoughts. By the same point of view Table 4.64 show mean score of arts faculty Students is 19.69, mean score of commerce faculty Students is 19.88 and mean score of science faculty Students is 20.15, it can be said there is no significant difference is existed among arts, commerce and science faculty on Conflictive thoughts. It can be seen in figure 4.64.There is no difference found in the scores of Conflictive thoughts. It means Students of arts, commerce and science faculty have similar level of Conflictive thoughts. So, the result is that Ho_{64} is accepted.

Figure No: 4.64
Showing Bar Graph with Means Scores of Conflictive thoughts of high school Students - Variable-A (Faculty)

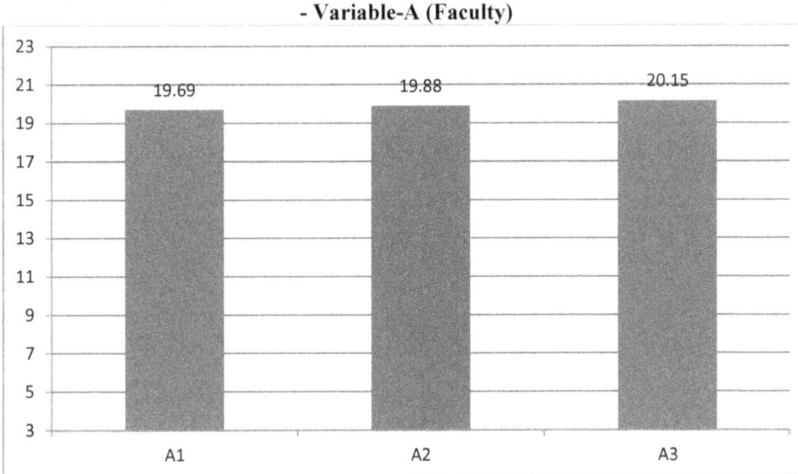

Table No: 4.65

Showing Means Scores of Conflictive thoughts of high school Students - Variable-B (Gender)

	B1	B2
Mean	18.88	20.94
N	360	360

F ratio for Bss (Gender) is 43.65, which is significant at 0.01 level. It means male and female Students of high school significantly differ on Conflictive thoughts. By the same point of view Table 4.65 show mean score of male Students is 18.88, and mean score of female Students is 20.94, it can be clearly said that significant difference is existed between male and female Students of high school on Conflictive thoughts. It can be seen in figure 4.65. Male and female Students of high school have different level of Conflictive thoughts; mean score of result indicates that female Students have higher Conflictive thoughts for suicidal tendency in compare to male Students. Female Students have to take care about many things like - family, social, academic, personal health and many other so it can be reason of conflict thoughts. So, the result is that Ho_{65} is rejected.

Figure No: 4.65

Showing Bar graph of Means Scores of Conflictive thoughts of high school Students - Variable-B (Gender)

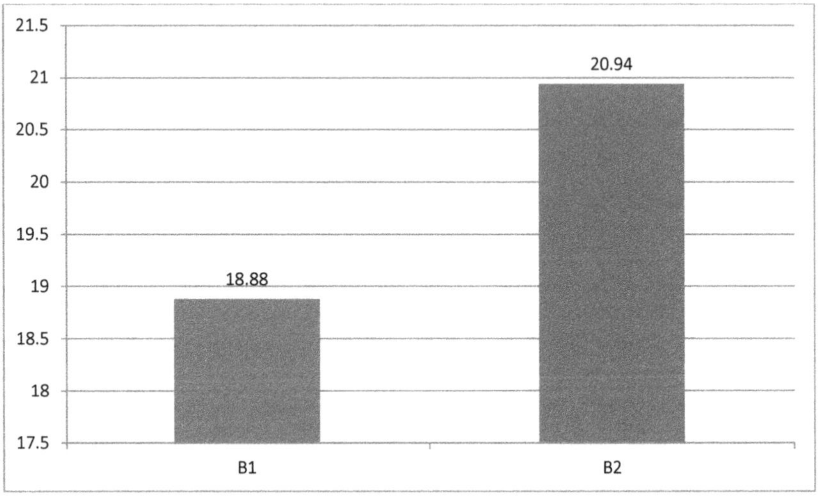

Table No: 4.66
Showing Means Scores of Conflictive thoughts of high school Students - Variable-C (Area)

	C1	C2
Mean	18.81	21.01
N	360	360

F ratio for Css (Area) is 49.71, which is significant at 0.01 level. It means high school Students of urban area and rural area significantly differ on Conflictive thoughts. By the same point of view Table 4.66 show the mean score of urban area Students is 18.81, mean score of rural area Students is 21.01. It can be clearly said that significant difference is existed among urban and rural area high school Students on Conflictive thoughts; mean score of result indicates that Students of rural area have more Conflictive thoughts in compare to urban area Students. It can be seen in figure 4.66. Students of rural area have to take care about the farming work as well as they do not have clear idea about the career so may they have more conflict thoughts. So, the result is that Ho_{66} is rejected.

Figure No: 4.66
Showing Bar Graph of Means Scores of Conflictive thoughts of high school Students - Variable-C (Area)

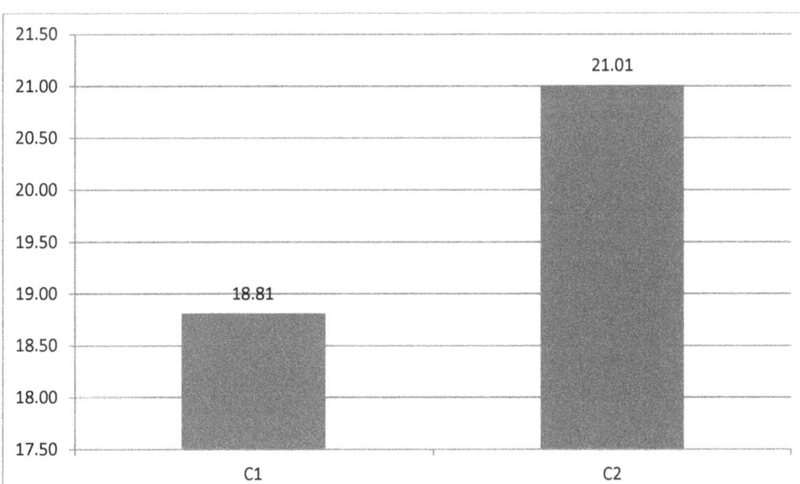

Table No: 4.67

Showing Means Scores of Conflictive thoughts of high school Students - Variable-A x B (Faculty x Gender)

		A1	A2	A3
B1	**Mean**	19.73	17.79	19.10
	N	120	120	120
B2	**Mean**	19.65	21.98	21.20
	N	120	120	120

F ratio for A x Bss (Faculty x Gender) is 15.54, which is significant at 0.01 level. It means faculty and gender of high school Students interact significantly each other significantly on Conflictive thoughts. By the same point of view Table 4.67 show the mean score of male Students of arts faculty is 19.73, mean score of male Students of commerce faculty is 17.79, mean score of male Students of science faculty is 19.10, mean score of female Students of arts faculty is 19.65, mean score of female Students of commerce faculty is 21.98, and mean score of female Students of science faculty is 21.20; which are not interacting each other significantly on Conflictive thoughts of high school Students. Mean score shows that female Students of commerce faculty have high level of Conflictive thoughts in compare to all other groups. It can be seen in figure 4.67. So, the result is that Ho_{67} is rejected.

Figure No: 4.67

Showing Bar Graph of Mean Scores of Conflictive thoughts of high school Students - Variable-A x B (Faculty x Gender)

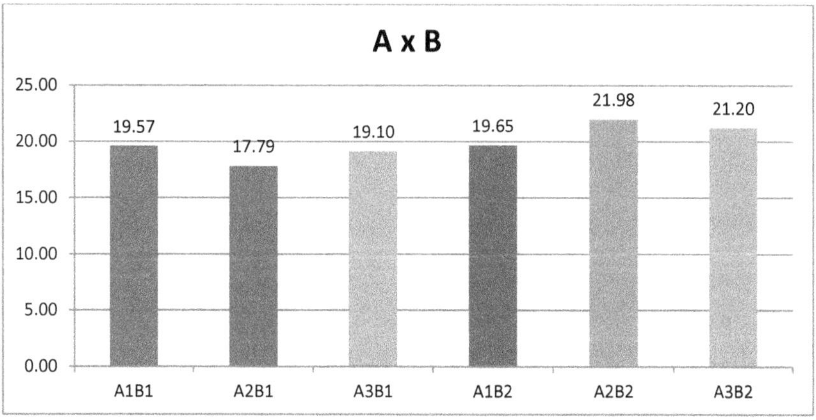

Table No: 4.68

Showing Means Scores of Conflictive thoughts of high school Students - Variable-A x C (Faculty x Area)

		A1	A2	A3
C1	**Mean**	18.93	18.67	18.83
	N	120	120	120
C2	**Mean**	20.46	21.11	21.48
	N	120	120	120

F ratio for A x Css (Faculty x Area) is 1.20, which is not significant. It means faculty and gender do not differ on Conflictive thoughts of high school Students. By the same point of view Table 4.68 show the mean score of arts Students of urban area is 18.93, mean score of commerce Students of urban area is 18.67, mean score of science Students of urban area is 18.83, mean score of arts Students of rural area is 20.46, mean score of commerce Students of rural area is 21.11, mean score of science Students of rural area is 21.48; which are not interacting each other significantly on Conflictive thoughts of high school Students. It means all group of faculty and gender has similar level of Conflictive thoughts. It can be seen in figure 4.68. So, the result is that Ho_{68} is accepted.

Figure No: 4.68

Showing Bar Graph of Mean Scores of Conflictive thoughts of high school Students - Variable-A x C (Faculty x Area)

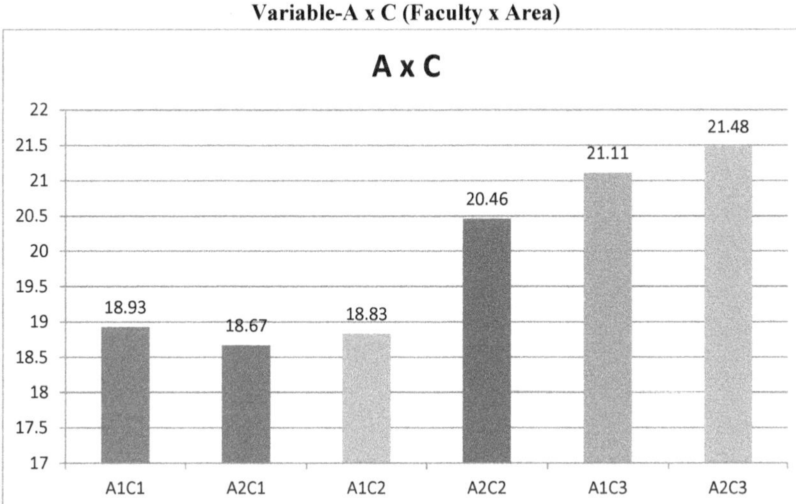

Table No: 4.69
Showing Means Scores of Conflictive thoughts of high school Students - Variable-B x C (Gender x Area)

		B1	B2
C1	Mean	16.90	20.71
	N	180	180
C2	Mean	20.85	21.18
	N	180	180

F ratio for B x Css (Gender x Area) is 30.96, which is significant at 0.01 level. It means gender and area interact significantly each other on Conflictive thoughts of high school Students. By the same point of view Table 4.69 shows the mean score of male Students of urban area is 16.90, mean score of female Students of urban area is 20.71, mean score of male Students of rural area is 20.85, mean score of female Students of rural area is 21.18, which are significantly interacting each other significantly on Conflictive thoughts of high school Students. It can be seen in figure 4.69. Mean score shows that female Students of rural area have higher level of Conflictive thoughts in compare to other group. So, the result is that Ho_{69} is rejected. Just because of social restriction conflictive thought can be high.

Figure No: 4.69
Showing Bar Graph of Mean Scores of Conflictive thoughts of high school Students - Variable-B x C (Gender x Area)

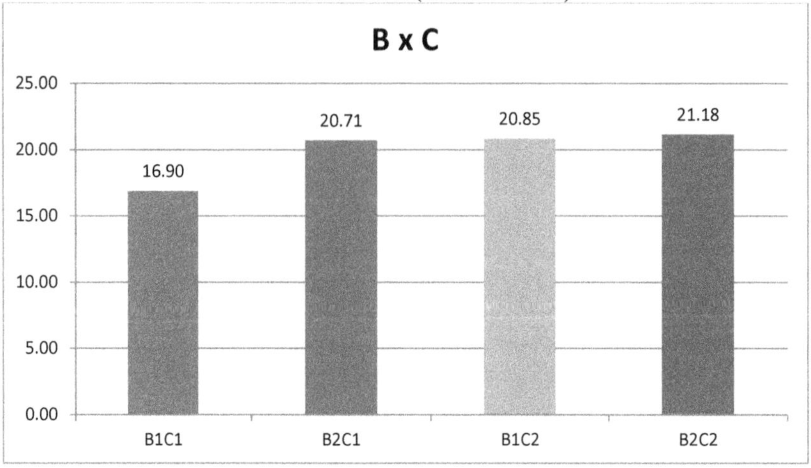

Table No: 4.70
Showing Means Scores of Conflictive thoughts of high school Students - Variable-A x B x C (Faculty x Gender x Area)

		A1		A2		A3	
		B1	**B2**	**B1**	**B2**	**B1**	**B2**
C1	**Mean**	18.35	19.50	15.28	22.05	17.07	20.58
	N	60	60	60	60	60	60
C2	**Mean**	21.12	19.80	20.30	21.92	21.13	21.82
	N	60	60	60	60	60	60

F ratio for A x B x Css (Faculty x Gender x Area) is 1.79, which is not significant. It means faculty, gender and area do not interact significantly each other on scores of Conflictive thoughts of high school Students. By the same point of view, table 4.70 shows the mean scores of male Students of urban area with arts faculty is 18.35, mean scores of female Students of urban area with arts faculty is 19.50, mean scores of male Students of urban area with commerce faculty is 15.28, mean scores of female Students of urban area with commerce faculty is 22.05, mean scores of male Students of urban area with science faculty is 17.07, mean scores of female Students of urban area with science faculty is 20.58, mean scores of male Students of rural area with arts faculty is 21.12, mean scores of female Students of rural area with arts faculty is 19.80, mean scores of male Students of rural area with commerce faculty is 20.30, mean scores of female Students of rural area with commerce faculty is 21.92, mean scores of male Students of rural area with science faculty is 21.13, mean scores of female Students of rural area with science faculty is 21.82, which do not differently interacting each other significantly on Conflictive thoughts of high school Students. It can be seen in figure 4.70. It means that all the groups of faculty, gender and area have similar level of Conflictive thoughts. So, the result is that Ho_{70} is accepted.

Figure No: 4.70
Showing Bar Graph of Means Scores of Conflictive thoughts of high school Students - Variable-A x B x C (Faculty x Gender x Area)

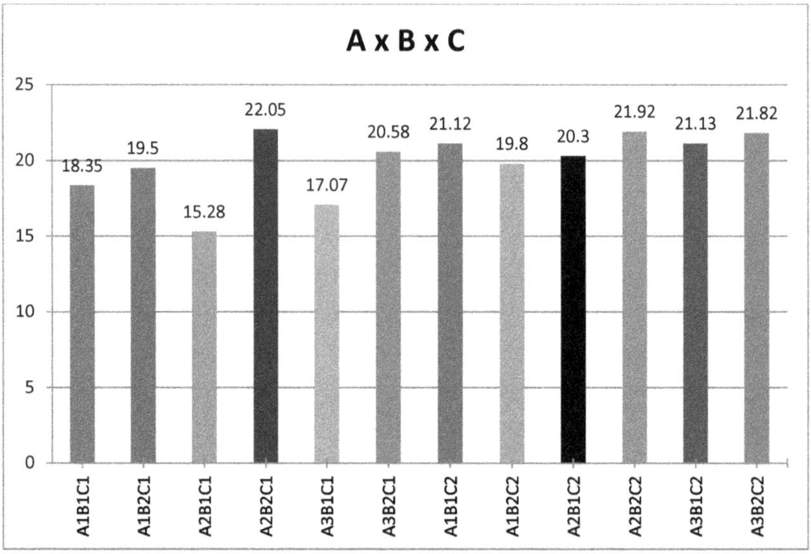

4.5.2.4 Result and Discussion on Self-harm tendency:

Table K: Showing Results of ANOVA of Self-harm tendency of high school Students:

Source of Variation	Sum of Square	Df	Mean sum of Square	F	Level of Significant
A (Faculty)	16.27	2	8.14	0.53	NS
B (Gender)	410.34	1	410.34	26.46	0.01
C (Area)	505.86	1	505.86	32.62	0.01
A x B	131.14	2	65.57	4.23	0.05
A x C	118.42	2	59.21	3.82	0.05
B x C	35.54	1	35.54	2.29	NS
A x B x C	34.24	2	17.12	1.10	NS
Error	10962.60	707	15.51		
Total	282330.00	719			

Significant level of 'F' value: 0.05 level 3.85 (df=1), 0.01 level 6.67 (df=1)
0.05 level 3.01 (df=2), 0.01 level 4.63 (df=2)

Table No: 4.71
Showing Means Scores of Self-harm tendency of high school Students - Variable-A (Faculty)

	A1	A2	A3
Mean	19.22	19.35	19.58
N	240	240	240

Results of ANOVA main and interaction group on Self-harm tendency of high school Students scores, Table K - consulted and it is found that the f ratio for Ass (faculty) is 0.53, which is not significant. It means higher secondary school Students from arts, commerce and science faculty do not significantly differ on score of Self-harm tendency. By the same point of view Table 4.71 show mean score of arts faculty Students is 19.22, mean score of commerce faculty Students is 19.35 and mean score of science faculty Students is 19.58, it can be said there is no significant difference is existed among arts, commerce and science faculty on Self-harm tendency. It can be seen in figure 4.71.There is no difference found in the scores of Self-harm tendency. It means Students of arts, commerce and science faculty have similar level of Self-harm tendency. So, the result is that Ho_{71} is accepted.

Figure No: 4.71
Showing Bar Graph with Means Scores of Self-harm tendency of high school Students - Variable-A (Faculty)

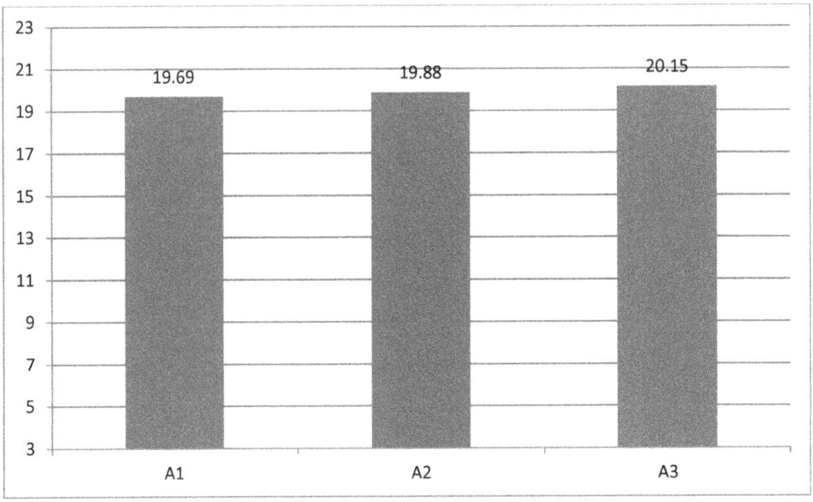

Table No: 4.72

Showing Means Scores of Self-harm tendency of high school Students - Variable-B (Gender)

	B1	B2
Mean	18.63	20.14
N	360	360

F ratio for Bss (Gender) is 26.46, which is significant at 0.01 level. It means male and female Students of high school significantly differ on Self-harm tendency. By the same point of view Table 4.72 show mean score of male Students is 18.63, and mean score of female Students is 20.14, it can be clearly said that significant difference is existed between male and female Students of high school on Self-harm tendency. It can be seen in figure 4.72. Male and female Students of high school have different level of Self-harm tendency; mean score of result indicates that female Students have higher Self-harm tendency for suicidal tendency in compare to male Students. Female mostly are not getting chance to interact with others and have to live alone in side of home so it may increase the self half behaviour tendency. So, the result is that Ho_{72} is rejected.

Figure No: 4.72

Showing Bar graph of Means Scores of Self-harm tendency of high school Students - Variable-B (Gender)

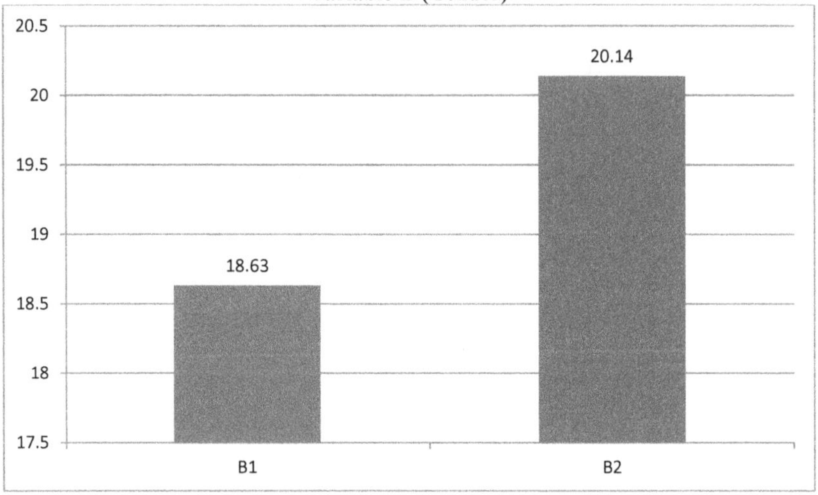

Table No: 4.73

Showing Means Scores of Self-harm tendency of high school Students - Variable-C (Area)

	C1	C2
Mean	18.54	20.22
N	360	360

F ratio for Css (Area) is 32.62, which is significant at 0.01 level. It means high school Students of urban area and rural area significantly differ on Self-harm tendency. By the same point of view Table 4.73 show the mean score of urban area Students is 18.54, mean score of rural area Students is 20.22. It can be clearly said that significant difference is existed among urban and rural area high school Students on Self-harm tendency; mean score of result indicates that Students of rural area have more Self-harm tendency in compare to urban area Students. It can be seen in figure 4.73. Students of rural area have less chance to get proper mental health counselling or professional help; even the social environment also narrow life style may lead to self half behaviour. So, the result is that Ho_{73} is rejected.

Figure No: 4.73

Showing Bar Graph of Means Scores of Self-harm tendency of high school Students - Variable-C (Area)

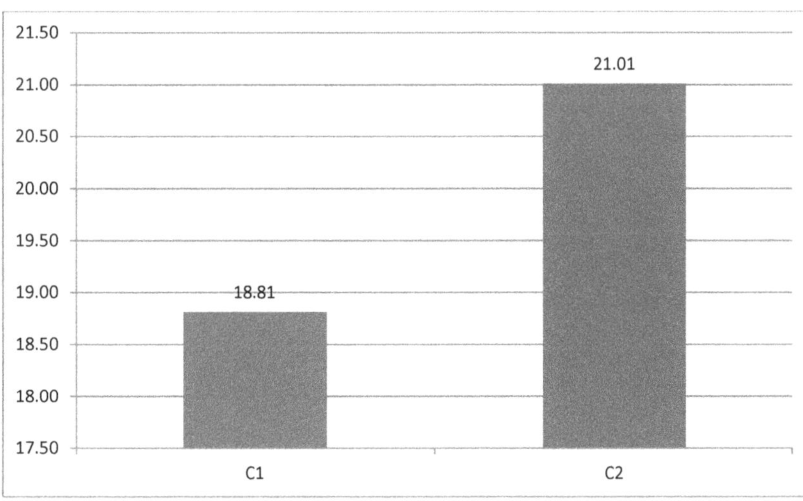

Table No: 4.74
Showing Means Scores of Self-harm tendency of high school Students - Variable-A x B (Faculty x Gender)

		A1	A2	A3
B1	**Mean**	18.96	18.04	18.88
	N	120	120	120
B2	**Mean**	19.48	20.65	20.28
	N	120	120	120

F ratio for A x Bss (Faculty x Gender) is 4.23, which is significant at 0.05 level. It means faculty and gender of high school Students interact significantly each other significantly on Self-harm tendency. By the same point of view Table 4.74 show the mean score of male Students of arts faculty is 18.96, mean score of male Students of commerce faculty is 18.04, mean score of male Students of science faculty is 18.88, mean score of female Students of arts faculty is 19.48, mean score of female Students of commerce faculty is 20.65, and mean score of female Students of science faculty is 20.68; which are not interacting each other significantly on Self-harm tendency of high school Students. Mean score shows that female Students of commerce faculty have high level of Self-harm tendency in compare to all other groups. It can be seen in figure 4.74. So, the result is that Ho_{74} is rejected.

Figure No: 4.74
Showing Bar Graph of Mean Scores of Self-harm tendency of high school Students - Variable-A x B (Faculty x Gender)

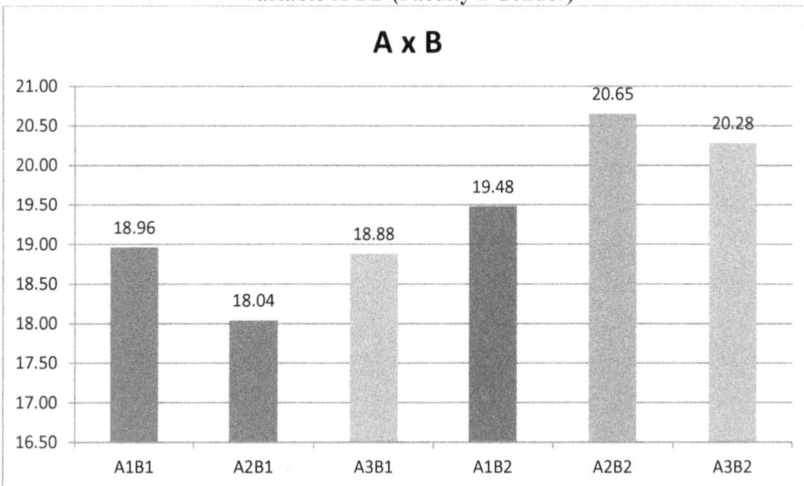

Table No: 4.75
Showing Means Scores of Self-harm tendency of high school Students - Variable-A x C (Faculty x Area)

		A1	A2	A3
C1	Mean	18.68	17.93	19.03
	N	120	120	120
C2	Mean	19.77	20.76	20.14
	N	120	120	120

F ratio for A x Css (Faculty x Area) is 3.82, which is significant at 0.05 level. It means faculty and gender differ significantly on Self-harm tendency of high school Students. By the same point of view Table 4.75 show the mean score of arts Students of urban area is 18.68, mean score of commerce Students of urban area is 17.93, mean score of science Students of urban area is 19.03, mean score of arts Students of rural area is 19.77, mean score of commerce Students of rural area is 20.76, mean score of science Students of rural area is 20.14; which are interacting each other significantly on Self-harm tendency of high school Students. Mean score indicates that commerce Students of rural area have high level of Self-harm tendency in compare to all other groups. It can be seen in figure 4.75. So, the result is that Ho_{75} is rejected.

Figure No: 4.75
Showing Bar Graph of Mean Scores of Self-harm tendency of high school Students - Variable-A x C (Faculty x Area)

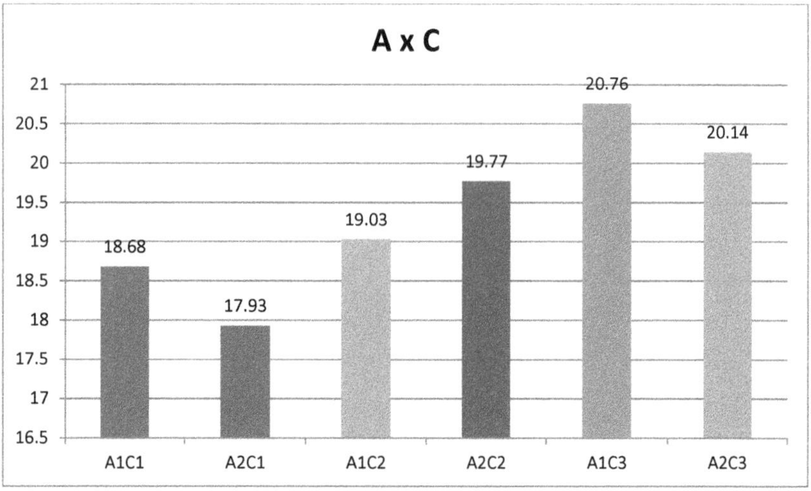

Table No: 4.76
Showing Means Scores of Self-harm tendency of high school Students - Variable-B x C (Gender x Area)

		B1	B2
C1	Mean	17.57	19.52
	N	180	180
C2	Mean	19.69	20.76
	N	180	180

F ratio for B x Css (Gender x Area) is 2.29, which is not significant. It means gender and area do not interact significantly each other on Self-harm tendency of high school Students. By the same point of view Table 4.76 shows the mean score of male Students of urban area is 17.57, mean score of female Students of urban area is 19.52, mean score of male Students of rural area is 19.69, mean score of female Students of rural area is 20.76, which are not significantly interacting each other significantly on Self-harm tendency of high school Students. It can be seen in figure 4.76. Mean score shows that Students with different gender and area have higher level of Self-harm tendency. So, the result is that Ho_{76} is accepted.

Figure No: 4.76
Showing Bar Graph of Mean Scores of Self-harm tendency of high school Students - Variable-B x C (Gender x Area)

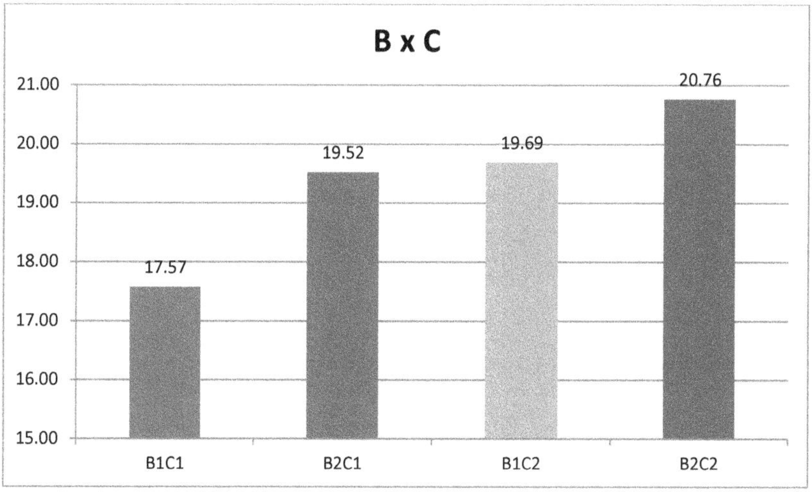

Table No: 4.77
Showing Means Scores of Self-harm tendency of high school Students - Variable-A x B x C (Faculty x Gender x Area)

		A1		A2		A3	
		B1	**B2**	**B1**	**B2**	**B1**	**B2**
C1	**Mean**	18.32	19.03	16.10	19.77	18.28	19.77
	N	60	60	60	60	60	60
C2	**Mean**	19.60	19.93	19.98	21.53	19.48	20.80
	N	60	60	60	60	60	60

F ratio for A x B x Css (Faculty x Gender x Area) is 1.10, which is not significant. It means faculty, gender and area do not interact significantly each other on scores of Self-harm tendency of high school Students. By the same point of view, table 4.77 shows the mean scores of male Students of urban area with arts faculty is 18.32, mean scores of female Students of urban area with arts faculty is 19.03, mean scores of male Students of urban area with commerce faculty is 16.10, mean scores of female Students of urban area with commerce faculty is 19.77, mean scores of male Students of urban area with science faculty is 18.28, mean scores of female Students of urban area with science faculty is 19.77, mean scores of male Students of rural area with arts faculty is 19.60, mean scores of female Students of rural area with arts faculty is 19.93, mean scores of male Students of rural area with commerce faculty is 19.98, mean scores of female Students of rural area with commerce faculty is 21.53, mean scores of male Students of rural area with science faculty is 19.48, mean scores of female Students of rural area with science faculty is 20.80, which do not differently interacting each other significantly on Self-harm tendency of high school Students. It can be seen in figure 4.77. It means that all the groups of faculty, gender and area have similar level of Self-harm tendency. So, the result is that Ho_{77} is accepted.

Figure No: 4.77
Showing Bar Graph of Means Scores of Self-harm tendency of high school Students - Variable-A x B x C (Faculty x Gender x Area)

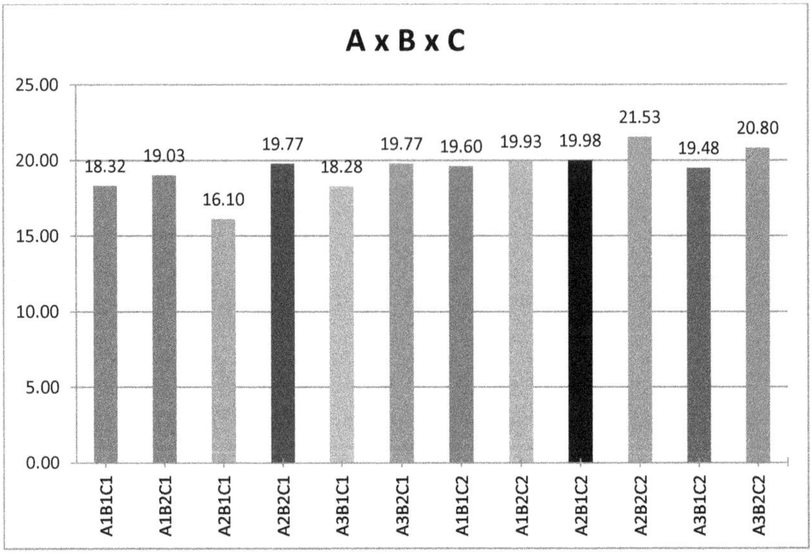

4.5.2.5 Result and Discussion on Suicidal tendency:

Table L: Showing Results of ANOVA of Suicidal tendency of high school Students:

Source of Variation	Sum of Square	Df	Mean sum of Square	F	Level of Significant
A (Faculty)	176.01	2	88.00	0.65	NS
B (Gender)	6208.13	1	6208.13	46.03	0.01
C (Area)	8120.37	1	8120.37	60.21	0.01
A x B	2937.08	2	1468.54	10.89	0.01
A x C	126.02	2	63.01	0.47	NS
B x C	3172.00	1	3172.00	23.52	0.01
A x B x C	208.10	2	104.05	0.77	NS
Error	95357.41	707	134.876		
Total	4550526.00	719			

Significant level of 'F' value: 0.05 level 3.85 (df=1), 0.01 level 6.67 (df=1)
0.05 level 3.01 (df=2), 0.01 level 4.63 (df=2)

Table No: 4.78
Showing Means Scores of Suicidal tendency of high school Students - Variable-A (Faculty)

	A1	A2	A3
Mean	77.86	79.03	78.71
N	240	240	240

Results of ANOVA main and interaction group on Suicidal tendency of high school Students scores, Table J - consulted and it is found that the f ratio for Ass (faculty) is 0.65, which is not significant. It means higher secondary school Students from arts, commerce and science faculty do not significantly differ on score of Suicidal tendency. By the same point of view Table 4.78 show mean score of arts faculty Students is 77.86, mean score of commerce faculty Students is 79.03 and mean score of science faculty Students is 78.71, it can be said there is no significant difference is existed among arts, commerce and science faculty on Suicidal tendency. It can be seen in figure 4.78.There is no difference found in the scores of Suicidal tendency. It means Students of arts, commerce and science faculty have similar level of Suicidal tendency. So, the result is that Ho_{78} is accepted.

Figure No: 4.78
Showing Bar Graph with Means Scores of Suicidal tendency of high school Students - Variable-A (Faculty)

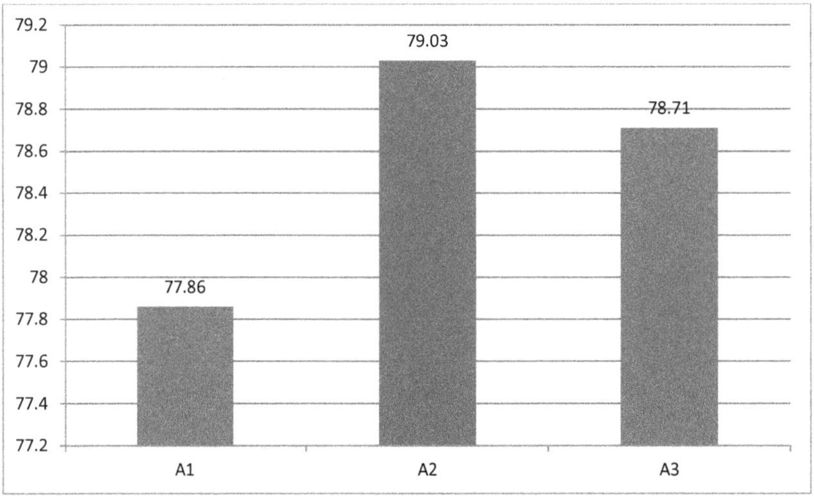

Table No: 4.79
Showing Means Scores of Suicidal tendency of high school Students - Variable-B (Gender)

	B1	B2
Mean	75.59	81.47
N	360	360

F ratio for Bss (Gender) is 46.03, which is significant at 0.01 level. It means male and female Students of high school significantly differ on Suicidal tendency. By the same point of view Table 4.79 show mean score of male Students is 75.59, and mean score of female Students is 81.47, it can be clearly said that significant difference is existed between male and female Students of high school on Suicidal tendency. It can be seen in figure 4.79. Male and female Students of high school have different level of Suicidal tendency; mean score of result indicates that female Students have higher Suicidal tendency for suicidal tendency in compare to male Students. Female are more emotional and unable to find the other solution for life so she may lead suicidal tendency. So, the result is that Ho_{79} is rejected.

Figure No: 4.79

Showing Bar graph of Means Scores of Suicidal tendency of high school Students - Variable-B (Gender)

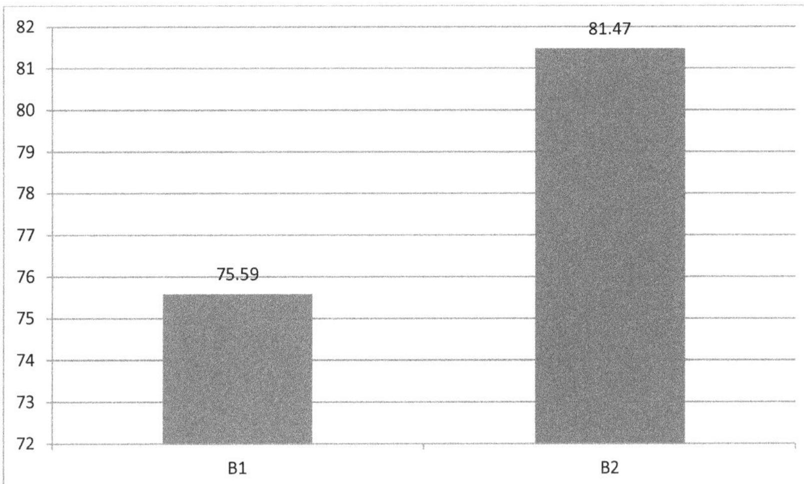

Table No: 4.80

Showing Means Scores of Suicidal tendency of high school Students - Variable-C (Area)

	C1	C2
Mean	75.17	81.89
N	360	360

F ratio for Css (Area) is 60.21, which is significant at 0.01 level. It means high school Students of urban area and rural area significantly differ on Suicidal tendency. By the same point of view Table 4.80 show the mean score of urban area Students is 75.17, mean score of rural area Students is 81.89. It can be clearly said that significant difference is existed among urban and rural area high school Students on Suicidal tendency; mean score of result indicates that Students of rural area have more Suicidal tendency in compare to urban area Students. It can be seen in figure 4.80. Students of rural area may frustrate from the factors which may affected to suicidal tendency. So, the result is that Ho_{80} is rejected.

Figure No: 4.80
Showing Bar Graph of Means Scores of Suicidal tendency of high school Students - Variable-C (Area)

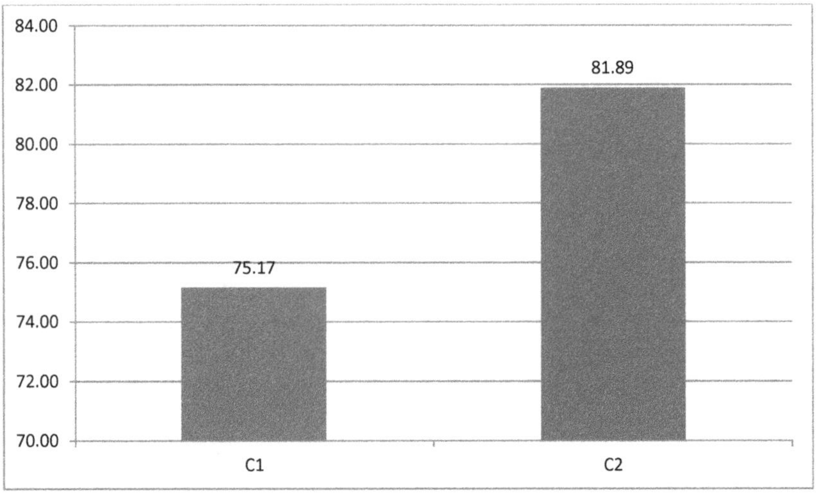

Table No: 4.81
Showing Means Scores of Suicidal tendency of high school Students - Variable-A x B (Faculty x Gender)

		A1	A2	A3
B1	**Mean**	77.28	73.52	75.98
	N	120	120	120
B2	**Mean**	78.43	84.54	81.44
	N	120	120	120

F ratio for A x Bss (Faculty x Gender) is 10.89, which is significant at 0.01 level. It means faculty and gender of high school Students interact significantly each other significantly on Suicidal tendency. By the same point of view Table 4.81 show the mean score of male Students of arts faculty is 77.28, mean score of male Students of commerce faculty is 73.52, mean score of male Students of science faculty is 75.98, mean score of female Students of arts faculty is 78.43, mean score of female Students of commerce faculty is 84.54, and mean score of female Students of science faculty is 81.44; which are not interacting each other significantly on Suicidal tendency of high school Students. Mean score shows that female Students of commerce faculty have high level of Suicidal tendency in compare to all other groups. It can be seen in figure 4.81. So, the result is that Ho_{81} is rejected.

Figure No: 4.81
Showing Bar Graph of Mean Scores of Suicidal tendency of high school Students - Variable-A x B (Faculty x Gender)

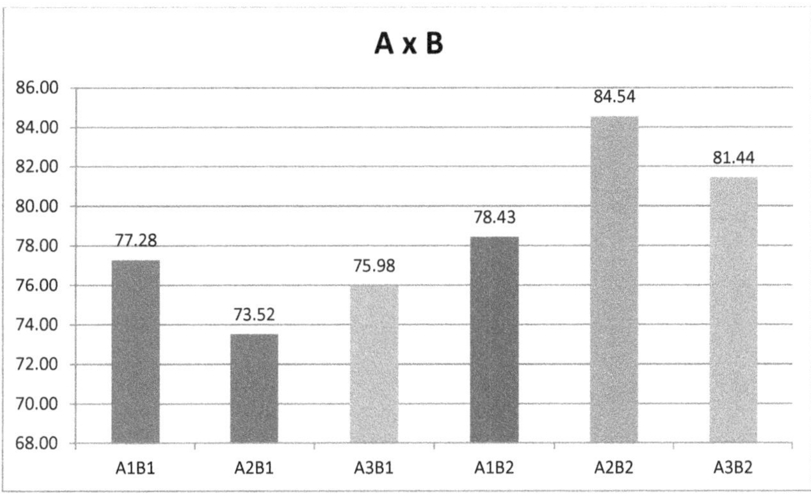

Table No: 4.82
Showing Means Scores of Suicidal tendency of high school Students - Variable-A x C (Faculty x Area)

		A1	A2	A3
C1	Mean	74.96	75.12	75.44
	N	120	120	120
C2	Mean	80.76	82.94	81.98
	N	120	120	120

F ratio for A x Css (Faculty x Area) is 0.47, which is not significant. It means faculty and gender do not differ on Suicidal tendency of high school Students. By the same point of view Table 4.82 show the mean score of arts Students of urban area is 74.96, mean score of commerce Students of urban area is 75.12, mean score of science Students of urban area is

75.44, mean score of arts Students of rural area is 80.76, mean score of commerce Students of rural area is 82.94, mean score of science Students of rural area is 81.98; which are not interacting each other significantly on Suicidal tendency of high school Students. It means all group of faculty and gender has similar level of Suicidal tendency. It can be seen in figure 4.82. So, the result is that Ho_{82} is accepted.

Figure No: 4.82

Showing Bar Graph of Mean Scores of Suicidal tendency of high school Students - Variable-A x C (Faculty x Area)

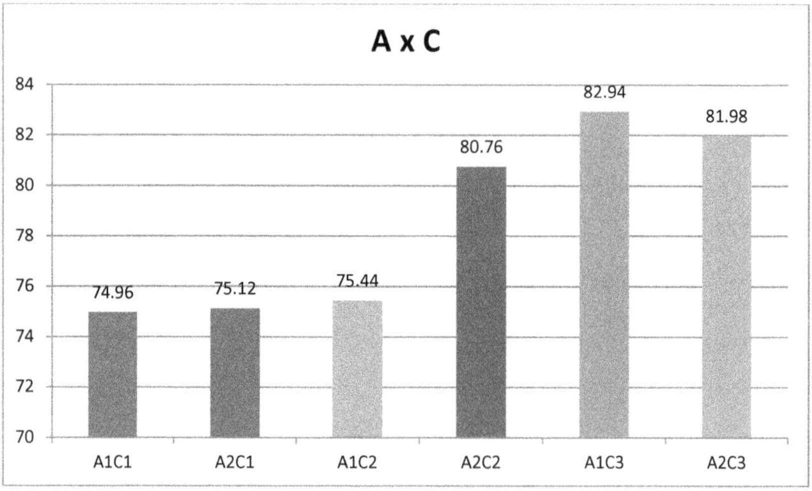

Table No: 4.83

Showing Means Scores of Suicidal tendency of high school Students - Variable-B x C (Gender x Area)

		B1	B2
C1	Mean	70.13	80.21
	N	180	180
C2	Mean	81.06	82.73
	N	180	180

F ratio for B x Css (Gender x Area) is 23.52, which is significant at 0.01 level. It means gender and area interact significantly each other on Suicidal tendency of high school Students. By the same point of view Table 4.83 shows the mean score of male Students of urban area is 70.13, mean score of female Students of urban area is 80.21, mean score of male Students of rural area is 81.06, mean score of female Students of rural area is 82.73, which are significantly interacting each other significantly on Suicidal tendency of high school Students. It can be seen in figure 4.83. Mean score shows that female Students of rural area have higher level of Suicidal tendency in compare to other group. So, the result is that Ho_{83} is rejected.

Figure No: 4.83
Showing Bar Graph of Mean Scores of Suicidal tendency of high school Students - Variable-B x C (Gender x Area)

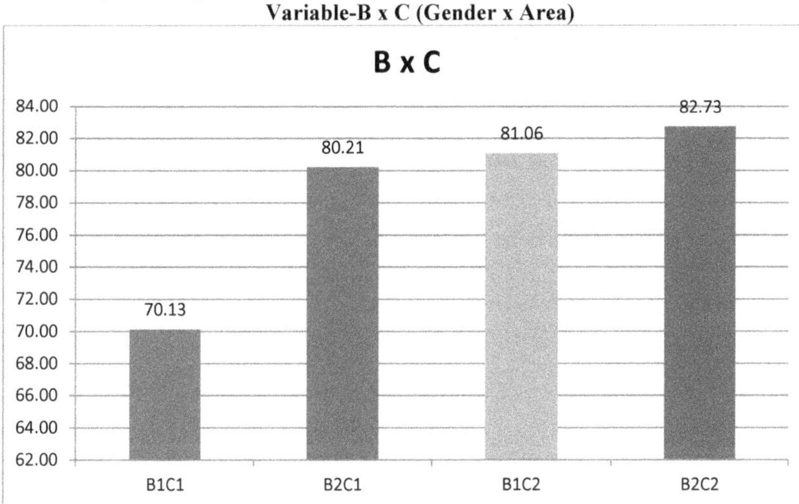

Table No: 4.84
Showing Means Scores of Suicidal tendency of high school Students - Variable-A x B x C (Faculty x Gender x Area)

		A1		A2		A3	
		B1	B2	B1	B2	B1	B2
C1	Mean	72.75	77.17	66.75	83.48	70.90	79.98
	N	60	60	60	60	60	60
C2	Mean	81.82	79.70	80.28	85.60	81.07	82.90
	N	60	60	60	60	60	60

F ratio for A x B x Css (Faculty x Gender x Area) is 0.77, which is not significant. It means faculty, gender and area do not interact significantly each other on scores of Suicidal tendency of high school Students. By the same point of view, table 4.84 shows the mean scores of male Students of urban area with arts faculty is 72.75, mean scores of female Students of urban area with arts faculty is 77.17, mean scores of male Students of urban area with commerce faculty is 66.75, mean scores of female Students of urban area with commerce faculty is 83.48, mean scores of male Students of urban area with science faculty is 70.90, mean scores of female Students of urban area with science faculty is 79.98, mean scores of male Students of rural area with arts faculty is 81.82, mean scores of female Students of rural area with arts faculty is 79.70, mean scores of male Students of rural area with commerce faculty is 80.28, mean scores of female Students of rural area with commerce faculty is 82.60, mean scores of male Students of rural area with science faculty is 81.07, mean scores of female Students of rural area with science faculty is 82.90, which do not differently interacting each other significantly on Suicidal tendency of high school Students. It can be seen in figure 4.84. It means that all the groups of faculty, gender and area have similar level of Suicidal tendency. So, the result is that Ho_{84} is accepted.

Figure No: 4.84
Showing Bar Graph of Means Scores of Suicidal tendency of high school Students - Variable-A x B x C (Faculty x Gender x Area)

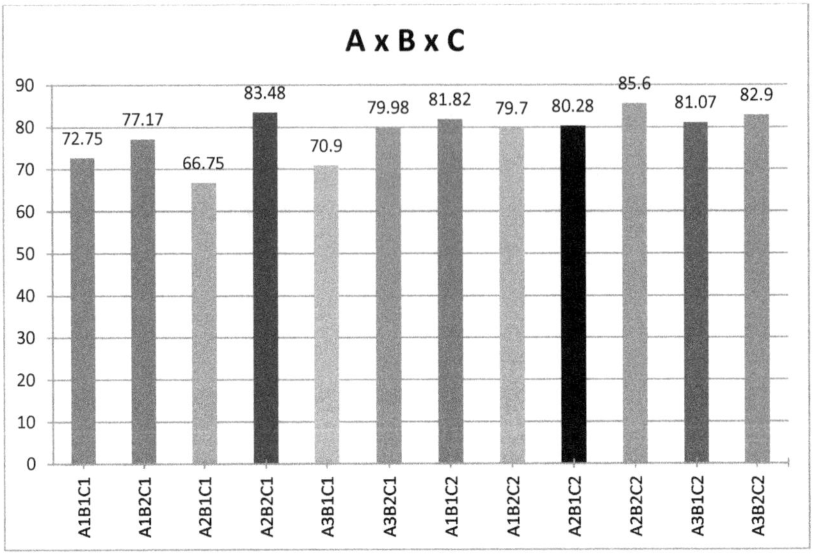

4.5.3 Result and Discussion of Emotional Intelligence:

The results and discussion of scores of five areas of emotional intelligence are described as under.

4.5.3.1 Result and Discussion on Intra-personal awareness:

Table M: Showing Results of ANOVA of Intra-personal awareness of high school Students:

Source of Variation	Sum of Square	Df	Mean sum of Square	F	Level of Significant
A (Faculty)	27.30	2	13.65	1.11	NS
B (Gender)	2.22	1	2.22	0.18	NS
C (Area)	20.00	1	20.00	1.63	NS
A x B	9.74	2	4.87	0.40	NS
A x C	1.23	2	0.62	0.05	NS
B x C	5.34	1	5.34	0.43	NS
A x B x C	0.21	2	0.11	0.01	NS
Error	8705.50	708	12.30		
Total	188702.00	720			

Significant level of 'F' value: 0.05 level 3.85 (df=1), 0.01 level 6.67 (df=1)
0.05 level 3.01 (df=2), 0.01 level 4.63 (df=2)

Table No: 4.85
Showing Means Scores of Intra-personal awareness of high school Students - Variable-A (Faculty)

	A1	A2	A3
Mean	15.56	16.03	15.83
N	240	240	240

Results of ANOVA main and interaction group on Intra-personal awareness of high school Students scores, Table M - consulted and it is found that the f ratio for Ass (faculty) is 1.11, which is not significant. It means higher secondary school Students from arts, commerce and science faculty do not significantly differ on score of Intra-personal awareness. By the same point of view Table 4.85 show mean score of arts faculty Students is 15.56, mean score of commerce faculty Students is 16.03 and mean score of science faculty Students is 15.83, it can be said there is no significant difference is existed among arts, commerce and science faculty on Intra-personal awareness. It can be seen in figure 4.85. There is no difference found in the scores of Intra-personal awareness. It means Students of arts, commerce and science faculty have similar level of Intra-personal awareness. So, the result is that Ho_{85} is accepted.

Figure No: 4.85
Showing Bar Graph with Means Scores of Intra-personal awareness of high school Students - Variable-A (Faculty)

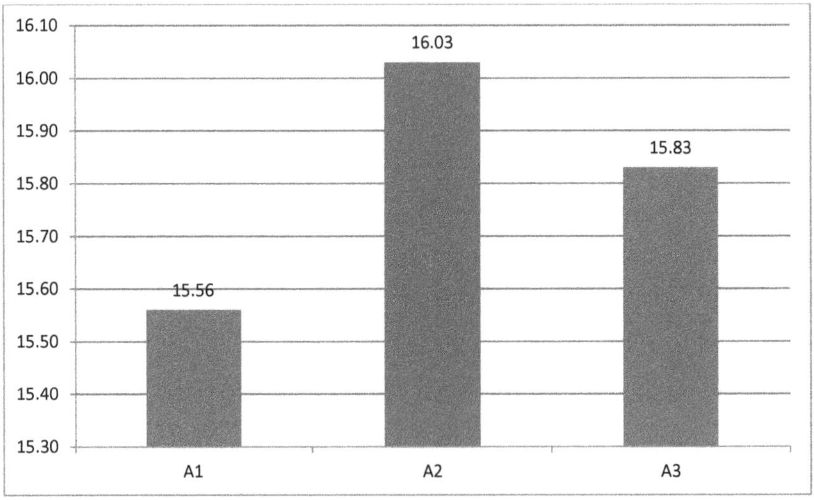

Table No: 4.86
Showing Means Scores of Intra-personal awareness of high school Students - Variable-B (Gender)

	B1	B2
Mean	15.86	15.75
N	360	360

F ratio for Bss (Gender) is 0.18, which is not significant. It means male and female Students of high school do not differ significantly on Intra-personal awareness. By the same point of view Table 4.86 show mean score of male Students is 15.86, and mean score of female Students is 15.75, it can be clearly said that no significant difference is existed between male and female Students of high school on Intra-personal awareness. It can be seen in figure 4.86. Male and female Students of high school have similar level of Intra-personal awareness. So, the result is that Ho_{86} is accepted.

Figure No: 4.86
Showing Bar graph of Means Scores of Intra-personal awareness of high school Students - Variable-B (Gender)

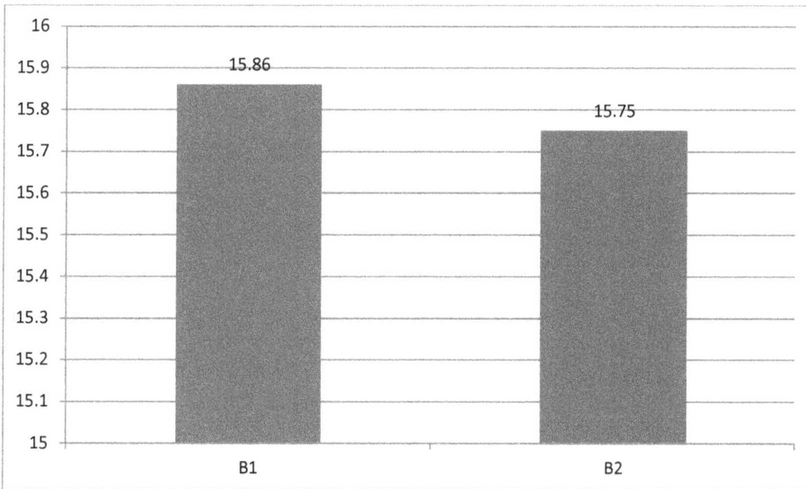

Table No: 4.87
Showing Means Scores of Intra-personal awareness of high school Students - Variable-C (Area)

	C1	C2
Mean	15.64	15.98
N	360	360

F ratio for Css (Area) is 1.63, which is not significant. It means high school Students of urban area and rural area do not differ significantly on Intra-personal awareness. By the same point of view Table 4.87 show the mean score of urban area Students is 15.64, mean score of rural area Students is 15.98. It can be clearly said that no significant difference is existed among urban and rural area high school Students on Intra-personal awareness. It can be seen in figure 4.87. So, the result is that Ho_{87} is accepted.

Figure No: 4.87
Showing Bar Graph of Means Scores of Intra-personal awareness of high school Students - Variable-C (Area)

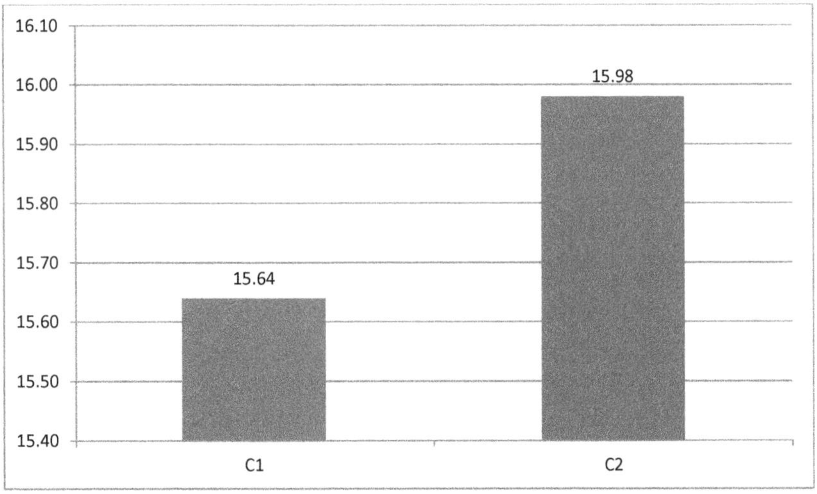

Table No: 4.88
Showing Means Scores of Intra-personal awareness of high school Students - Variable-A x B (Faculty x Gender)

		A1	A2	A3
B1	Mean	15.71	15.93	15.96
	N	120	120	120
B2	Mean	15.41	16.14	15.71
	N	120	120	120

F ratio for A x Bss (Faculty x Gender) is 0.40, which is not significant. It means faculty and gender of high school Students do not interact each other significantly on Intra-personal awareness. By the same point of view Table 4.88 show the mean score of male Students of arts faculty is 15.71, mean score of male Students of commerce faculty is 15.93, mean score of male Students of science faculty is 15.96, mean score of female Students of arts faculty is 15.41, mean score of female Students of commerce faculty is 16.14, and mean score of female Students of science faculty is 15.71; which are not interacting each other significantly on Intra-personal awareness of high school Students. It can be seen in figure 4.88. So, the result is that Ho_{88} is accepted.

Figure No: 4.88
Showing Bar Graph of Mean Scores of Intra-personal awareness of high school Students - Variable-A x B (Faculty x Gender)

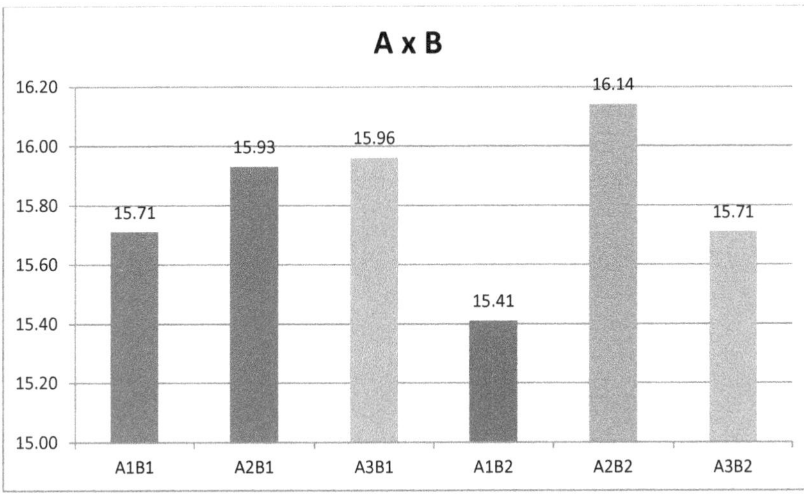

Table No: 4.89
Showing Means Scores of Intra-personal awareness of high school Students - Variable-A x C (Faculty x Area)

		A1	A2	A3
C1	**Mean**	15.43	15.81	15.69
	N	120	120	120
C2	**Mean**	15.69	16.26	15.98
	N	120	120	120

F ratio for A x Css (Faculty x Area) is 0.05, which is not significant. It means faculty and gender do not differ on Intra-personal awareness of high school Students. By the same point of view Table 4.89 show the mean score of arts Students of urban area is 15.43, mean score of commerce Students of urban area is 15.81, mean score of science Students of urban area is 15.69, mean score of arts Students of rural area is 15.69, mean score of commerce

Students of rural area is 16.26, mean score of science Students of rural area is 15.98; which are not interacting each other significantly on Intra-personal awareness of high school Students. It means all group of faculty and gender have similar level of Intra-personal awareness. It can be seen in figure 4.89. So, the result is that Ho_{89} is accepted.

Figure No: 4.89
Showing Bar Graph of Mean Scores of Intra-personal awareness of high school Students - Variable-A x C (Faculty x Area)

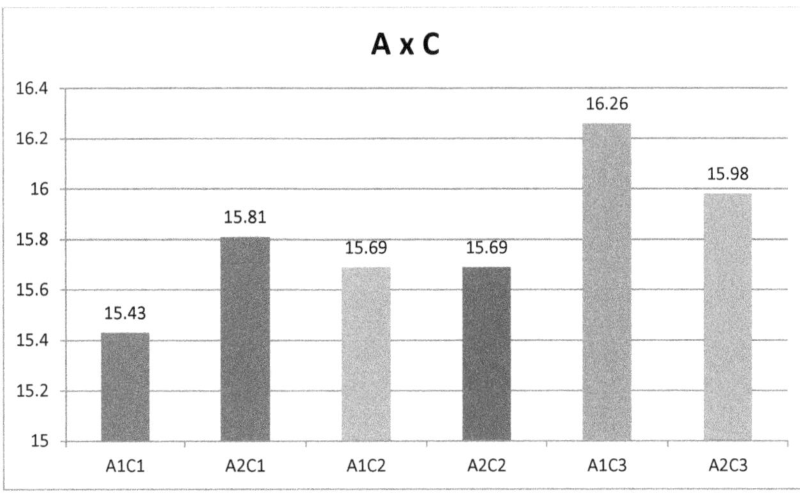

Table No: 4.90
Showing Means Scores of Intra-personal awareness of high school Students - Variable-B x C (Gender x Area)

		B1	B2
C1	Mean	15.78	15.50
	N	180	180
C2	Mean	15.94	16.06
	N	180	180

F ratio for B x Css (Gender x Area) is 0.43, which is not significant. It means gender and area do not interact each other on Intra-personal awareness of high school Students. By the same point of view Table 4.90 shows the mean score of male Students of urban area is

15.78, mean score of female Students of urban area is 15.50, mean score of male Students of rural area is 15.94, mean score of female Students of rural area is 16.06, which are not differently interacting each other significantly on Intra-personal awareness of high school Students. It can be seen in figure 4.90. It means all group of gender and area have similar level of Intra-personal awareness. So, the result is that Ho_{90} is accepted.

Figure No: 4.90
Showing Bar Graph of Mean Scores of Intra-personal awareness of high school Students - Variable-B x C (Gender x Area)

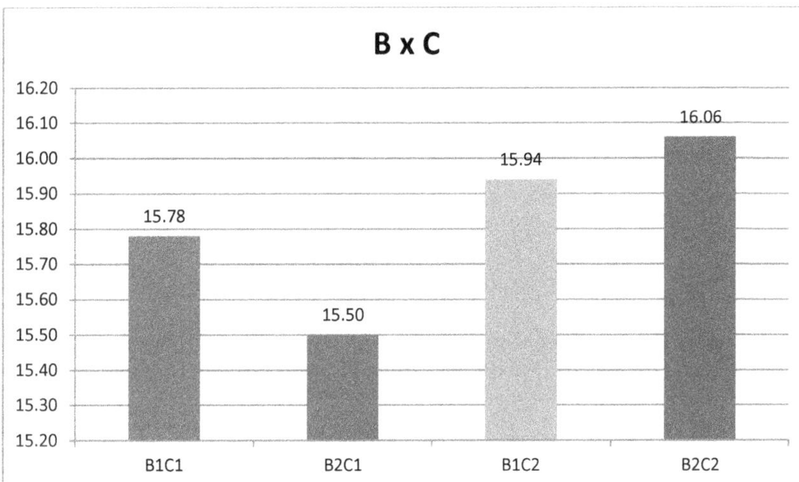

Table No: 4.91
Showing Means Scores of Intra-personal awareness of high school Students - Variable-A x B x C (Faculty x Gender x Area)

		A1		A2		A3	
		B1	**B2**	**B1**	**B2**	**B1**	**B2**
C1	**Mean**	15.68	15.17	15.77	15.85	15.90	15.48
	N	60	60	60	60	60	60
C2	**Mean**	15.73	15.65	16.08	16.43	16.02	15.93
	N	60	60	60	60	60	60

F ratio for A x B x Css (Faculty x Gender x Area) is 0.01, which is not significant. It means faculty, gender and area do not interact significantly each other on scores of Intra-personal awareness of high school Students. By the same point of view, table 4.91 shows the mean scores of male Students of urban area with arts faculty is 15.68, mean scores of female Students of urban area with arts faculty is 15.17, mean scores of male Students of urban area with commerce faculty is 15.77, mean scores of female Students of urban area with commerce faculty is 15.85, mean scores of male Students of urban area with science faculty is 15.90, mean scores of female Students of urban area with science faculty is 15.48, mean scores of male Students of rural area with arts faculty is 15.73, mean scores of female Students of rural area with arts faculty is 15.65, mean scores of male Students of rural area with commerce faculty is 16.08, mean scores of female Students of rural area with commerce faculty is 16.43, mean scores of male Students of rural area with science faculty is 16.02, mean scores of female Students of rural area with science faculty is 15.93, which do not differently interacting each other significantly on Intra-personal awareness of high school Students. It can be seen in figure 4.91. It means that all the groups of faculty, gender and area have similar level of Intra-personal awareness. So, the result is that Ho_{91} is accepted.

Figure No: 4.91
Showing Bar Graph of Means Scores of Intra-personal awareness of high school Students - Variable-A x B x C (Faculty x Gender x Area)

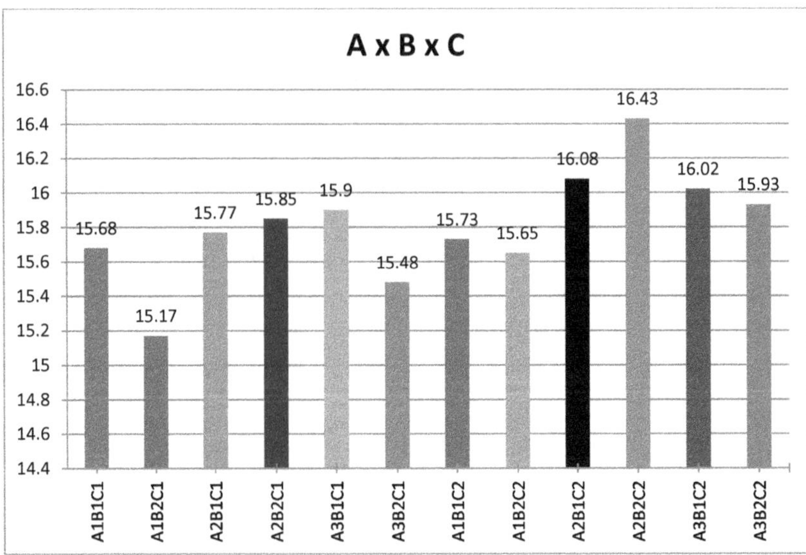

4.5.3.2 Result and Discussion on Inter-personal awareness:

Table N: Showing Results of ANOVA of Inter-personal awareness of high school Students:

Source of Variation	Sum of Square	Df	Mean sum of Square	F	Level of Significant
A (Faculty)	11.20	2	5.60	1.33	NS
B (Gender)	2.11	1	2.11	0.50	NS
C (Area)	0.01	1	0.01	0.00	NS
A x B	32.23	2	16.12	3.84	0.05
A x C	11.74	2	5.87	1.40	NS
B x C	32.51	1	32.51	7.74	0.01
A x B x C	27.30	2	13.65	3.25	0.05
Error	2975.08	708	4.20		
Total	181225.00	720			

Significant level of 'F' value: 0.05 level 3.85 (df=1), 0.01 level 6.67 (df=1)
0.05 level 3.01 (df=2), 0.01 level 4.63 (df=2)

Table No: 4.92
Showing Means Scores of Inter-personal awareness of high school Students - Variable-A (Faculty)

	A1	A2	A3
Mean	15.60	15.70	15.90
N	240	240	240

Results of ANOVA main and interaction group on Inter-personal awareness of high school Students scores, Table N - consulted and it is found that the f ratio for Ass (faculty) is 1.33, which is not significant. It means higher secondary school Students from arts, commerce and science faculty do not significantly differ on score of Inter-personal awareness. By the same point of view Table 4.92 show mean score of arts faculty Students is 15.60, mean score of commerce faculty Students is 15.70 and mean score of science faculty Students is 15.90, it can be said there is no significant difference is existed among arts, commerce and science faculty on Inter-personal awareness. It can be seen in figure 4.92. There is no difference found in the scores of Inter-personal awareness. It means

Students of arts, commerce and science faculty have similar level of Inter-personal awareness. So, the result is that Ho_{92} is accepted.

Figure No: 4.92
Showing Bar Graph with Means Scores of Inter-personal awareness of high school Students - Variable-A (Faculty)

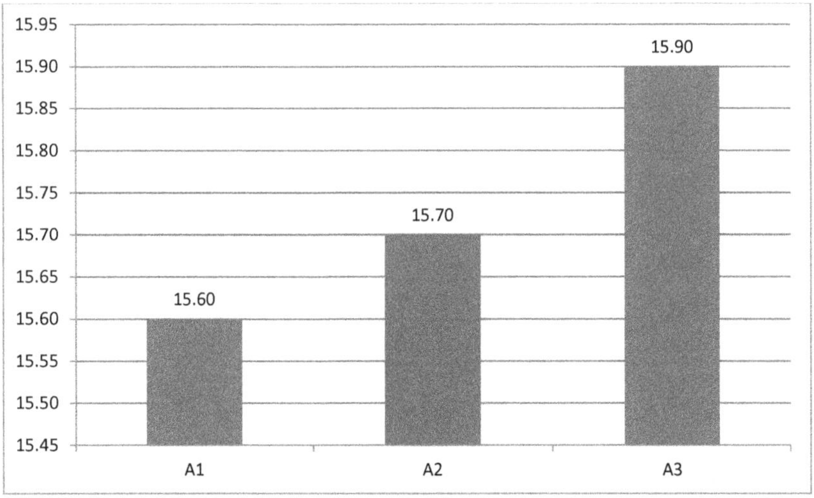

Table No: 4.93
Showing Means Scores of Inter-personal awareness of high school Students - Variable-B (Gender)

	B1	B2
Mean	15.78	15.68
N	360	360

F ratio for Bss (Gender) is 0.50, which is not significant. It means male and female Students of high school do not differ significantly on Inter-personal awareness. By the same point of view Table 4.93 show mean score of male Students is 15.78, and mean score of female Students is 15.68, it can be clearly said that no significant difference is existed between male and female Students of high school on Inter-personal awareness. It can be seen in figure 4.93. Male and female Students of high school have similar level of Inter-personal awareness. So, the result is that Ho_{93} is accepted.

Figure No: 4.93
Showing Bar graph of Means Scores of Inter-personal awareness of high school Students - Variable-B (Gender)

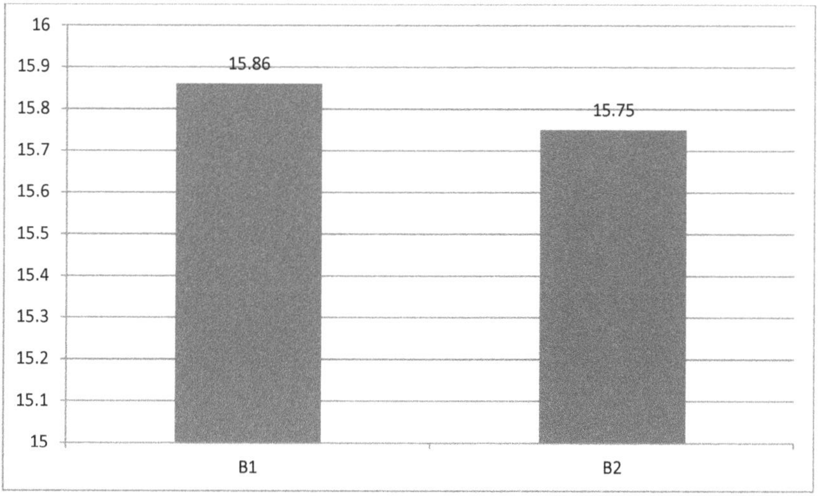

Table No: 4.94
Showing Means Scores of Inter-personal awareness of high school Students - Variable-C (Area)

	C1	C2
Mean	15.73	15.73
N	360	360

F ratio for Css (Area) is 0.00, which is not significant. It means high school Students of urban area and rural area do not differ significantly on Inter-personal awareness. By the same point of view Table 4.94 show the mean score of urban area Students is 15.73, mean score of rural area Students is 15.73. It can be clearly said that no significant difference is existed among urban and rural area high school Students on Inter-personal awareness. It can be seen in figure 4.94. So, the result is that Ho_{94} is accepted.

Figure No: 4.94
Showing Bar Graph of Means Scores of Inter-personal awareness of high school Students - Variable-C (Area)

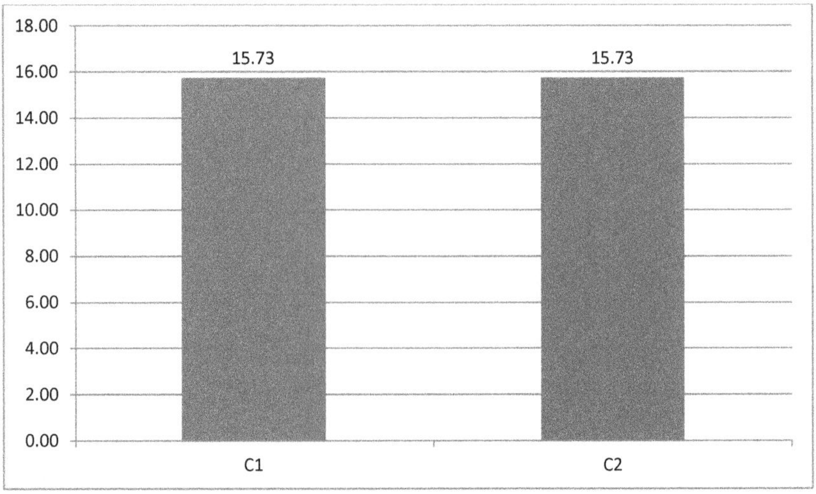

Table No: 4.95
Showing Means Scores of Inter-personal awareness of high school Students - Variable-A x B (Faculty x Gender)

		A1	A2	A3
B1	**Mean**	15.88	15.81	15.67
	N	120	120	120
B2	**Mean**	15.32	15.58	16.13
	N	120	120	120

F ratio for A x Bss (Faculty x Gender) is 3.84, which is significant at 0.05 level. It means faculty and gender of high school Students interact each other significantly on Inter-personal awareness. By the same point of view Table 4.95 show the mean score of male Students of arts faculty is 15.88, mean score of male Students of commerce faculty is 15.81, mean score of male Students of science faculty is 15.67, mean score of female Students of arts faculty is 15.32, mean score of female Students of commerce faculty is 15.58, and mean score of female Students of science faculty is 16.13; which are interacting each other significantly on Inter-personal awareness of high school Students. Mean score indicates that female Students of science faculty have high inter-personal awareness in compare to all other groups. It can be seen in figure 4.95. So, the result is that Ho_{95} is rejected.

Figure No: 4.95
Showing Bar Graph of Mean Scores of Inter-personal awareness of high school Students - Variable-A x B (Faculty x Gender)

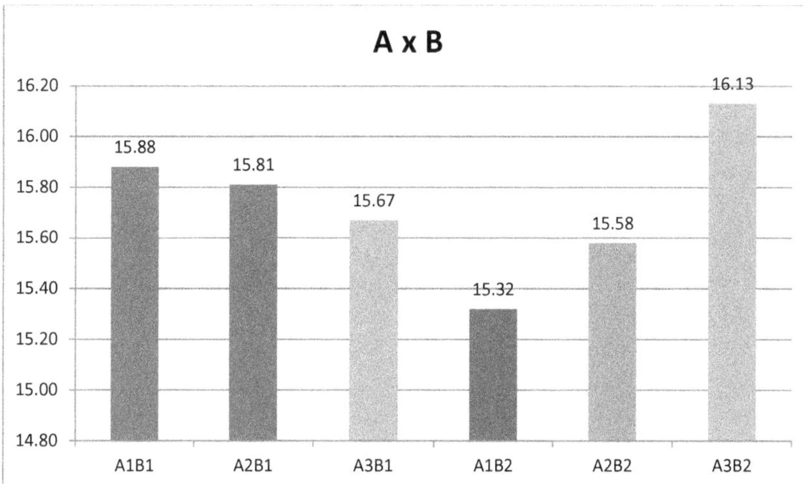

Table No: 4.96
Showing Means Scores of Inter-personal awareness of high school Students - Variable-A x C (Faculty x Area)

		A1	A2	A3
C1	**Mean**	15.78	15.60	15.81
	N	120	120	120
C2	**Mean**	15.42	15.79	15.98
	N	120	120	120

F ratio for A x Css (Faculty x Area) is 1.40, which is not significant. It means faculty and gender do not differ on Inter-personal awareness of high school Students. By the same point of view Table 4.96 show the mean score of arts Students of urban area is 15.78, mean score of commerce Students of urban area is 15.60, mean score of science Students of urban area is 15.81, mean score of arts Students of rural area is 15.42, mean score of commerce Students of rural area is 15.79, mean score of science Students of rural area is 15.98; which are not interacting each other significantly on Inter-personal awareness of high school Students. It means all group of faculty and gender have similar level of Inter-personal awareness. It can be seen in figure 4.96. So, the result is that Ho_{96} is accepted.

Figure No: 4.96

Showing Bar Graph of Mean Scores of Inter-personal awareness of high school Students - Variable-A x C (Faculty x Area)

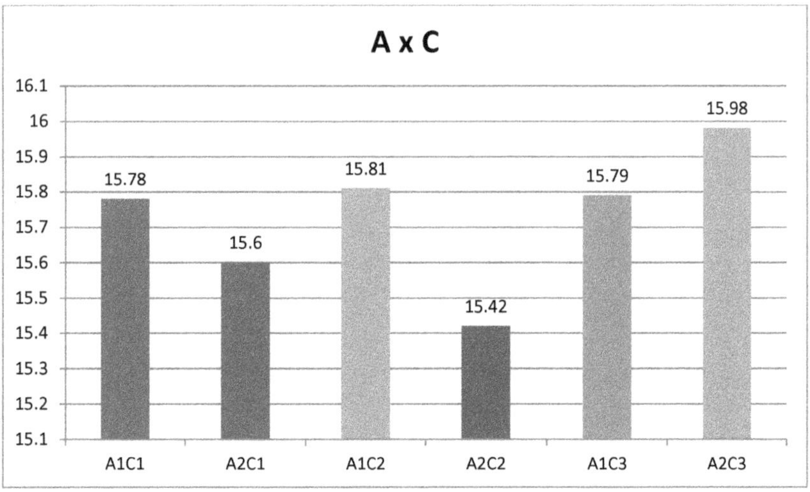

Table No: 4.97

Showing Means Scores of Inter-personal awareness of high school Students - Variable-B x C (Gender x Area)

		B1	B2
C1	Mean	15.99	15.46
	N	180	180
C2	Mean	15.57	15.89
	N	180	180

F ratio for B x Css (Gender x Area) is 7.74, which is significant at 0.01 level. It means gender and area interact significantly each other on Inter-personal awareness of high school Students. By the same point of view Table 4.97 shows the mean score of male Students of urban area is 15.99, mean score of female Students of urban area is 15.46, mean score of male Students of rural area is 15.57, mean score of female Students of rural area is 15.89, which are differently interacting each other significantly on Inter-personal awareness of high school Students. It can be seen in figure 4.97. Mean score shows that male Students of urban area have high level of Inter-personal awareness in compare to all other groups. So, the result is that Ho_{97} is rejected.

Figure No: 4.97
Showing Bar Graph of Mean Scores of Inter-personal awareness of high school Students - Variable-B x C (Gender x Area)

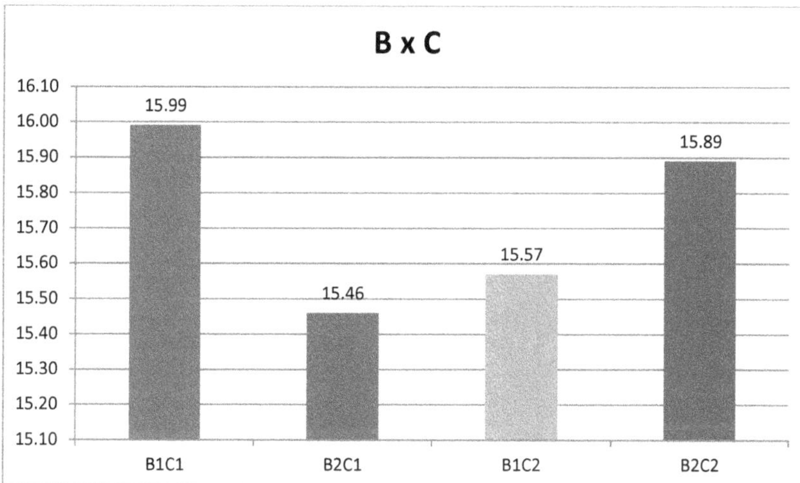

Table No: 4.98
Showing Means Scores of Inter-personal awareness of high school Students - Variable-A x B x C (Faculty x Gender x Area)

		A1		A2		A3	
		B1	**B2**	**B1**	**B2**	**B1**	**B2**
C1	**Mean**	16.52	15.03	15.90	15.30	15.57	16.05
	N	60	60	60	60	60	60
C2	**Mean**	15.23	15.60	15.72	15.87	15.77	16.20
	N	60	60	60	60	60	60

F ratio for A x B x Css (Faculty x Gender x Area) is 3.25, which is significant at 0.05 level. It means faculty, gender and area interact significantly each other on scores of Inter-personal awareness of high school Students. By the same point of view, table 4.98 shows the mean scores of male Students of urban area with arts faculty is 16.52, mean scores of female Students of urban area with arts faculty is 15.03, mean scores of male Students of urban area with commerce faculty is 15.90, mean scores of female Students of urban area with commerce faculty is 15.30, mean scores of male Students of urban area with science faculty is 15.57, mean scores of female Students of urban area with science faculty is 16.05, mean scores of male Students of rural area with arts faculty is 15.23, mean scores of female Students of rural area with arts faculty is 15.60, mean scores of male Students of rural area with commerce faculty is 15.72, mean scores of female Students of rural area with commerce faculty is 15.87, mean scores of male Students of rural area with science faculty is 15.77, mean scores of female Students of rural area with science faculty is 16.20, which are differently interacting each other significantly on Inter-personal awareness of high school Students. It can be seen in figure 4.98. Mean score indicates that male Students of arts faculty who lives in urban area have higher score on Inter-personal awareness in compare to all other groups. So, the result is that Ho_{98} is rejected.

Figure No: 4.98
Showing Bar Graph of Means Scores of Inter-personal awareness of high school Students - Variable-A x B x C (Faculty x Gender x Area)

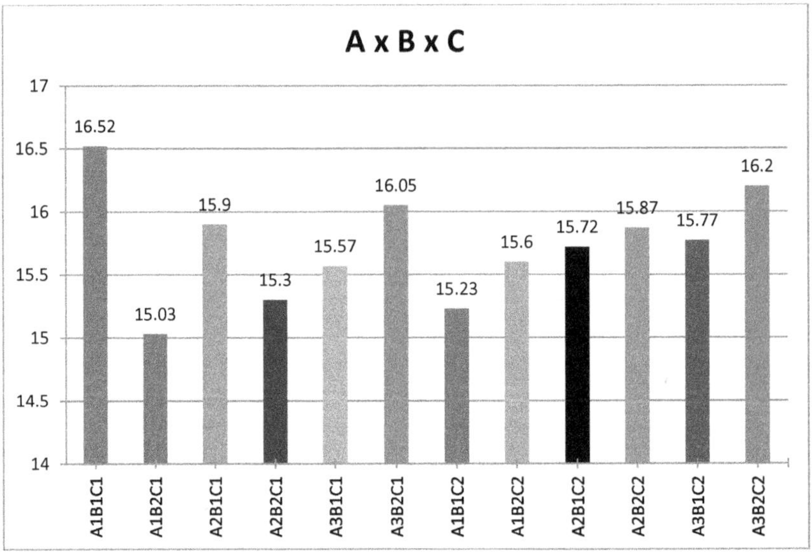

4.5.3.3 Result and Discussion on Intra-personal management:

Table O: Showing Results of ANOVA of Intra-personal management of high school Students:

Source of Variation	Sum of Square	Df	Mean sum of Square	F	Level of Significant
A (Faculty)	19.08	2	9.54	1.04	NS
B (Gender)	15.02	1	15.02	1.64	NS
C (Area)	26.45	1	26.45	2.88	NS
A x B	9.67	2	4.84	0.53	NS
A x C	12.48	2	6.24	0.68	NS
B x C	9.34	1	9.34	1.02	NS
A x B x C	30.97	2	15.49	1.69	NS
Error	6505.00	708	9.19		
Total	183348.00	720			

Significant level of 'F' value: 0.05 level 3.85 (df=1), 0.01 level 6.67 (df=1)
0.05 level 3.01 (df=2), 0.01 level 4.63 (df=2)

Table No: 4.99
Showing Means Scores of Intra-personal management of high school Students - Variable-A (Faculty)

	A1	A2	A3
Mean	15.61	15.50	15.89
N	240	240	240

Results of ANOVA main and interaction group on Intra-personal management of high school Students scores, Table O - consulted and it is found that the f ratio for Ass (faculty) is 1.04, which is not significant. It means higher secondary school Students from arts, commerce and science faculty do not significantly differ on score of Intra-personal management. By the same point of view Table 4.99 show mean score of arts faculty Students is 15.61, mean score of commerce faculty Students is 15.50 and mean score of science faculty Students is 15.89, it can be said there is no significant difference is existed among arts, commerce and science faculty on Intra-personal management. It can be seen in figure 4.99. There is no difference found in the scores of Intra-personal management. It means Students of arts, commerce and science faculty have similar level of Intra-personal management. So, the result is that Ho_{99} is accepted.

Figure No: 4.99
Showing Bar Graph with Means Scores of Intra-personal management of high school Students - Variable-A (Faculty)

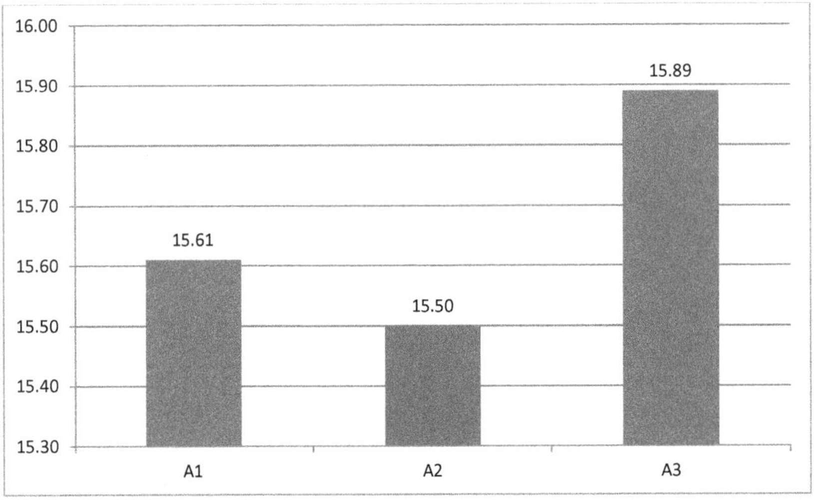

Table No: 4.100
Showing Means Scores of Intra-personal management of high school Students - Variable-B (Gender)

	B1	B2
Mean	15.81	15.52
N	360	360

F ratio for Bss (Gender) is 1.64, which is not significant. It means male and female Students of high school do not differ significantly on Intra-personal management. By the same point of view Table 4.100 show mean score of male Students is 15.81, and mean score of female Students is 15.52, it can be clearly said that no significant difference is existed between male and female Students of high school on Intra-personal management. It can be seen in figure 4.100. Male and female Students of high school have similar level of Intra-personal management. So, the result is that Ho_{100} is accepted.

Figure No: 4.100
Showing Bar graph of Means Scores of Intra-personal management of high school Students - Variable-B (Gender)

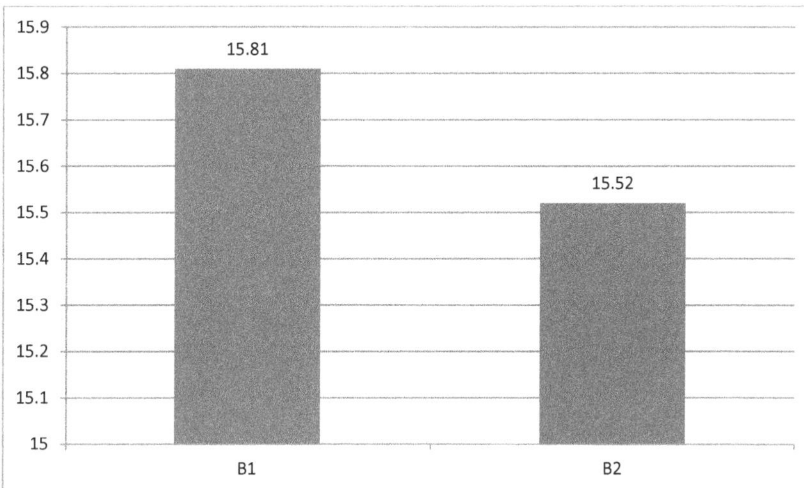

Table No: 4.101
Showing Means Scores of Intra-personal management of high school Students - Variable-C (Area)

	C1	C2
Mean	15.86	15.48
N	360	360

F ratio for Css (Area) is 2.88, which is not significant. It means high school Students of urban area and rural area do not differ significantly on Intra-personal management. By the same point of view Table 4.101 show the mean score of urban area Students is 15.86, mean score of rural area Students is 15.48. It can be clearly said that no significant difference is existed among urban and rural area high school Students on Intra-personal management. It can be seen in figure 4.101. So, the result is that Ho_{101} is accepted.

Figure No: 4.101
Showing Bar Graph of Means Scores of Intra-personal management of high school Students - Variable-C (Area)

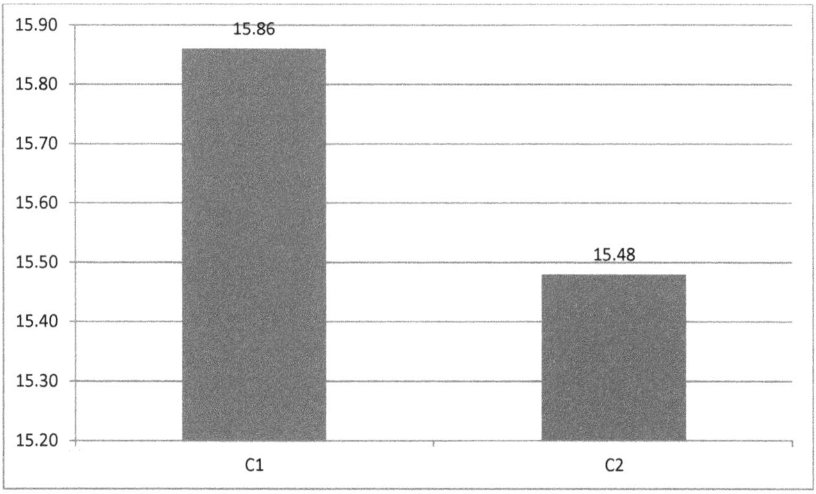

Table No: 4.102
Showing Means Scores of Intra-personal management of high school Students - Variable-A x B (Faculty x Gender)

		A1	A2	A3
B1	Mean	15.68	15.81	15.95
	N	120	120	120
B2	Mean	15.55	15.19	15.83
	N	120	120	120

F ratio for A x Bss (Faculty x Gender) is 0.53, which is not significant. It means faculty and gender of high school Students do not interact each other significantly on Intra-personal management. By the same point of view Table 4.102 show the mean score of male Students of arts faculty is 15.68, mean score of male Students of commerce faculty is 15.81, mean score of male Students of science faculty is 15.95, mean score of female Students of arts faculty is 15.55, mean score of female Students of commerce faculty is 15.19, and mean score of female Students of science faculty is 15.83; which are not interacting each other significantly on Intra-personal management of high school Students. It can be seen in figure 4.102. So, the result is that Ho_{102} is accepted.

Figure No: 4.102
Showing Bar Graph of Mean Scores of Intra-personal management of high school Students - Variable-A x B (Faculty x Gender)

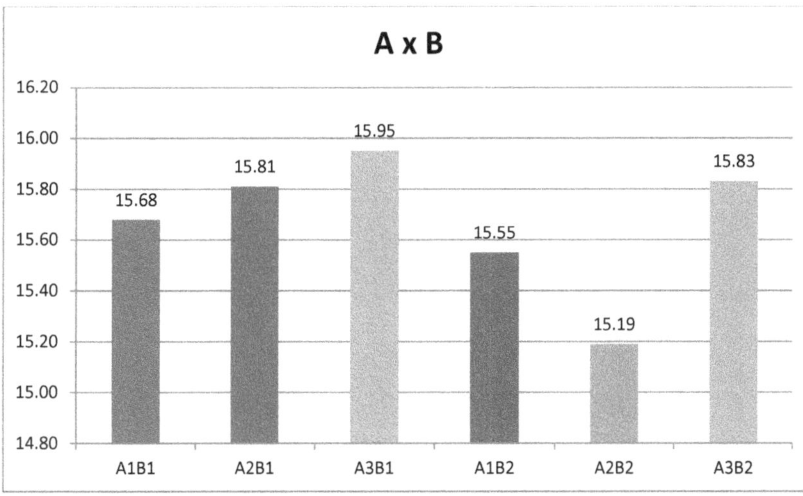

Table No: 4.103
Showing Means Scores of Intra-personal management of high school Students - Variable-A x C (Faculty x Area)

		A1	A2	A3
C1	Mean	15.63	15.83	16.13
	N	120	120	120
C2	Mean	15.60	15.18	15.65
	N	120	120	120

F ratio for A x Css (Faculty x Area) is 0.68, which is not significant. It means faculty and gender do not differ on Intra-personal management of high school Students. By the same point of view Table 4.103 show the mean score of arts Students of urban area is 15.63, mean score of commerce Students of urban area is 15.83, mean score of science Students of urban area is 16.13, mean score of arts Students of rural area is 15.60, mean score of commerce Students of rural area is 15.18, mean score of science Students of rural area is 15.65; which are not interacting each other significantly on Intra-personal management of high school Students. It means all group of faculty and gender have similar level of Intra-personal management. It can be seen in figure 4.103. So, the result is that Ho_{103} is accepted.

Figure No: 4.103
Showing Bar Graph of Mean Scores of Intra-personal management of high school Students - Variable-A x C (Faculty x Area)

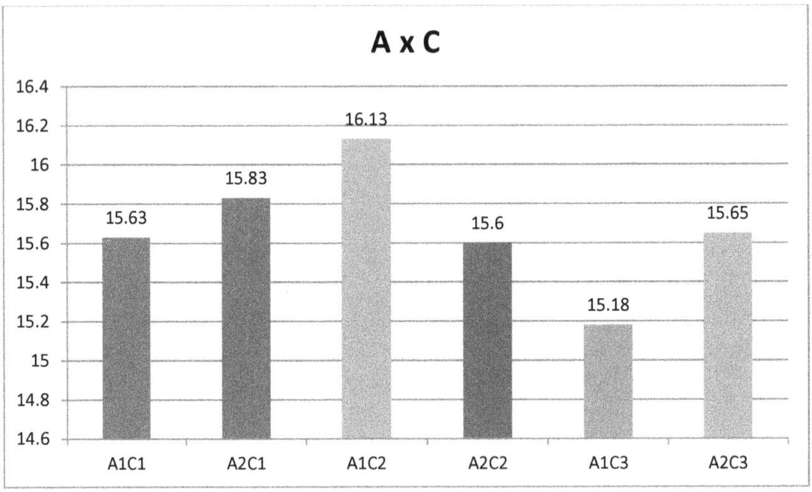

Table No: 4.104
Showing Means Scores of Intra-personal management of high school Students - Variable-B x C (Gender x Area)

		B1	B2
C1	Mean	15.89	15.83
	N	180	180
C2	Mean	15.73	15.22
	N	180	180

F ratio for B x Css (Gender x Area) is 1.02, which is not significant. It means gender and area do not interact each other on Intra-personal management of high school Students. By the same point of view Table 4.104 shows the mean score of male Students of urban area is 15.89, mean score of female Students of urban area is 15.83, mean score of male Students of rural area is 15.73, mean score of female Students of rural area is 15.22, which are not differently interacting each other significantly on Intra-personal management of high school Students. It can be seen in figure 4.104. It means all group of gender and area have similar level of Intra-personal management. So, the result is that Ho_{104} is accepted.

Figure No: 4.104
Showing Bar Graph of Mean Scores of Intra-personal management of high school Students - Variable-B x C (Gender x Area)

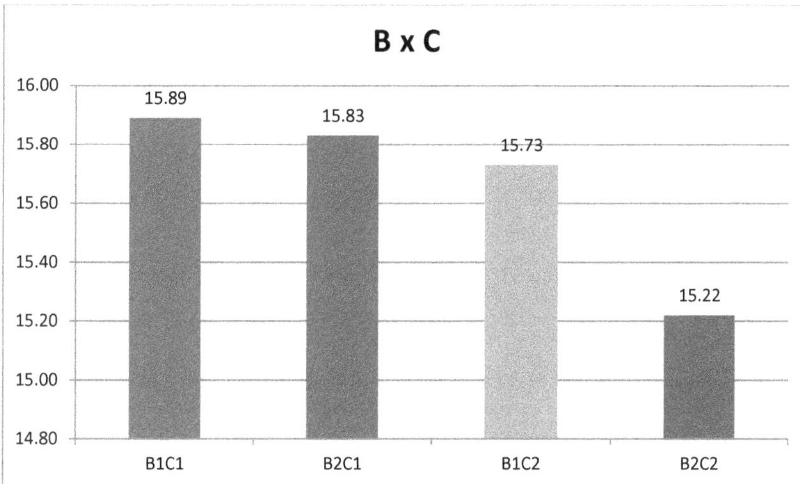

Table No: 4.105
Showing Means Scores of Intra-personal management of high school Students - Variable-A x B x C (Faculty x Gender x Area)

		A1		A2		A3	
		B1	**B2**	**B1**	**B2**	**B1**	**B2**
C1	**Mean**	15.87	15.38	15.88	15.77	15.92	16.33
	N	60	60	60	60	60	60
C2	**Mean**	15.48	15.72	15.73	14.62	15.98	15.32
	N	60	60	60	60	60	60

F ratio for A x B x Css (Faculty x Gender x Area) is 1.69, which is not significant. It means faculty, gender and area do not interact significantly each other on scores of Intra-personal management of high school Students. By the same point of view, table 4.105 shows the mean scores of male Students of urban area with arts faculty is 15.87, mean scores of female Students of urban area with arts faculty is 15.38, mean scores of male Students of urban area with commerce faculty is 15.88, mean scores of female Students of urban area with commerce faculty is 15.77, mean scores of male Students of urban area with science faculty is 15.92, mean scores of female Students of urban area with science faculty is 16.33, mean scores of male Students of rural area with arts faculty is 15.48, mean scores of female Students of rural area with arts faculty is 15.72, mean scores of male Students of rural area with commerce faculty is 15.73, mean scores of female Students of rural area with commerce faculty is 14.62, mean scores of male Students of rural area with science faculty is 15.98, mean scores of female Students of rural area with science faculty is 15.32, which do not differently interacting each other significantly on Intra-personal management of high school Students. It can be seen in figure 4.105. It means that all the groups of faculty, gender and area have similar level of Intra-personal management. So, the result is that Ho_{105} is accepted.

Figure No: 4.105
Showing Bar Graph of Means Scores of Intra-personal management of high school Students - Variable-A x B x C (Faculty x Gender x Area)

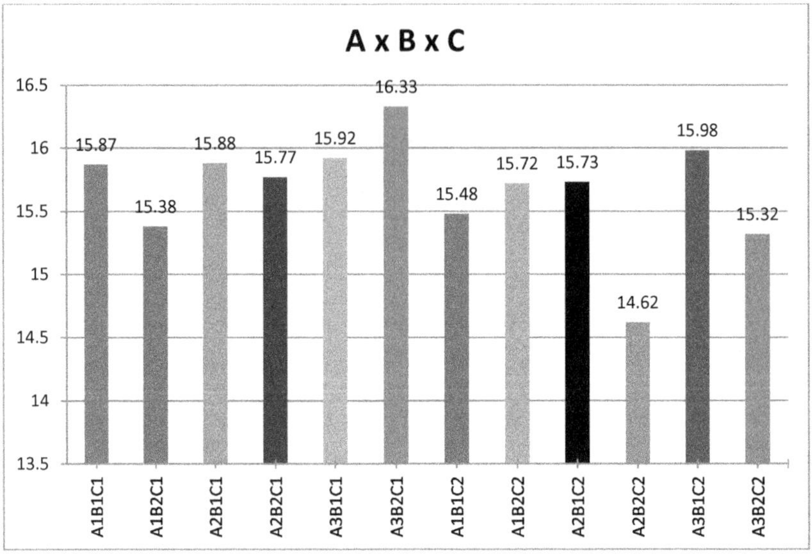

4.5.3.4 Result and Discussion on Inter-personal management:

Table P: Showing Results of ANOVA of Inter-personal management of high school Students:

Source of Variation	Sum of Square	Df	Mean sum of Square	F	Level of Significant
A (Faculty)	0.18	2	0.09	0.01	NS
B (Gender)	94.61	1	94.61	11.85	0.01
C (Area)	0.50	1	0.50	0.06	NS
A x B	13.36	2	6.68	0.84	NS
A x C	49.95	2	24.98	3.13	0.05
B x C	103.51	1	103.51	12.96	0.01
A x B x C	74.43	2	37.21	4.66	0.01
Error	5653.95	708	7.986		
Total	180929.00	720			

Significant level of 'F' value: 0.05 level 3.85 (df=1), 0.01 level 6.67 (df=1)
0.05 level 3.01 (df=2), 0.01 level 4.63 (df=2)

Table No: 4.106
Showing Means Scores of Inter-personal management of high school Students - Variable-A (Faculty)

	A1	A2	A3
Mean	15.57	15.61	15.58
N	240	240	240

Results of ANOVA main and interaction group on Inter-personal management of high school Students scores, Table P - consulted and it is found that the f ratio for Ass (faculty) is 0.01, which is not significant. It means higher secondary school Students from arts, commerce and science faculty do not significantly differ on score of Inter-personal management. By the same point of view Table 4.106 show mean score of arts faculty Students is 15.57, mean score of commerce faculty Students is 15.61 and mean score of science faculty Students is 15.58, it can be said there is no significant difference is existed among arts, commerce and science faculty on Inter-personal management. It can be seen in figure 4.106. There is no difference found in the scores of Inter-personal management. It means Students of arts, commerce and science faculty have similar level of Inter-personal management. So, the result is that Ho_{106} is accepted.

Figure No: 4.106
Showing Bar Graph with Means Scores of Inter-personal management of high school Students - Variable-A (Faculty)

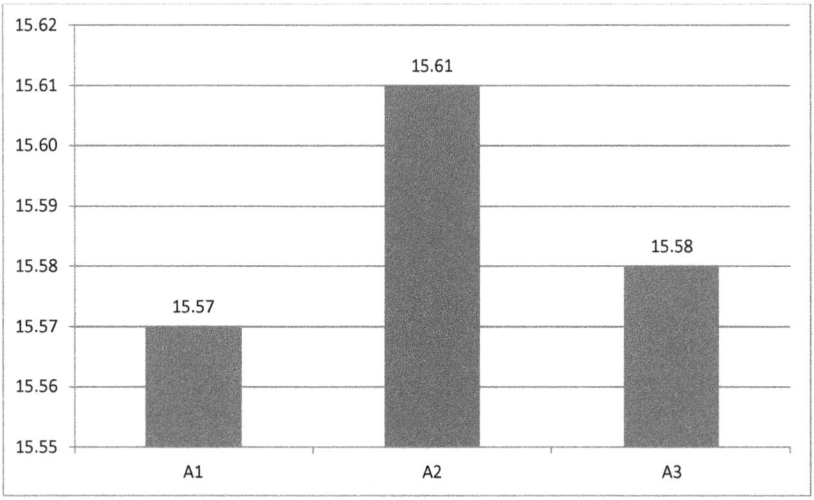

Table No: 4.107
Showing Means Scores of Inter-personal management of high school Students - Variable-B (Gender)

	B1	B2
Mean	15.95	15.23
N	360	360

F ratio for Bss (Gender) is 11.85, which is significant at 0.01 level. It means male and female Students of high school differ significantly on Inter-personal management. By the same point of view Table 4.107 show mean score of male Students is 15.95, and mean score of female Students is 15.23, it can be clearly said that there is significant difference is existed between male and female Students of high school on Inter-personal management. It can be seen in figure 4.107. Male Students have Inter-personal management in compare to female Students. Male mostly connected with external society and they can interact easily with any person so it can lead to high inter-personal management .So, the result is that Ho_{107} is rejected.

Figure No: 4.107
Showing Bar graph of Means Scores of Inter-personal management of high school Students - Variable-B (Gender)

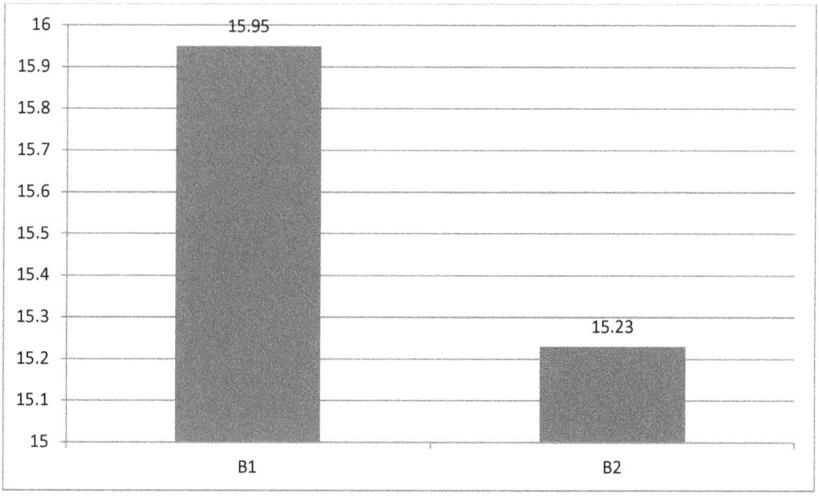

Table No: 4.108
Showing Means Scores of Inter-personal management of high school Students - Variable-C (Area)

	C1	C2
Mean	15.61	15.56
N	360	360

F ratio for Css (Area) is 0.06, which is not significant. It means high school Students of urban area and rural area do not differ significantly on Inter-personal management. By the same point of view Table 4.108 show the mean score of urban area Students is 15.61, mean score of rural area Students is 15.56. It can be clearly said that no significant difference is existed among urban and rural area high school Students on Inter-personal management. It can be seen in figure 4.108. So, the result is that Ho_{108} is accepted.

Figure No: 4.108
Showing Bar Graph of Means Scores of Inter-personal management of high school Students - Variable-C (Area)

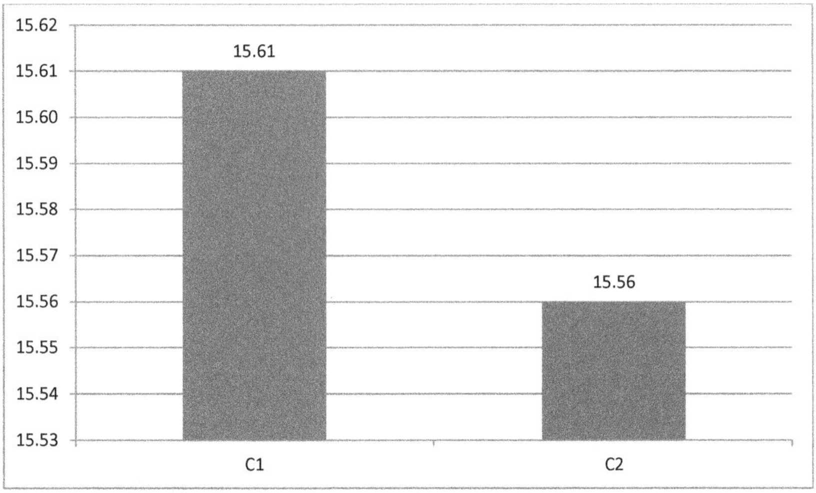

Table No: 4.109
Showing Means Scores of Inter-personal management of high school Students - Variable-A x B (Faculty x Gender)

		A1	A2	A3
B1	**Mean**	15.74	16.05	16.06
	N	120	120	120
B2	**Mean**	15.40	15.17	15.11
	N	120	120	120

F ratio for A x Bss (Faculty x Gender) is 0.84, which is not significant. It means faculty and gender of high school Students do not interact each other significantly on Inter-personal management. By the same point of view Table 4.109 show the mean score of male Students of arts faculty is 15.74, mean score of male Students of commerce faculty is 16.05, mean score of male Students of science faculty is 16.06, mean score of female Students of arts faculty is 15.40, mean score of female Students of commerce faculty is 15.17, and mean score of female Students of science faculty is 15.11; which are not interacting each other significantly on Inter-personal management of high school Students. It can be seen in figure 4.109. So, the result is that Ho_{109} is accepted.

Figure No: 4.109

Showing Bar Graph of Mean Scores of Inter-personal management of high school Students - Variable-A x B (Faculty x Gender)

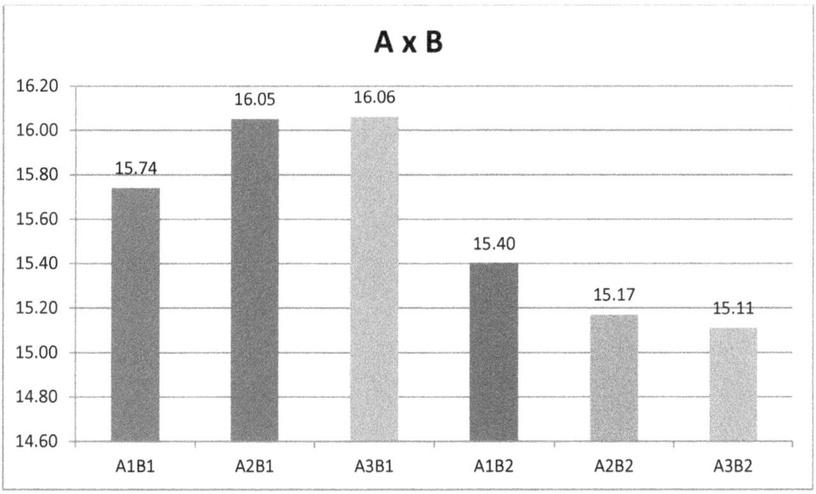

Table No: 4.110

Showing Means Scores of Inter-personal management of high school Students - Variable-A x C (Faculty x Area)

		A1	A2	A3
C1	**Mean**	15.56	15.33	15.95
	N	120	120	120
C2	**Mean**	15.58	15.88	15.22
	N	120	120	120

F ratio for A x Css (Faculty x Area) is 3.13, which is significant at 0.05 level. It means faculty and gender differ significantly on Inter-personal management of high school Students. By the same point of view Table 4.110 show the mean score of arts Students of urban area is 15.56, mean score of commerce Students of urban area is 15.33, mean score of science Students of urban area is 15.95, mean score of arts Students of rural area is 15.58, mean score of commerce Students of rural area is 15.88, mean score of science Students of rural area is 15.22; which are interacting each other significantly on Inter-personal management of high school Students. Mean score indicates that rural Students of commerce faculty have high inter-personal management in compare to all other groups. It can be seen in figure 4.110. So, the result is that Ho_{110} is rejected.

Figure No: 4.110

Showing Bar Graph of Mean Scores of Inter-personal management of high school Students - Variable-A x C (Faculty x Area)

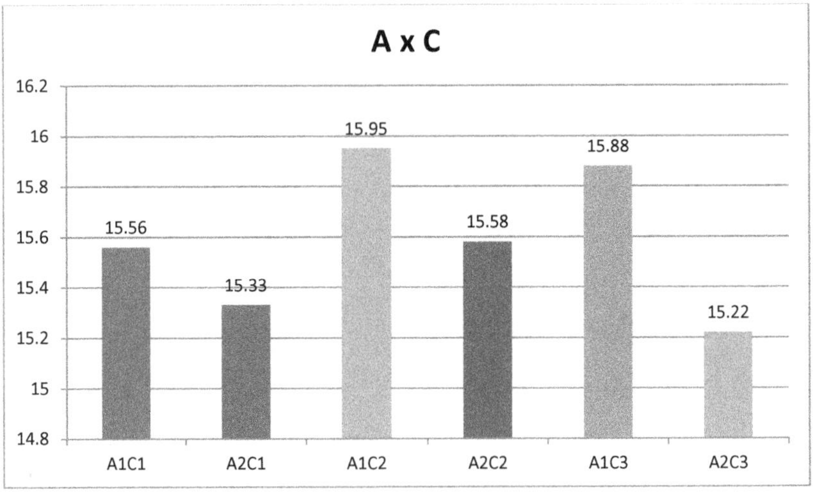

Table No: 4.111

Showing Means Scores of Inter-personal management of high school Students - Variable-B x C (Gender x Area)

		B1	B2
C1	Mean	16.36	14.87
	N	180	180
C2	Mean	15.54	15.58
	N	180	180

F ratio for B x Css (Gender x Area) is 12.96, which is significant at 0.01 level. It means gender and area interact significantly each other on Inter-personal management of high school Students. By the same point of view Table 4.111 shows the mean score of male Students of urban area is 16.36, mean score of female Students of urban area is 14.87, mean score of male Students of rural area is 15.54, mean score of female Students of rural area is 15.58, which are differently interacting each other significantly on Inter-personal management of high school Students. It can be seen in figure 4.111. Mean score shows that male Students of urban area have high level of Inter-personal management in compare to all other groups. So, the result is that Ho_{111} is rejected.

Figure No: 4.111
Showing Bar Graph of Mean Scores of Inter-personal management of high school Students - Variable-B x C (Gender x Area)

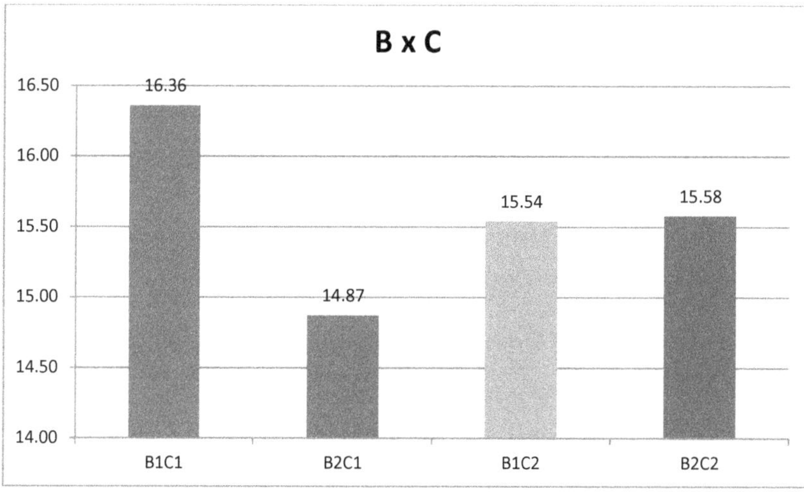

Table No: 4.112
Showing Means Scores of Inter-personal management of high school Students - Variable-A x B x C (Faculty x Gender x Area)

		A1		A2		A3	
		B1	**B2**	**B1**	**B2**	**B1**	**B2**
C1	**Mean**	16.32	14.80	16.40	14.27	16.35	15.55
	N	60	60	60	60	60	60
C2	**Mean**	15.17	16.00	15.70	16.07	15.77	14.67
	N	60	60	60	60	60	60

F ratio for A x B x Css (Faculty x Gender x Area) is 4.66, which is significant at 0.01 level. It means faculty, gender and area interact significantly each other on scores of Inter-personal management of high school Students. By the same point of view, table 4.112 shows the mean scores of male Students of urban area with arts faculty is 16.32, mean scores of female Students of urban area with arts faculty is 14.80, mean scores of male Students of urban area with commerce faculty is 16.40, mean scores of female Students of urban area with commerce faculty is 14.27, mean scores of male Students of urban area with science faculty is 16.35, mean scores of female Students of urban area with science faculty is 15.55, mean scores of male Students of rural area with arts faculty is 15.17, mean scores of female Students of rural area with arts faculty is 16.00, mean scores of male Students of rural area with commerce faculty is 15.70, mean scores of female Students of rural area with commerce faculty is 16.07, mean scores of male Students of rural area with science faculty is 15.77, mean scores of female Students of rural area with science faculty is 14.67, which are differently interacting each other significantly on Inter-personal management of high school Students. It can be seen in figure 4.112. Mean score indicates that male Students of arts faculty who lives in urban area have higher score on Inter-personal management in compare to all other groups. So, the result is that Ho_{112} is rejected.

Figure No: 4.112
Showing Bar Graph of Means Scores of Inter-personal management of high school Students - Variable-A x B x C (Faculty x Gender x Area)

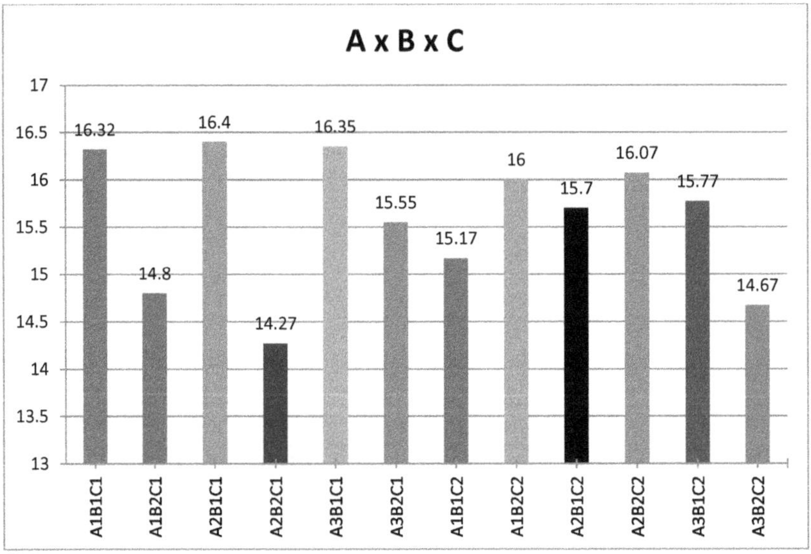

4.5.3.5 Result and Discussion on Emotional intelligence:

Table Q: Showing Results of ANOVA of Emotional intelligence of high school Students:

Source of Variation	Sum of Square	Df	Mean sum of Square	F	Level of Significant
A (Faculty)	90.03	2	45.01	0.75	NS
B (Gender)	273.80	1	273.80	4.57	0.05
C (Area)	1.80	1	1.80	0.03	NS
A x B	13.11	2	6.55	0.11	NS
A x C	50.06	2	25.03	0.42	NS
B x C	228.94	1	228.94	3.83	NS
A x B x C	313.55	2	156.78	2.62	NS
Error	42379.47	708	59.86		
Total	2882162.00	720			

Significant level of 'F' value: 0.05 level 3.85 (df=1), 0.01 level 6.67 (df=1)
0.05 level 3.01 (df=2), 0.01 level 4.63 (df=2)

Table No: 4.113
Showing Means Scores of Emotional intelligence of high school Students - Variable-A (Faculty)

	A1	A2	A3
Mean	62.34	62.84	63.20
N	240	240	240

Results of ANOVA main and interaction group on Emotional intelligence of high school Students scores, Table Q - consulted and it is found that the f ratio for Ass (faculty) is 0.75, which is not significant. It means higher secondary school Students from arts, commerce and science faculty do not significantly differ on score of Emotional intelligence. By the same point of view Table 4.113 show mean score of arts faculty Students is 62.34, mean score of commerce faculty Students is 62.84 and mean score of science faculty Students is 63.20, it can be said there is no significant difference is existed among arts, commerce and science faculty on Emotional intelligence. It can be seen in figure 4.113. There is no difference found in the scores of Emotional intelligence. It means Students of arts, commerce and science faculty have similar level of Emotional intelligence. So, the result is that Ho_{113} is accepted.

Figure No: 4.113
Showing Bar Graph with Means Scores of Emotional intelligence of high school Students - Variable-A (Faculty)

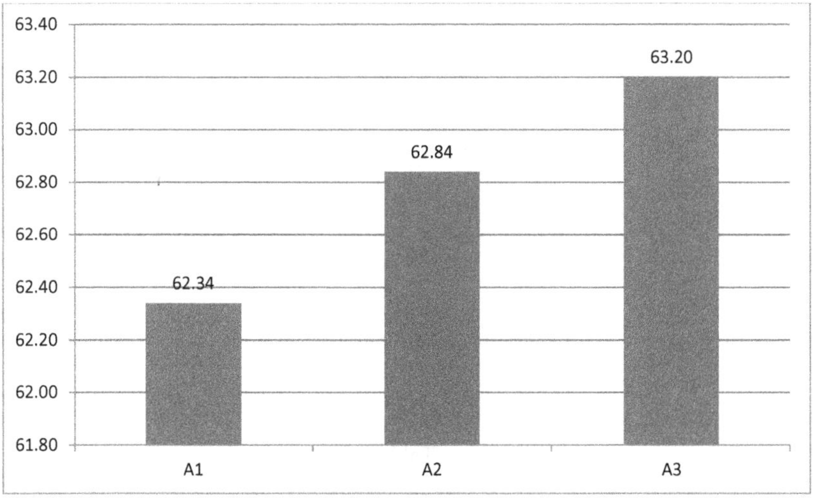

Table No: 4.114
Showing Means Scores of Emotional intelligence of high school Students - Variable-B (Gender)

	B1	B2
Mean	63.41	62.18
N	360	360

F ratio for Bss (Gender) is 4.57, which is significant at 0.05 level. It means male and female Students of high school differ significantly on Emotional intelligence. By the same point of view Table 4.114 show mean score of male Students is 63.41, and mean score of female Students is 62.18, it can be clearly said that significant difference is existed between male and female Students of high school on Emotional intelligence. It can be seen in figure 4.114. Male Students have high level of Emotional intelligence in compare to female

Students. Female are mostly more emotional in compare to male. So, the result is that Ho_{114} is rejected.

Figure No: 4.114
Showing Bar graph of Means Scores of Emotional intelligence of high school Students - Variable-B (Gender)

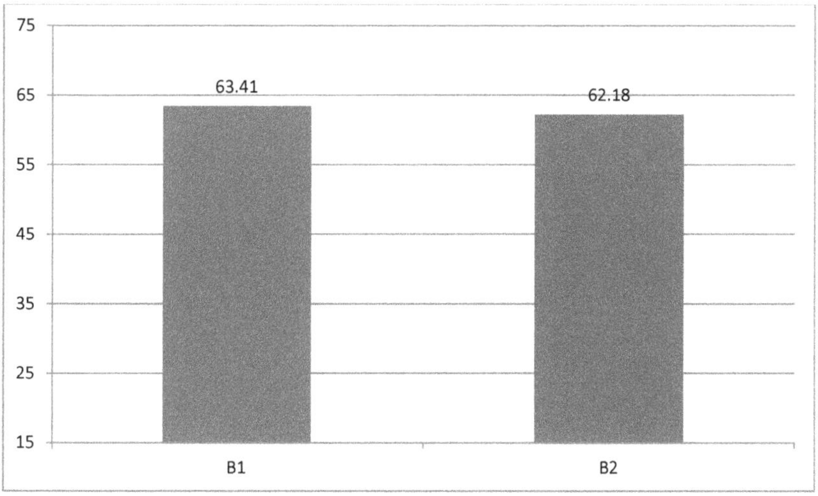

Table No: 4.115
Showing Means Scores of Emotional intelligence of high school Students - Variable-C (Area)

	C1	C2
Mean	62.84	62.74
N	360	360

F ratio for Css (Area) is 0.03, which is not significant. It means high school Students of urban area and rural area do not differ significantly on Emotional intelligence. By the same point of view Table 4.115 show the mean score of urban area Students is 62.84, mean score of rural area Students is 62.74. It can be clearly said that no significant difference is existed among urban and rural area high school Students on Emotional intelligence. It can be seen in figure 4.115. So, the result is that Ho_{115} is accepted.

Figure No: 4.115
Showing Bar Graph of Means Scores of Emotional intelligence of high school Students - Variable-C (Area)

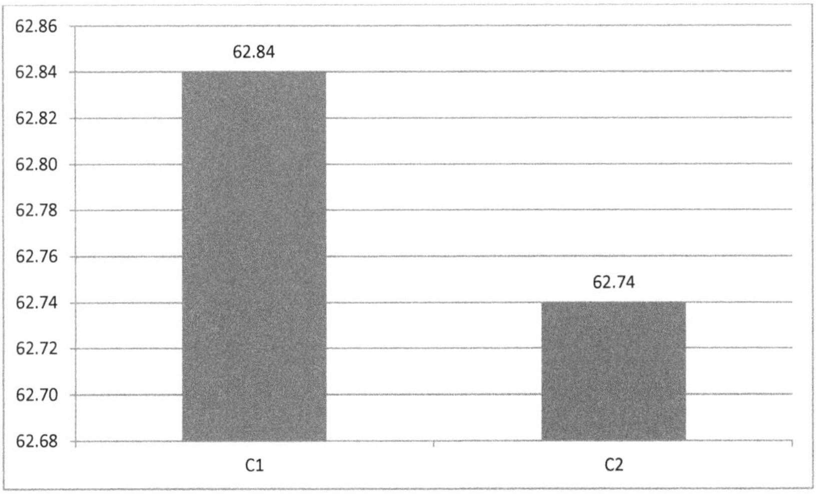

Table No: 4.116
Showing Means Scores of Emotional intelligence of high school Students - Variable-A x B (Faculty x Gender)

		A1	A2	A3
B1	**Mean**	63.00	63.59	63.63
	N	120	120	120
B2	**Mean**	61.68	62.08	62.77
	N	120	120	120

F ratio for A x Bss (Faculty x Gender) is 0.11, which is not significant. It means faculty and gender of high school Students do not interact each other significantly on Emotional intelligence. By the same point of view Table 4.116 show the mean score of male Students of arts faculty is 63, mean score of male Students of commerce faculty is 63.59, mean score of male Students of science faculty is 63.63, mean score of female Students of arts faculty is 61.68, mean score of female Students of commerce faculty is 62.08, and mean score of female Students of science faculty is 62.77; which are not interacting each other significantly on Emotional intelligence of high school Students. It can be seen in figure 4.116. So, the result is that Ho_{116} is accepted.

Figure No: 4.116
Showing Bar Graph of Mean Scores of Emotional intelligence of high school Students - Variable-A x B (Faculty x Gender)

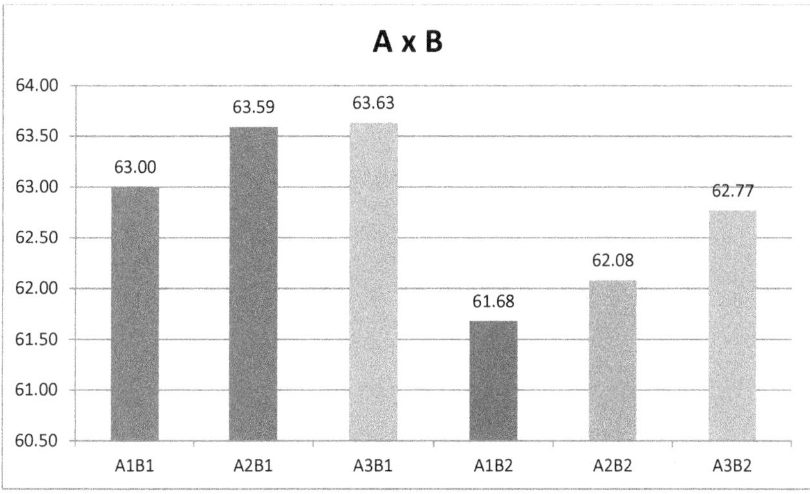

Table No: 4.117
Showing Means Scores of Emotional intelligence of high school Students - Variable-A x C (Faculty x Area)

		A1	A2	A3
C1	**Mean**	62.38	62.57	63.58
	N	120	120	120
C2	**Mean**	62.29	63.11	62.83
	N	120	120	120

F ratio for A x Css (Faculty x Area) is 0.42, which is not significant. It means faculty and gender do not differ on Emotional intelligence of high school Students. By the same point of view Table 4.117 show the mean score of arts Students of urban area is 62.38, mean score of commerce Students of urban area is 62.57, mean score of science Students of urban area is 63.58, mean score of arts Students of rural area is 62.29, mean score of commerce Students of rural area is 63.11, mean score of science Students of rural area is 62.83; which are not interacting each other significantly on Emotional intelligence of high school Students. It means all group of faculty and gender has similar level of Emotional intelligence. It can be seen in figure 4.117. So, the result is that Ho_{117} is accepted.

Figure No: 4.117
Showing Bar Graph of Mean Scores of Emotional intelligence of high school Students - Variable-A x C (Faculty x Area)

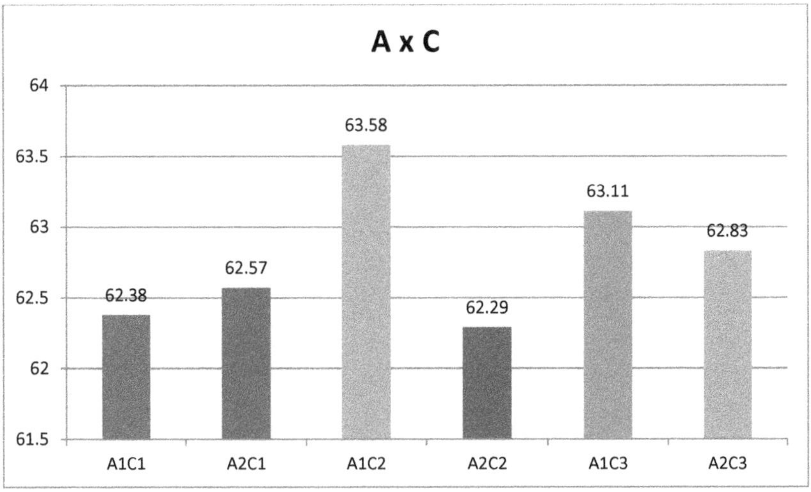

Table No: 4.118
Showing Means Scores of Emotional intelligence of high school Students - Variable-B x C (Gender x Area)

		B1	B2
C1	**Mean**	64.02	61.66
	N	180	180
C2	**Mean**	62.79	62.69
	N	180	180

F ratio for B x Css (Gender x Area) is 3.83, which is not significant. It means gender and area do not interact each other on Emotional intelligence of high school Students. By the same point of view Table 4.118 shows the mean score of male Students of urban area is 64.02, mean score of female Students of urban area is 61.66, mean score of male Students of rural area is 62.79, mean score of female Students of rural area is 62.69, which are not differently interacting each other significantly on Emotional intelligence of high school Students. It can be seen in figure 4.118. It means all group of gender and area have similar level of Emotional intelligence. So, the result is that Ho_{118} is accepted.

Figure No: 4.118
Showing Bar Graph of Mean Scores of Emotional intelligence of high school Students - Variable-B x C (Gender x Area)

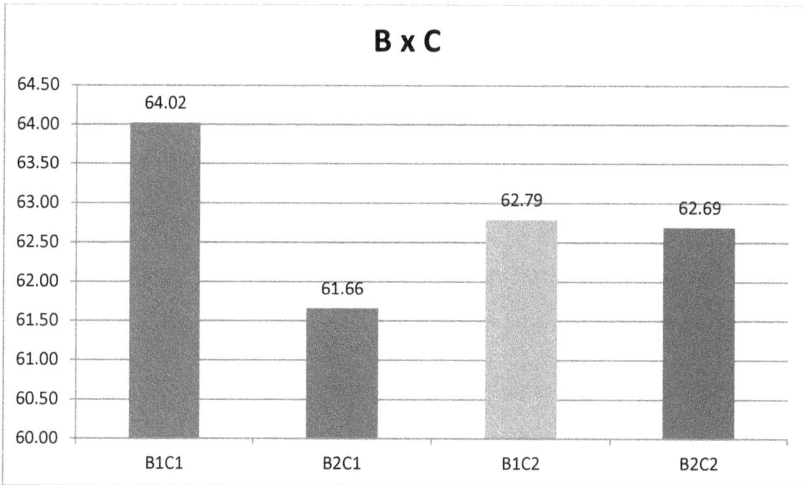

Table No: 4.119
Showing Means Scores of Emotional intelligence of high school Students - Variable-A x B x C (Faculty x Gender x Area)

		A1		A2		A3	
		B1	**B2**	**B1**	**B2**	**B1**	**B2**
C1	**Mean**	64.38	60.38	63.95	61.18	63.73	63.42
	N	60	60	60	60	60	60
C2	**Mean**	61.62	62.97	63.23	62.98	63.53	62.12
	N	60	60	60	60	60	60

F ratio for A x B x Css (Faculty x Gender x Area) is 2.62, which is not significant. It means faculty, gender and area do not interact significantly each other on scores of

Emotional intelligence of high school Students. By the same point of view, table 4.119 shows the mean scores of male Students of urban area with arts faculty is 64.38, mean scores of female Students of urban area with arts faculty is 60.38, mean scores of male Students of urban area with commerce faculty is 63.95, mean scores of female Students of urban area with commerce faculty is 61.18, mean scores of male Students of urban area with science faculty is 63.73, mean scores of female Students of urban area with science faculty is 63.42, mean scores of male Students of rural area with arts faculty is 61.62, mean scores of female Students of rural area with arts faculty is 62.97, mean scores of male Students of rural area with commerce faculty is 63.23, mean scores of female Students of rural area with commerce faculty is 62.98, mean scores of male Students of rural area with science faculty is 63.53, mean scores of female Students of rural area with science faculty is 62.12, which do not differently interacting each other significantly on Emotional intelligence of high school Students. It can be seen in figure 4.119. It means that all the groups of faculty, gender and area have similar level of Emotional intelligence. So, the result is that Ho_{119} is accepted.

Figure No: 4.119
Showing Bar Graph of Means Scores of Emotional intelligence of high school Students - Variable-A x B x C (Faculty x Gender x Area)

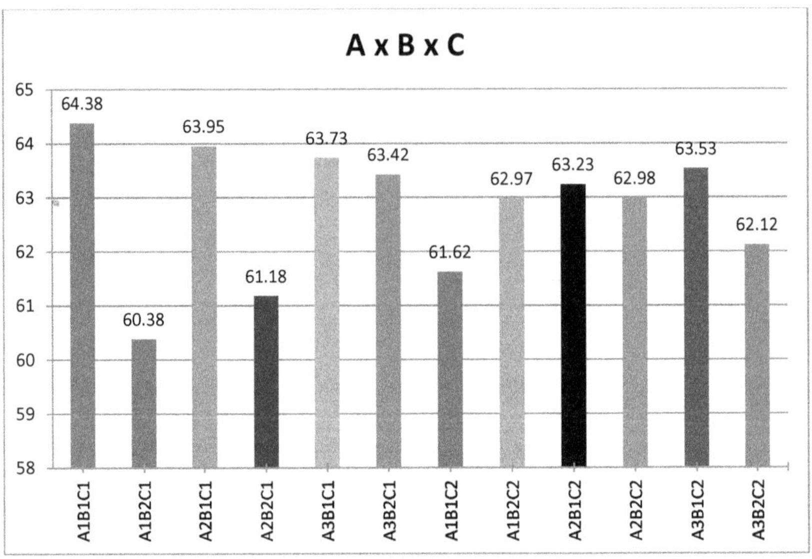

4.5.4 Result and Discussion of Correlation:

Table - 4.120: Showing correlation between mental health and suicidal tendency of high school Students.

Variables	Correlation value of 'r'	df	Inference
Mental Health Suicidal Tendency	0.038	718	Significance

0.103>* *Significant at 0.01 level 0.073>*significant at 0.05 level

Table 4.120 shows that, the calculate value of coefficient of correlation (r) came out to be 0.038 which indicates that there is a no correlation between mental health and suicidal tendency of high school Students. Thus the null hypothesis "There is no significant correlation between mental health and suicidal tendency of high school Students." is accepted. The result is that Ho_{120} is accepted.

Table - 4.121: Showing correlation between mental health and Emotional intelligence of high school Students.

Variables	Correlation value of 'r'	Df	Inference
Mental Health Emotional Intelligence	0.075*	718	Significance

0.103>* *Significant at 0.01 level 0.073>*significant at 0.05 level

Table 4.121 shows that, the calculate value of coefficient of correlation (r) came out to be 0.075 which indicates that there is a positive correlation between mental health and emotional intelligence of high school Students, which is significant at 0.05 level of confidence. Thus the null hypothesis "There is no significant correlation between mental health and emotional intelligence of high school Students." is rejected. Therefore it is concluded that there is significant positive correlation between high school Students's mental health and emotional intelligence. The result is that Ho_{121} is rejected.

Table - 4.122: Showing correlation between suicidal tendency and emotional intelligence of high school Students.

Variables	Correlation value of 'r'	Df	Inference
Suicidal tendency Emotional intelligence	0.055	718	Significance

0.103>* *Significant at 0.01 level 0.073>*significant at 0.05 level

Table 4.122 shows that, the calculate value of coefficient of correlation (r) came out to be 0.055 which indicates that there is a no correlation between suicidal tendency and emotional intelligence of high school Students. Thus the null hypothesis "There is no significant correlation between suicidal tendency and emotional intelligence of high school Students." is accepted. The result is that Ho_{122} is accepted.

In chapter four the examination of information through use of measurable deduction, testing hypothesis, discoveries of the exploration and elucidation of result is detailed. The reader is now referred to chapter fifth with conclusions, implications of the present examination and recommendations for further investigates.

CPSIA information can be obtained
at www.ICGtesting.com
Printed in the USA
LVHW081151241122
733912LV00015B/664

9 781805 450320